BRACE BY WIRE TO FLY-BY-WIRE

80 YEARS OF THE ROYAL AIR FORCE 1918-1998

Commemorating the 80th Anniversary of
The Royal Air Force

Compiled by PETER R. MARCH

BRACE BY WIRE TO FLY-BY-WIRE

80 YEARS OF THE ROYAL AIR FORCE 1918-1998

Publishing Director: PAUL A. BOWEN
Managing Editor: PETER R. MARCH
Editorial Research: BRIAN S. STRICKLAND
Art Consultant: WILFRED HARDY GAvA
Art Research: WING COMMANDER K. BURFORD, RAF
Design: GRAHAM FINCH
RAFBFE Publishing Unit: CHERYL CLIFTON & CLAIRE LOCK
Sponsorship Manager: CLIVE ELLIOTT

Published by The Royal Air Force Benevolent Fund Enterprises
Bader House, RAF Fairford, Glos GL7 4DL, England

Produced in Hong Kong by Jade Productions

© The Royal Air Force Benevolent Fund Enterprises 1993, 1998

First edition, 1993 – ISBN 0 9516581 3 1
Second, revised and enlarged edition, 1998 – ISBN 1 899808 06 X

SOLD FOR THE BENEFIT OF THE ROYAL AIR FORCE BENEVOLENT FUND

Cover painting: 21st Century Team by Wilfred Hardy GAvA.
A Eurofighter FGA1 in the colours of No 74 Squadron operating with an E-3D Sentry AEW1 of No 8 Squadron. Specially commissioned by The Royal Air Force Benevolent Fund Enterprises to mark the 80th Anniversary of The Royal Air Force.

CONTENTS

YORK HOUSE
ST. JAMES'S PALACE
LONDON S.W. 1

The modern RAF is forever indebted to the dashing young men who took off from fields on the Western Front to fly their fragile machines into the world's first aerial combat. High above the mud and carnage of the Great War, the new Warriors on the Wing served with distinction and daring. When Sir Hugh, later Lord, Trenchard established the Royal Air Force on 1 April 1918, he knew he could rely on this legacy of elan, team spirit and gallantry.

Indeed, the eighty years of history of the RAF has always been distinguished by a willingness to meet new challenges. Between the wars, in very different times, the Service safeguarded the far flung outposts of empire. Through the hard-won victory of World War II, the perils of the Cold War, countless humanitarian and peace-keeping missions, and the long range sorties of the Falkland and Gulf Wars, the Royal Air Force has earned world-wide admiration and respect.

The work of the RAF Benevolent Fund is a constant reminder that this has not been achieved without great personal sacrifice. Success for this excellent new version of 'Brace by Wire to Fly-by-Wire' seems assured. For the men and women of the Royal Air Force who turn to the Fund in times of crises, it also means a vital contribution to their present, and future, well-being.

HRH The Duke of Kent, KG
President
The Royal Air Force Benevolent Fund

1O DOWNING STREET
LONDON SW1A 2AA

FROM THE PRIME MINISTER

For eighty years the Royal Air Force has been a source of pride to the British people and, when confronted with a threat to national or global security, fearless defenders of freedom. It is also the world's oldest independent air force, setting the highest standards of efficiency and gallantry for all those who were to follow.

As we pay tribute to the RAF in its 80th year, we also celebrate the young airmen and women who have acted as our guardians across the ages. The common thread which so firmly binds the World War I bi-plane pilot to today's Tornado pilot gives the Service its strength and constancy.

Another enduring link is the Royal Air Force Benevolent Fund, formed in 1919 as a compassionate response to the hardship faced by the families of young airmen who have been lost or wounded in the Great War. This work continues as tirelessly as ever, each year bringing care and relief to many thousands of veterans and serving personnel.

Let us fly the flag for the Royal Air Force in 1998, remembering the past but also looking forward to the challenges of the 21st century.

Tony Blair

With true vision at a critical time, the Royal Air Force was created out of the air arms of the Royal Navy and the Army 80 years ago. Its genesis was challenged frequently in the early years but the force of the original arguments and the determination of Viscount Trenchard fortunately held sway. Today the Royal Air Force has capabilities that could not have been imagined in 1918, and the foresight of the creators of the Royal Air Force has been amply justified.

This book is in part a tribute to the remarkable machines which the Royal Air Force has flown over these years; it is also a tribute to the Servicemen and women who have crewed, maintained and supported them over the greater part of this century. In 1919, Trenchard established the Royal Air Force Benevolent Fund which has been a staunch support to these people and their dependants ever since. This new edition of 'Brace by Wire to Fly-by-Wire' is an excellent way of recognising and continuing our support for the outstanding work of the Benevolent Fund.

General Sir Charles Guthrie
Chief of the Defence Staff

The original 'Brace by Wire to Fly-by-Wire' was a fine tribute to 75 years of RAF history by some of the most distinguished aviation artists of recent years. How appropriate that the book should now be reissued in updated form to coincide with the Service's 80th Anniversary, and to celebrate the RAF Benevolent Fund's own 80th Anniversary. I know it will be welcomed both by those with a specialist interest in the history of military aviation and by the wider public. The pictures capture the skill and daring of the pilots, whether in the challenges of early flying, in the emotional and physical demands of warfare, or in the demanding environment of the fast jet cockpit. They provide a record of the ingenuity and perseverance of the aircraft and aero-engine designers who have pushed forward the boundaries of flight to a point scarcely imaginable in 1918. And they bear witness to the way in which air power has come to exercise a decisive influence over the conduct of warfare. The book is testimony to the skill of those artists who have made the history of aviation their speciality; but it is also a fitting tribute to all those men and women who in their different ways have contributed to the distinguished history of the RAF.

It is fitting too on this anniversary, that sales of this book should contribute to the work of the RAF Benevolent Fund. From its foundation in 1919, the Fund has supported those serving in or retired from the Service together with their relatives in their time of need, whether this need arises from physical injury, from emotional trauma or from wider hardship. For the RAF, the Fund is an embodiment of that family ethos on which the Service has prospered. For the wider community it is a means of acknowledging the service given by those now in need of help. The success of this book will make a welcome contribution to the much needed work of the Fund and I commend it to you.

Richard Johns

Sir Richard Johns
Air Chief Marshal
Chief of the Air Staff

Viscount Trenchard of Wolfeton
GCB, OM, GCVO, DSO (1873–1956)
by O. Birley
By kind permission of the Royal
Air Force Club

These pages generously
donated by the Course
Members of No 85 Advanced
Staff Course, RAF Staff
College, Bracknell.

THE ROYAL AIR FORCE BENEVOLENT FUND

When the Royal Air Force came into being on 1 April 1918, formed from the wartime amalgamation of the Royal Flying Corps and the Royal Naval Air Service, it joined two sister Services which were steeped in centuries of tradition. It had to win its spurs, yet it was hardly six months old when the Great War ended on 11 November 1918. Armistice Day found the new Service with a legacy of 16,000 casualties, leaving 2,600 widows and dependants, and 7,500 totally or badly incapacitated officers and men. In those days there were no Social Security payments, pensions were pitiful and the outlook for families with no bread-winner or whose bread-winner was disabled or out of work, was very bleak.

This was the sombre back-drop against which Lord Trenchard determined to honour those who had died in the air war and to succour those who had suffered, together with their dependants. So it was that in October 1919, together with a few influential friends, he founded what was to become the Royal Air Force Benevolent Fund. It is therefore felt appropriate to mark the 80th Anniversary in some positive way to benefit the Fund, hence the publication of this book celebrating 80 years of the Royal Air Force and its Benevolent Fund.

The Fund has come a long way from its beginnings in 1919, when for its first year the welfare expenditure was £919. In the years that have followed, the Royal Air Force has not only won its spurs, it has forged proud traditions – but at a terrible cost. Those years have seen dramatic changes. Aircraft technology has developed at an almost unimaginable rate, while conditions of service, pensions and social security have all improved dramatically. But some things have not changed. One of these is the spirit and dedication of the men and women who serve, or have served, in the Royal Air Force. Another, sadly, is the need for some of these to be helped over difficult times, since no Government can institute and maintain a system that copes adequately with all eventualities. During those intervening years the remit of the Fund was extended to what it is today, that is, irrespective of rank or sex, relieving distress or need amongst past and present members of the Royal Air Force, the Women's Services, the Royal Auxiliary Air Force and the Reserve Forces, including their widows, children and other dependants. Since 1918, the Fund's total expenditure over its lifetime has reached more than £164 million, spent helping some 900,000 people.

Those enormous sums of money are understandable when you consider that our Grants Committees deal with over 100 new cases each week. Moreover, eligibility for help from the Fund lasts for life and we still have people who fought in World War 1 on our books. As well as those, some 1.7 million men and women served in the Royal Air Force during World War 2. A large number of these are still with us, now mostly in their late seventies and more vulnerable to the vicissitudes of life with every passing year. Numerically this group made up the majority of last year's beneficiaries and the help we gave them varied from a small grant to buy a warm winter coat to helping to re-roof a pensioner's house. Some of them also found a safe haven in our two residential homes. Help for serving members covers a wide spectrum too, extending as far as providing housing for life for a widow of someone killed in the Service and helping to educate the children through to university, if appropriate.

The money comes into our London Headquarters at 67 Portland Place (for which we pay only a peppercorn rent) from two main sources. The serving members of the Royal Air Force have given marvellous support to their Benevolent Fund. They and their families raise funds in a variety of ways on their Stations and in their neighbourhoods, and 80% of them voluntarily donate half-a-day's pay a year. For the rest of the money we rely on the generosity of the public through covenants, donations, legacies and attendance at events such as the Fund's Royal International Air Tattoo and RAF Massed Bands Concerts, all finally 'topped up' by our investment income.

Sir Winston Churchill once called the Fund "part of the conscience of the British Nation" and on another occasion Sir Arthur Bryant wrote "in the last resort, all national security, active or passive, depends on the readiness of men to sacrifice themselves for the defence of their Country. That readiness has been shown by the officers and men of the Royal Air Force ever since it came into existence in 1918. The confidence that their countrymen would look after their dependants in the event of their full sacrifice being accepted was, and still is, a most vital factor in the formation and preservation of the Service's morale. The Royal Air Force Benevolent Fund is the permanent guarantee that the confidence shall never be misplaced".

These are indeed heavy responsibilities, but with the continuing help of our many stalwart supporters, especially those who have contributed to this publication, we are confident we can live up to them.

1918

The birth of the Royal Air Force as an independent, third arm of the British Services had been considered by various committees but met much opposition. The public furore over German air raids on London in 1917 gave an impetus to the development of new and different tactics and strategies. Lieutenant General Jan Smuts who came to England as the South African Government's representative on the Imperial War Cabinet, acted with characteristic speed, foresight and application to produce a report in August 1917, recommending a single Air Force to cover all the flying activities of the nation at war. With reluctant acceptance of this the Air Force (Constitution) Bill was passed on 29 November 1917. The first Air Council was formed on 3 January 1918, but friction continued, especially amongst the senior personnel selected to implement the formation.

On 1 April 1918 the Royal Flying Corps and the Royal Naval Air Service ceased to exist, both becoming integral parts of the new Royal Air Force, the world's first independent air arm. The first Chief of the Air Staff Major-General Hugh Trenchard resigned his post on 13 April after a disagreement with Lord Rothermere, Secretary of State for Air. He assumed command of the Independent Air Force (the long-range bomber force) established in France, in June 1918. Fortunately, the logistics of aircraft production had been solved by the middle of 1918 when the 'last great battle on the Western Front' began. By August there were 800 British aircraft lined up for battle against some 350 German machines. When the RAF was formed the war was expected to continue for some years. The collapse of Germany seven months after the formation of the Service gave the RAF little chance to show what it could really do compared with what had been achieved by the RFC and RNAS.

---

2 January: The Air Ministry was formed. On the following day the first Air Council was established.

1 April: The Royal Air Force was formed by the amalgamation of the Royal Flying Corps and Royal Naval Air Service. The Women's Royal Air Force was also formed. On the Western Front, the RAF destroyed 23 enemy aircraft and eight balloons for the loss of 18 of its own aircraft.

21 April: Captain A R Brown of No 209 Squadron shot down the German ace, Baron Manfred von Richthofen.

May: Britain sent a seaborne expedition to Murmansk and Archangel in Northern Russia to prevent Germany from establishing U-boat bases there, to help the Czech forces in their drive on Vladivostock and to deny the resource of Western Siberia to Germany. It included an RAF flight of DH4s later supplemented by the seaplane carrier HMS *Campania*.

13 May: It was announced that a 'long-range bomber force' was to be established, with the title the Independent Air Force, for the strategic bombing of Germany.

28 May: In answer to Colonel T E Lawrence's request for heavy bomber support a Handley Page O/400 left Cranwell, England for Egypt. Piloted by Brigadier General A E Borton, it eventually reached Ramleh on 29 August, after delays in Egypt.

June: The Royal Air Force Nursing Service was formed.

6 June: Trenchard took command of the Independent Air Force to operate without reference to the Army and Navy. It provided a bombing force of nine squadrons equipped with

DH4s, DH9s, DH9As, FE2Bs and Handley Page O/100s.

18 June: Sopwith Camels from HMS *Furious* engaged in first air-combat between carrier and land based aircraft over the Skaggerak.

July: The RAF completed the first flight from England (Cranwell) to Egypt (Cairo), with Major A S C MacLaren flying a Handley Page O/400.

July: Major James McCudden VC was killed in a flying accident in France.

24/25 July: The RAF's first heavy bomb (1,650lb named 'SN') was dropped from a Handley Page O/400 of No 214 Squadron piloted by Sergeant Dell, on a target at Middelkirke, Belgium.

26 July: Major Edward Mannock VC was reported missing whilst on a patrol over the Western Front.

5 August: During the last airship raid on London one German Zeppelin was shot down.

11 August: The German Navy Zeppelin L53 (LZ100) was shot down by Flight Sub Lieutenant Stuart Culley, who had taken off from a lighter towed behind a destroyer.

16 August: The first massed low-level attack was made by 65 RAF aircraft on the German airfield at Haubourdin.

21 September: RAF aircraft, in support of General Allenby's flying campaign in Palestine, attacked and destroyed the retreating Turkish Seventh Army at Wadi el Far'a.

October: HMS *Argus,* the first aircraft carrier equipped to recover landplanes, joined the Grand Fleet. It was armed with

Sopwith Cuckoo torpedo bombers, which were to have been used against the Wilhelmshaven naval base.

26 October: The Inter-Allied Independent Air Force was created with Marshal Foch as Supreme Commander and Major General Hugh Trenchard as Commander-in-Chief.

11 November: The Armistice was declared – the First World War was over. The RAF had 22,647 aircraft of all types on charge, of which 103 were airships, while front-line strength was 3,300. Resources included 133 squadrons and 15 flights overseas, 55 squadrons at home, 75 training squadrons and depots, 401 airfields at home and 274 abroad. Personnel totals were 27,333 officers and 263,837 other ranks, with approximately 25,000 in the Women's Royal Air Force The aircraft industry was producing about 3,500 machines a month.

29 November: Brigadier General A E Borton left England in an HP O/400 for Egypt, to survey the air-mail route to India.

13 December: Major A S C MacLaren and Captain R Halley, with Brigadier General N D McEwen on board, set out from Martlesham, Suffolk for Karachi, India in the Handley Page V/1500 *Old Carthusian.* They arrived on 30 December.

Frank Wootton's painting depicts an airfield in France in April 1918, the month in which the Royal Air Force was formed. It is published by kind permission of The Greenwich Workshop, Inc., Trumbull, CT 06611, USA. For information on limited edition fine art prints call 010–1–203–371–6568.

These pages generously donated by SNECMA

April Morning, France 1918 by Frank Wootton FPGAvA

In a statement after the end of the war, the Chief of Air Staff said "The first duty of the RAF is to garrison the British Empire". A plan for the permanent peace-time organisation of the RAF was presented to both Houses of Parliament. At home, this provided for: two squadrons (increasing to four) as a striking force; one Army co-operation flight for each Army Division; one or more squadrons for artillery co-operation; one reconnaissance and spotting squadron, half a torpedo squadron, an aeroplane fighting flight, a flying boat flight and a float seaplane flight for Fleet co-operation. Overseas, there was provision for eight squadrons and one depot in India, seven squadrons and one depot in Egypt, three squadrons and one depot in Mesopotamia, one seaplane flight in Malta, one seaplane flight in Alexandria and another aboard a carrier in the Mediterranean. The Sopwith Snipe was introduced as a successor to the Camel, but arrived too late to see service in the war. The DH9 bomber was to have replaced the DH4 but was hampered by an unreliable engine.

A large proportion of squadrons were reduced to cadre strength, and then disbanded. Senior officers in both the War Office and the Admiralty were waiting to split up the RAF and resume control over their own air services. Fortunately, Winston Churchill came on the scene, and he was able to maintain a separate air force. He also invited Trenchard back into the post of Chief of Air Staff. Trenchard knew that the new service could only survive if it built up its own traditions on sound foundations; therefore he declined offers made by the Army and Navy to provide training in their cadet and staff colleges. Trenchard ensured that the building of the new Royal Air Force Cadet College at Cranwell went ahead, and inaugurated the Halton apprenticeship scheme for boy entrants (who were known as 'Trenchard's Brats'). He also introduced the scheme for a territorial arm which was eventually to become the Auxiliary Air Force. It was on this foundation that the peacetime RAF was to be built.

January: The third Afghan War broke out on the North-West frontier of India. Six squadrons of Bristol Fighters, DH9As and DH10s were involved.

10 January: Regular passenger and mail services were started between London and Paris by No 2 (Communications) Squadron. The RAF service lasted until September, mainly for the benefit of the Peace Conference at Versailles. Aircraft used were DH4As, with enclosed accommodation, aft of the pilot, for two passengers.

11 January: Major General Sir Hugh Trenchard was re-appointed as Chief of Air Staff and Major General F H Sykes transferred as Controller-General of Civil Aviation in the Dept of Civil Aviation at the Air Ministry.

14 January: Winston Churchill became Secretary of State for War and Air.

February: The Director General of Production and Research (Major General E L Ellington) was appointed to the Air Council.

February: An express parcel air service commenced between Folkestone and Ghent, started by Air Transport and Travel Ltd, to carry food and clothing to Belgium. The flying was carried out by RAF pilots in DH9s.

March: An RAF Air Mail Service was inaugurated between Folkestone and Cologne for the Army of Occupation. This service was discontinued in August 1919 after 749 flights.

6 March: Airship R-33 was launched at Howden.

April: No 58 Squadron moved to Egypt from France with its Handley Page O/400s.

24 May: A Handley Page V/1500 bomber attacked the Afghan capital, Kabul.

14–15 June: Captain John Alcock and Lieutenant Arthur Whitten Brown made the first non-stop crossing of the Atlantic in a Vickers Vimy bomber. They flew from St John's, Newfoundland to Clifden, County Galway, Ireland in a total flying time of 16hr 27min.

July: The Vickers Vimy bomber entered service with No 58 Squadron at Heliopolis in Egypt.

9–13 July: The first two-way airship crossing of the Atlantic was completed by Squadron Leader G H Scott and a crew of 30 in Airship R-34. They flew from East Fortune, Scotland to New York and back to Pulham, Norfolk.

18 July: Britain's top ranking ace of WW1, Major Edward 'Mick' Mannock, was posthumously awarded the VC.

August: A Handley Page V/1500 of No 274 Squadron made a round-Britain flight in 12hr 28min.

4 August: New rank titles, exclusive to the RAF, came into force.

15 September: The Coastal Area was formed to control all units working with the Royal Navy. The remaining portion at home was organised into Southern Area and Northern Area.

19 September: A Handley Page O/400 dropped sixteen 112-lb bombs on the Turkish main telephone exchange at El Affule on the eve of General Allenby's famed offensive. The RAF also strafed the retreating Turkish Eighth Army on the Tulkeram–Nablus road.

21 September: For the first time, a major ground force (the retreating Turkish Seventh Army) was virtually annihilated by aircraft alone. With this attack, the campaign in Palestine and Syria was brought close to an end.

23 October: The RAF Benevolent Fund was founded by Trenchard to cater for the needs of all those within or attached to the new Service, whose lives were tragically affected by the misfortunes of peace or war.

December: By December, the RAF's 188 operational squadrons had been reduced to 12, of which one was in Germany with the Rhineland occupational forces, nine in the Middle East and two at home. In addition, there was a small number of aircraft for service with the Fleet. Personnel strength was reduced to 31,500 officers and men.

'Preparing the Atlantic Vimy' by Ray Tootall shows the famous Vickers Vimy being readied for the first direct Atlantic flight from Newfoundland to Co. Galway, Ireland on 14–15 June 1919. The aircraft is currently exhibited in the Science Museum, South Kensington.

These pages generously donated by Timet UK Ltd

Preparing the Atlantic Vimy by R. C. Tootall GAvA

The RAF continued to have a hard time after the Armistice and subsequent demobilisation, recession and uncertainty. The controversy about the organisation and control of the air arms was constantly brought before the Government. Trenchard was fortunate in that the Admiralty and the War Office had little inclination to co-operate with each other. First one attacked, and then the other, and the arguments they put forward were ill-informed and often contradictory. The greatest strength of air power – its remarkable flexibility – was clearly underlined. Trenchard wasted no time in making it clear that this would be lost if the RAF was divided and specialised for co-operation with the Army and Navy; arguing that it was this very weakness that had brought about the formation of the RAF two years earlier. The weakest point in the Chief of the Air Staff's defence was the fact that the RAF had been superimposed, on an older, outmoded pattern of defence. The turn of events in the Middle East gave Trenchard the opportunity he was seeking. Flexible air operations depended upon a mobile ground operation and with this the RAF was able to switch forces from one end of the Middle East to the other, as well as continuing action on the North-West Frontier of India. The first example of this flexibility came in 1920 in British Somaliland where a small force of RAF DH9As successfully bombed the 'Mad Mullah' forcing him to flee with his tribesmen from the country. This operation proved to be far cheaper, quicker and more effective than that planned by the Army. It was a major factor in assuring the long-term future of the RAF.

The first RAF Tournament at Hendon in July allowed the public to see RAF equipment, from wartime veteran aircraft to new designs, that were just entering service when the Armistice was declared. Successful fighters, like the Sopwith Camel and Royal Aircraft Factory SE5a, were all but replaced by Sopwith's more powerful fighter, the Snipe. Army co-operation work was being taken over by surplus Bristol Fighter two-seaters, though some RE8s remained. The Handley Page O/400s were being replaced by the Vickers Vimy, which came to fame when Alcock and Brown crossed the Atlantic in 1919. The DH9A, subsequently re-engined with a 420hp Liberty powerplant, became the definitive light bomber. The Sopwith Cuckoo became the principal torpedo-bomber, while coastal units forged on with Felixstowe flying-boats and a variety of floatplanes. The ubiquitous Avro 504K continued as the RAF's trainer, remaining in this role until the end of the decade.

January–February: The RAF's first 'little war' operation provided air support for the Camel Corps in British Somaliland. RAF units, commanded by Group Captain R Gordon, were the 'main instrument and factor' in the overthrow of the 'Mad Mullah'. Action was concluded in three weeks after the Mullah had defied military power since 1900.

21 January: RAF DH9As bombed the 'Mad Mullah' and his rebels and persuaded them to flee from British Somaliland.

21 January: No 1 Squadron re-formed in India with Sopwith Snipes and Nighthawks. Other squadrons followed during 1920, reversing the mass disbanding of fighter and bomber squadrons of the previous year.

February: A group of 235 'Boy Mechanics' commenced training under Trenchard's apprentice scheme.

1 February: The first RAF operational unit (No 14 Squadron) was established at Ramleh in Palestine, operating Bristol F2Bs. Half of the squadron was based at Amman in Transjordan. No 14 Squadron was regularly involved in reconnaissance flights and bombing action during the next 16 years against dissident tribesmen, while supporting the Transjordan Frontier Force and RAF ground patrols.

4 February: Squadron Leader Christopher Q Brand and Lieutenant Colonel Pierre van Ryneveld took off from Brooklands in a Vickers Vimy bomber in an attempt to make the first flight from England to South Africa. They crashed at Bulawayo, in Southern Rhodesia, on 6 March, and the final leg of the flight was made in a DH9.

5 February: The RAF College was formally opened, with a first entry of 52 cadets, occupying temporary wooden huts at Cranwell.

March: The School of Special Flying was moved from Gosport to merge with the RAF Central Flying School at RAF Upavon.

8 March: The total uniformed strength of the RAF was now reduced to 29,730.

1 April: The RAF Central Band was formed at Uxbridge.

1 April: The Women's Royal Air Force was disbanded.

5 May: RAF operations in support of the Indian Army succeeded in quelling an uprising on the North West Frontier.

3 July: The first RAF Tournament at Hendon attracted 60,000 spectators. These events were later known as Pageants, and finally as Displays.

19 July: The Vickers R-80 Airship, designed as an innovative streamlined shape by Barnes Wallis, made its first flight.

20 August: The prototype Fairey IIID (N9450, c/n F344), developed as a general purpose land or floatplane, made its first flight at Hamble. It was initially powered by a Rolls-Royce Eagle VIII engine of 575hp. Initially known as the Fairey IIIC (Improved), 207 were produced for the RAF for use in the bomber and reconnaissance roles.

18 October: No 8 Squadron was re-formed with DH9As at Helwan, Egypt.

November: A specification for a new heavy bomber for the RAF was issued by the Air Ministry (Spec. 2/20). The Avro Aldershot and DH Derby were built for competitive trials.

December: By now the RAF had over 500 Sopwith Snipes, of which two-thirds had been delivered directly from the manufacturer to store.

The first catapult trials from HMS Slinger with a Fairey N9 Seaplane are captured by Colin Ashford in this historic painting which is reproduced here by kind permission of the Royal Air Force Museum, Hendon.

First Catapult Trials with Fairey N9 Seaplane by C. J. Ashford GAvA, FCIAD

Most of the emerging states in the Middle East were poorly organised, politically backward and economically weak. The League of Nations gave mandates to some developed countries to supervise the emergent states. The mandates for Palestine and Transjordan, together with Iraq, were allocated to Great Britain. This arrangement was not recognised by Turkey, and some Arab states, resulting in considerable unrest, riots and border incursions. The estimated cost of the forces needed to subdue the dissidents, and to carry out the mandatory responsibilities was unacceptably high, in both financial and manpower resources. Trenchard proposed that a system of air control should be tried: if successful it would cut the cost to a small fraction of the that expended on land forces. The Air Staff was confident that the risk would be small. It was agreed to try the system out in Iraq and Jordan and, if successful, to extend it to other suitable areas. The British Cabinet agreed that the RAF should take over the policing of Iraq from the Army. Winston Churchill called a conference in Cairo and told all concerned that this plan, despite protests, would be put into effect, and that the RAF would take control from the Army for a period of 18 months, from March 1921.

In 1921 it was decided that Singapore should become the main base for the Royal Navy in the Far East. Trenchard proposed that it should also become a major air base, as Singapore Island could best be defended by an air striking force, able to attack at sea. It would also be able to give strong support to the Army, if an attack should come overland through Malaya. The Army believed that an overland attack could be ruled out, because of the Malayan terrain. The Navy, having no faith in the offensive power of aircraft, considered that a powerful battery of 15-inch guns would provide the only reliable defence. A battle of words between Admiral Beatty and Trenchard reached deadlock in mid-year and Lord Balfour with his Committee of Imperial Defence was called in to adjudge the claims and counter-claims. Fortunately for the RAF, he favoured maintaining an autonomous air force.

Later in 1921, the Geddes Inquiry (known as the *Geddes Axe*) into government expenditure almost halted the building programme on which the RAF was dependent. Most squadrons were still flying WW1 aircraft, the only exception being two transport squadrons, Nos 45 and 70, which operated the Vickers Vernon.

January: A decision was taken to allow the Airship Service of the RAF to lapse. (In 1920 the Air Ministry had decided, on the grounds of financial stringency and the proven superiority of the aeroplane, to abandon its proposed plan to lay down one new rigid airship every two years.)

January: Airship R-34 was seriously damaged when it struck a hill in thick fog. It returned to its Howden base, where groundcrew caused further damage. Finally, it was caught by gusting winds, plunged to the ground and was totally destroyed.

23 February: No 8 Squadron arrived in Iraq from Egypt, to undertake the RAF's overall policing and security responsibilities.

March: Developed from the ABC Dragonfly engined Siddeley Deasy, the first Armstrong Siddeley Jaguar powered Armstrong Whitworth Siskin (C4541) made its debut. This resulted in the Siskin II the following year and production of the all-metal Siskin III in 1923.

1 April: No 45 Squadron was re-formed at Helwan, Egypt and equipped with Vimy transports.

5 April: Captain the Honourable F E Guest was appointed as Secretary of State for Air.

19 April: The first Short-designed and built flying-boat flew as the N.3 Cromarty.

1 May: No 1 (Fighter) Squadron was moved from Bangalore to Hinaidi, Iraq with Sopwith Snipes to assist in the policing of this desert country.

3 June: Vickers Vimys of Nos 45 and 70 Squadrons began weekly airmail services over the 840 miles (1,352 km) between Cairo and Baghdad. Navigation was by following tracks ploughed across the Syrian Desert. This service continued until taken over by Imperial Airways in 1927.

8 June: RAF DH9As of Nos 30 and 47 Squadrons became involved in the regular airmail service between Cairo and Baghdad.

31 August: The first Vickers Vernon (J6864), a purpose-designed biplane troop carrier, was delivered to the RAF. It was powered by two Rolls-Royce Eagle VIII engines which were to prove inadequate for the high temperatures in the Middle East.

24 August: Airship R-38 broke up during trials over the Humber, near Hull, with the loss of 43 lives, including those of 16 Americans.

September: The last Avro 504J (100hp Gnome Monosoupape) was retired from RAF service, leaving over 900 of the more powerful Avro 504Ks still in service.

October: Air Vice-Marshal Sir John Salmond assumed command of all forces in Iraq, as the RAF took over policing duties.

October: The last Handley Page O/400, serving with No 216 Squadron, was withdrawn from service at Heliopolis. It was subsequently replaced by the Vickers Vimy for the squadron's bomber-transport duties.

December: At the end of the year the RAF had 532 Sopwith Snipes on strength, including 400 in storage.

The de Havilland DH10 Amiens twin-engined bomber in Keith Woodcock's painting is in the markings of No 216 Squadron, that was based at Abu Sueir and Heliopolis in 1921. Today 'Two-sixteen' operates Lockheed Tristars in the passenger/freight and tanker roles from Royal Air Force Brize Norton, Oxford.

DH10s of No 216 Squadron by Keith Woodcock GMA, GAvA

Throughout 1922 the arguments about the Army and RN operating their own air arms rumbled on in Parliament and Whitehall. The Chanak Crisis in Turkey was, however, an important factor which united the Chiefs of Staff in their preparations for a possible war. The same crisis forced a general election, and, with a new prime minister, the whole question of the desirability of maintaining an independent Air Force was raised again. It was the pace of overseas developments and pressures on the British government, with its responsibilities in the Middle East and India, that gave the RAF fresh opportunities to prove itself.

The RAF took over complete responsibility for the control of Iraq from October 1922, and the method of air policing which the Service adopted was quickly shown to be relatively cheap and very effective. The usual method of Army policing involved a large number of troops holding down comparatively small groups of very mobile dissident tribesmen. The RAF conducted its campaign quite differently. It delivered a note to the villagers stating that unless they stopped fighting, their village would be bombed on a particular day. They were given adequate time to vacate the village. Once several camps had been bombed after the dissidents had fled, the RAF's message was widely heeded. Using air reconnaissance, the RAF was able to pursue fleeing tribesmen with no risk of being ambushed or attacked in hostile territory. The success of this strategy quickly provided a more stable situation at a fraction of the cost and effort. Land forces were soon withdrawn, except for one mixed Brigade of British and Indian troops. Some native levies and four squadrons of armoured cars also remained, the latter manned by the RAF.

The strength of the RAF was much reduced; the Air Estimates were less than £16 million, a quarter of the funds available in the first post-war year. Apart from training establishments, there were only four Army Co-operation squadrons in England, with five squadrons in the Near East, four in Iraq, four in India and one in the Far East. In addition, there were a few float-plane or flying-boat squadrons for sea reconnaissance and coastal patrol. The RAF's total aircraft strength was under 1000 aircraft, of which only 420 were assigned to front-line squadrons.

January: De Havilland DH10 Amiens aircraft were used by No 60 Squadron to bomb rebel tribesmen on the North West frontier of India.

January: The first Westland Walrus, a modified DH9A, entered service with No 3 Squadron, at that time based at RAF Leuchars for Fleet co-operation duties.

9 February: The formation of the RAF Reserve was announced.

March: The Vickers Vernon, the first aircraft specifically designed for troop-carrying duties entered service with No 45 Squadron at Hinaidi. The Vernon replaced the Vickers Vimy.

March: The independent air force status of the RAF was confirmed by the Cabinet.

4 April: The RAF Staff College opened at Andover, Hants. The first Commandant was Air Commodore H R M Brooke-Popham.

June: No 216 Squadron replaced its last DH10 Amiens with the Vickers Vimy.

24 June: Two new aircraft appeared at the RAF Tournament at Hendon – the Westland Weasel and the Sopwith Dragon single-seat biplane fighters.

27 July: The final Bristol F2B Fighters, in service in Europe for army co-operation duties, were retired when No 12 Squadron disbanded at Bickendorf in Germany.

22 August: The prototype Vickers Victoria troop-carrier (J6860) made its first flight from Brooklands. A maximum speed of 106mph was achieved on this flight.

September: RAF aircraft including Fairey IIIDs, Nieuport Nightjars (No 203 Squadron), Bristol F2Bs (Nos 4 and 208 Squadrons), De Havilland DH9As (No 207 Squadron) and Sopwith Snipes (Nos 25 and 56 Squadrons) arrived in the Dardanelles to face the Turks in the Chanak Crisis.

1 October: RAF Iraq Command was formed to take over military control of Iraq under the command of Air Vice-Marshal Sir John Salmond.

November: No 70 Squadron based at Hinaidi, Iraq also received its first Vickers Vernon transports, which it used for regular mail services between Cairo and Baghdad.

8 November: No 3 Squadron moved to Gosport and received its first Avro Bison I reconnaissance aircraft.

24 November: The prototype Vickers Virginia (J6856) made its maiden flight at Brooklands. It was delivered to Martlesham Heath for trials on 11 December.

28 November: The prototype Fairey Flycatcher biplane fighter made its first flight. The production Flycatcher became the first Fleet Air Arm fighter to be specifically strengthened for catapulting so it could be launched from warships without carrier-type decks.

15 December: The Avro Aldershot II bomber was flown for the first time by H. J. 'Bert' Hinkler at Hamble. This version had a longer fuselage and was ordered into limited production for the RAF.

One of the most famous training aircraft to have been used by the RAF, the Avro 504K, remained in service with the Central Flying School and Nos 1–5 Flying Training Schools. Air Vice-Marshal Norman Hoad's painting depicts aircraft of No 4 FTS based at Abu Sueir, Egypt in 1922. Now based at RAF Valley, No 4 FTS operates BAe Hawks for advanced and tactical weapons training.

Avro 504Ks of No 4 FTS at Abu Sueir, Egypt by Air Vice-Marshal Norman Hoad CVO, CBE, AFC*, GAvA

In 1923 Lord Balfour was again called upon to head the committee which had, once more, to arbitrate between Trenchard (Royal Air Force) and Beatty (Royal Navy). The Navy somewhat overstated its case, which contributed to the recommendations going in favour of retaining the Royal Air Force – but also made some important suggestions to improve naval/air co-operation. Beatty and the Board of Admiralty threatened to resign en masse if the government took up the Balfour Committee's recommendations. However, when the Cabinet endorsed the recommendations, the threat was shown to be a bluff. The wrangle was settled – at least for the time being. This allowed Trenchard to concentrate upon the more positive task of building up the Royal Air Force to meet its increasing commitments.

In June 1923, following the Salisbury Report, the Prime Minister authorised a Home Defence Force of 52 squadrons, a far cry from the two which Trenchard had allowed himself only three years before. However, even a decade later, these 52 squadrons had not materialised.

The hostile activities of Sheikh Mahmud in Kurdistan had been a constant problem since WW1. The Sheikh was originally appointed by the British, only to be dismissed when he revolted. By early 1923 he had gathered a large force which advanced on Kirkuk in North-East Iraq. The RAF immediately flew in troops to bolster the garrison, arriving in sufficient time to fight off the attackers. From then on, Mahmud was harassed by the RAF and had to resort to making occasional raids over the border from Persia. These raids continued sporadically throughout the 1920s, but never became a serious threat whilst the RAF had control over Iraq. To maintain this, Air Marshal Sir John Salmond formed a large Headquarters at Hinaidi airfield, where some five squadrons were stationed. There was also a squadron at Shaibah, further down the Persian Gulf, plus one Mosul in the north, and another at Kirkuk in the north-east. In 1923, there was a serious Turkish attempt to reoccupy the northern province of Iraq – the Mosul Vilayet. The attack was dealt with effectively in a brief but brilliant campaign, using the RAF as the spear-head; this action decisively ended the threat to Iraq's external security.

---

9 January: The C4 autogiro, designed by Don Juan de la Cierva, made its first flight, marking the beginning of widespread interest in gyroplanes.

February: A considerable force of Kurds and hill Arabs began advancing on Kirkuk. The RAF responded by mounting the first-ever airlift of troops by Vernons of Nos 45 and 70 Squadrons.

9 February: A Reserve of Air Force officers was formed.

March: Developed from the Fairey Pintail amphibian, the prototype Fairey Fawn (J6907), a two-seat day bomber designed to Air Ministry Specification 20/23, was first flown by Vincent Nicholl.

14 March: The Air Minister, Sir Samuel Hoare said of the RAF, "we must keep it a *corps d'élite*; highly trained, well equipped and capable, as far as possible, of quick expansion".

April: Aircraft from eight RAF squadrons (Nos 1, 6, 8, 30, 45, 55, 70 and 84 Squadrons) were engaged in action against Sheikh Mahmud's forces in Mesopotamia.

April: The last de Havilland DH10 Amiens in front-line service with the RAF (No 60 Squadron at Risalpur, India) were replaced by DH9As for bombing raids on rebel tribesmen on the North-West Frontier.

May: The Air Minister was given a seat in the Cabinet for the first time.

May: Nieuport Nighthawks were sent to Mesopotamia for service trials under tropical conditions.

7 May: The prototype Armstrong Whitworth Siskin III (J6583) was first flown. With a total of 62 ordered, the production Siskin became only the second newly-designed and built fighter to enter RAF service since the end of WW1.

June: The RAF Nursing Service became Princess Mary's RAF Nursing Service.

June: A prototype Gloster Grebe (J6969) single-seat fighter version of the Grouse, made its first flight and was demonstrated at the Hendon Air Pageant. It was immediately ordered into full production for the RAF, to replace (with the AW Siskin) the Sopwith Snipe.

20 June: An interim report of the committee, (Chairman, Marquis of Salisbury) set up to enquire into the question of National and Imperial Service, was published. The Prime Minister, acting on the committee's recommendations, advocated a Home Defence Force of 52 squadrons.

23 June: Flight Lieutenant W H Longton RAF won the first Grosvenor Challenge Cup for British aircraft, of under 150hp, flying a Sopwith Gnu.

August: After the unsuccessful Jaguar engined Hawker Woodcock I was rejected by the RAF, the redesigned Woodcock II prototype (J6988) powered by a Bristol Jupiter engine was flown. It went into limited production as a night fighter.

October: Gloster Grebe fighters entered service with a flight of No 111 Squadron at RAF Duxford. The Grebe replaced the Sopwith Snipe and was the first new RAF fighter since 1918.

October: The Handley Page W.8d/HP24 Hyderabad prototype (J6994) twin-engined night bomber made its first flight. After service trials at Martlesham Heath, it was ordered into production for the RAF.

2 October: The prototype de Havilland DH53 Humming Bird flew for the first time. The company's first light aircraft, it was designed and built as a small single-seater powered by a 750cc Douglas converted motorcycle engine. It was produced to compete in the Lympne Motor Glider Competitions, and two were used by the RAF for parasite experiments with the R-33 airship.

Specially commissioned for the Royal Air Force Benevolent Fund's 75th Anniversary, Anthony Cowland's Wisps of Silver *shows Sopwith Snipes of No 41 Squadron that re-formed at RAF Northolt on 1 April 1923 with a flight of these biplane fighters. The squadron is today equipped with SEPECAT Jaguar GR1As and based at RAF Coltishall, Norfolk.*

Wisps of Silver by Anthony R. G. Cowland GAvA

Trenchard's Short Service Commission Scheme came into being at the outset of 1924, with the Air Ministry calling for 400 officers. It was also in this year that the first positive steps were taken to advance the research and development side of the RAF with the setting up of the Aeroplane and Armament Experimental Establishment (A&AEE) at Martlesham Heath. Also introduced was the Marine Aircraft Experimental Establishment at Felixstowe, a base where all the flying-boat development work had started during WW1, and which was now officially recognised and expanded. It was to these two establishments that a new generation of aircraft, to replace the remaining veterans from WW1, was taken to be evaluated by specially trained RAF crews. As a consequence of the adoption of the Balfour Committee's recommendations, the Fleet Air Arm of the Royal Air Force was formed. Instead of returning to the original RNAS squadrons, now renumbered in the 200 series, the whole organisation was set up on the basis of Fleet Flights, numbered in the 400 series. These were principally based at Leuchars in Scotland, and Gosport in Hampshire. At first, there were six Fleet Fighter Flights with the Nieuport Nightjar and/or Fairey Flycatcher. The three Fleet Spotter Reconnaissance Flights were equipped with the Westland Walrus (basically a DH9A modified for naval operations) at Gosport. The flying boat flight at Leuchars had the Supermarine Seagull amphibian, together with two flights of Parnell Panther spotter aircraft. At Gosport, there were two torpedo bomber reconnaissance flights with the Blackburn Dart, and at Calshot seaplane base was the sole Flying Boat Flight, equipped with the Felixstowe F5.

The RAF's Iraq operations had been so successful that a similar policy was laid down for other areas where Britain had mandates for supervision. As a result a similar, but smaller, organisation was set up in Palestine in April 1924. In the Far East, the Air Ministry decided that an overland attack on Singapore was impossible and concluded that a sea defence force of fighters, army co-operation and sea reconnaissance aircraft, and torpedo bombers, backed by a battery of 6-inch guns, would provide a far cheaper and much more flexible defence. During this controversy, the Government suspended the Singapore defence scheme in the hope of encouraging general disarmament. This gesture produced no noticeable response and it was decided, three years later, to go ahead with the scheme, by building a battery of three 15-inch guns and leaving open the question of providing aircraft or further heavy guns.

Also in 1924, the Government adopted what was known as the 'ten year rule', indicating that there would be no major war for ten years. When any defence project was planned, the Treasury would ask whether it could be completed in ten years. No project could take longer than that and would not be authorised if it did. The rule considerably reduced and delayed Trenchard's expansion schemes for the re-equipment of the RAF, bringing development to almost a complete standstill.

---

3 January: The Air Ministry called for 400 officers required for flying duties for the Short Service Commission Scheme.

23 January: Lord Thompson became Secretary of State for Air.

29 January: The first production Fairey Fawn, J7182, made its maiden flight at Northolt. The Fawn had the distinction of being the first post-war light day bomber to enter RAF service. Seventy production Fawns were built.

20 March: The Aeroplane and Armament Experimental Establishment (A&AEE) was formed at RAF Martlesham Heath, Suffolk.

24 March: The first production Siskin III (J6981) made its maiden flight at Coventry.

25 March: A Vickers Vulture II took off from the Calshot seaplane base to attempt a round-the-world flight.

April: The list of squadrons equipped with Sopwith Snipes had grown to ten – Nos 3, 17, 19, 23, 25, 29, 32, 56 and 111 Squadrons based in Britain, and No 1 Squadron in Iraq.

1 April: The Fleet Air Arm of the RAF was formed, comprising RAF units normally embarked on HM aircraft carriers and fighting ships. The flights were allocated numbers in the 400 series: 401+ for Fleet fighters, 420+ for Fleet spotters, 440+ for Fleet reconnaissance and 460+ for Fleet torpedo bomber Flights.

1 April: Palestine Command was formed.

1 April: The Marine Aircraft Experimental Establishment was officially created at Felixstowe.

5 April: The second Vickers Virginia (J6857) entered flight test. After taking part in the programme, it was delivered to No 7 (Bomber) Squadron, at RAF Bircham Newton, for service trials.

20 April: The first flight of a Fairey IIID seaplane (N9634) took place in Singapore, operating from HMS *Pegasus*.

May: The Armstrong Whitworth Siskin III fighter entered service with No 41 Squadron at RAF Northolt.

June: Fairey Flycatchers equipped Nos 401, 403, 405 and 406 Flights, replacing all of the former carrier based catapult fighters in service on the aircraft carriers HMS *Argus*, *Courageous*, *Eagle*, *Furious*, *Glorious* and *Hermes*.

24 July: Six RAF squadrons were in action again on the North West Frontier of India at South Waziristan.

September: All RAF Fleet Fighter flights had been re-equipped with the Fairey Flycatcher.

October: The Gloster Grebe fighter entered service with No 25 Squadron at RAF Hawkinge.

3 October: The first flight of a Vickers Virginia, with Rolls-Royce Condor engines.

December: The Vickers Virginia bomber entered service with No 7 Squadron at RAF Bircham Newton and No 58 Squadron at RAF Worthy Down.

Bristol Fighters, painted here by Robin Smith, served as fighters from April 1917, and for Army Co-operation after World War 1. The type was operated at home until 1927 and the last unit overseas, No 6 Squadron, finally replaced them with Gordons in June 1932. An improved version, the Mk III, was first flown in 1924.

These pages generously donated by Courage Ltd

Bristol Fighters by Robin Smith GAvA

Trenchard's new look at the Home Defence line-up, which was now entitled Air Defence of Great Britain (ADGB), emerged in 1925. This had four divisions (the Bombing Area, Fighting Area, Special Reserve and Auxiliary Air Force). The last two arose from Trenchard's desire to exploit the potential of retired officers and airmen by creating the equivalent of a Territorial Army. Together with others of a high quality, these personnel took up military aviation as a weekend occupation. The Special Reserve Squadrons, of which there were at one time five, were approximately one-third regular personnel and two-thirds local volunteers. The Auxiliary Air Force comprised 16 squadrons, each having a small core of regulars, with the remainder being 'weekend airmen'. They were based at military airfields, adjoining areas of population, where they would find volunteers, and units were associated with the local county or city. The first to form was No 602 (Auxiliary) Squadron (City of Glasgow) which was inaugurated on 12 September 1925. By the end of the following month, three others had formed, two at RAF Northolt – No 600 (City of London) and No 601 (County of London) and one at Turnhouse – No 603 (City of Edinburgh).

Another of Trenchard's ideas came to fruition in 1925. He was constantly striving to attract the finest type of officer into the RAF for permanent commissions, despite intense competition from the older services. He set up, at selected universities, what were known as University Air Squadrons (UASs), with the aim of providing undergraduates with early training in flying and RAF topics and the opportunity of moving into the RAF as a career. Not only did these Air Squadrons provide good officers for the RAF, but they also played a prominent part in spreading 'air-mindedness' amongst one of the most important sectors of the nation. The first two University Air Squadrons were formed during 1925 at Oxford and Cambridge and by the late 1930s the scheme was to spread to many other universities.

---

3 January: The prototype Fairey Fox two-seat day bomber first flew. It so impressed Trenchard that he ordered sufficient aircraft for a complete squadron.

25 January: The Air Defence of Great Britain Command was formed, comprising Bombing Area, Fighting Area and Special Reserve and Auxiliary Air Force units of the RAF plus Army Anti-Aircraft Artillery, Searchlight and Listening Posts.

February: Powered by a Bristol Jupiter engine, the prototype Gloster Gamecock single-seat fighter (J7497) made its maiden flight.

22 February: The first of a long line of de Havilland Moths, the Cirrus Moth, was flown for the first time. This version and the re-engined Genet and Gipsy Moths were later used by the Central Flying School and other Flying Training Schools.

9 March: Aircraft from Nos 5, 20, 27 and 60 Squadrons re-commenced bombing attacks against rebels at Waziristan on the North West Frontier.

10 March: The first Supermarine Southampton flying boat (N9896) made its maiden flight at Calshot. The initial order for six aircraft was completed by October, when further production was initiated.

10 May: The prototype Armstrong Whitworth Atlas (J8675) army co-operation aircraft first flew. It was designed to replace the veteran Bristol Fighter in this role.

15 May: The first Special Reserve Unit, No 502 (Ulster) Squadron, was formed at Aldergrove, Northern Ireland.

July: The Hawker Woodcock II, the very first single-seat fighter to be produced by the Hawker Company, entered service with No 3 Squadron at RAF Upavon. The type was a replacement for the 1918-vintage Sopwith Snipe and a total of 62 was delivered to the RAF over a two-year period. It was powered by a 420hp Bristol Jupiter IV engine and had a maximum speed of 138mph. Its armament was twin Vickers guns.

18 July: The role of the RAF as an imperial sword of judgement was demonstrated (literally) when a low-flying Bristol F2B Fighter decapitated a Turkish cavalryman who was part of a unit trying to infiltrate British-controlled Iraq.

August: The Supermarine Southampton flying boat entered service with No 480 (Coastal Reconnaissance) Flight at RAF Calshot. It superseded the Felixstowe flying boats of 1918 vintage and became famous for long-distance formation flights. The RAF received 56 Southamptons during the period 1925–1933 and these served until 1936. Powered by two 520hp Napier Lion V engines, the Southampton had a top speed of 108mph, carried a crew of five and had three Lewis guns in the bows and amidships.

12 September: The first Auxiliary Air Force squadron was formed at Renfrew – No 602 (City of Glasgow).

1 October: The first University Air Squadron was formed at Cambridge. Oxford UAS followed on 11 October.

14 October: The first English Auxiliary Air Force squadrons formed at RAF Northolt; No 600 (City of London) and No 601 (County of London (Bomber)) Squadrons. By 25 October the first four Auxiliary Air Force squadrons were operating de Havilland DH9As and Avro 504K/Ns.

21 October: The first Armstrong Whitworth Siskin IIIA was flown at Coventry. Over 400 of the type were eventually delivered to the RAF.

22 October: No 1 Apprentices Wing was formed at RAF Halton.

27 October: Three DH9As made the first Cairo to Kano (Nigeria) flight, returning on 19 November.

29 October: The Observer Corps was formed.

December: No 99 Squadron at RAF Bircham Newton became the first RAF squadron to be equipped with the Handley Page Hyderabad, which was the last RAF heavy bomber in squadron service to be constructed of wood. A total of 38 was eventually delivered. It supplanted the large single-engined Aldershot bomber.

The popular air shows at RAF Hendon in the inter-war years produced many notable displays by RAF solo and formation performers. Kenneth McDonough's painting shows Gloster Grebe IIs of No 56 Squadron at this event. Today, the squadron operates Panavia Tornado F3s as the F3 Operational Conversion Unit at RAF Coningsby, Lincoln.

Gloster Grebe IIs of No 56 Squadron at the Hendon Air Tournament by Kenneth McDonough GAvA

Both the Geddes Committee (1921) and the Colwyn Committee (1925), which were tasked with making economies in Government spending and on defence on particular, received advice, which they did not accept, that the RAF should be carved up and the operation of aircraft returned to the Army and Navy. Such surgery, whatever its merits, would have been fatal to the RAF. In the Air Estimates for 1926, the RAF asked for £16 million. The Cabinet, acting under the influence of the Locarno talks, decided to delay completion of the recently approved air defence plan for 52 squadrons of fighters and bombers by up to five years. The RAF's record overseas was a major factor in securing its position. However, it was operating on a shoestring budget, with old aircraft against targets that could not fight back. In Iraq and Egypt and, subsequently, in Palestine and India, the RAF had developed a system of air control which proved more effective, and far less expensive in lives and material, than more traditional methods using ground forces.

On the basis of its performance overseas, Trenchard was able to argue convincingly that the RAF was a powerful money-saver. The theory was sound but the doctrine of air substitution made many enemies for the RAF. This was particularly so in India, where the Army kept the RAF on a 'very tight rein'. The Treaty of Locarno, signed in London in December 1925, bound the Western Powers to keep the peace and to unite against an aggressor. At the end of 1926, the RAF had about 720 front-line aircraft in 61 squadrons and two coastal reconnaissance flights. These squadrons included 25 for home defence (less than half of the planned number), nine in the Fleet Air Arm, and five Auxiliary squadrons.

January: The Vickers Victoria entered RAF service with No 216 Squadron in Egypt (and with No 70 Squadron in August). It was a replacement for the Vernon troop carrier and it bore the same relationship to the Virginia bomber as the Vernon transport had to the Vimy bomber. Total production, which ended in 1933, was 94. They remained in both squadrons until replaced by Valentias in 1936. Few Victorias operated in the UK but one was used by the CFS. With a crew of two and capacity for 22 troops, the final Mark VI version was powered by two Bristol Pegasus engines of 622hp and had a top speed of 130mph.

February: The Government once again stated that there would be no further consideration of separate air arms for the Army and Navy.

March: The Gloster Gamecock, the RAF's last biplane fighter of wooden construction, entered service with No 43 Squadron at RAF Henlow. Production for the RAF totalled 91 and the Gamecock remained in service until 1931, when it was replaced by the Bulldog. A 425hp Bristol Jupiter VI gave it a top speed of 155mph and armament was two Vickers guns.

1 March: The start of the first Cairo to Cape Town flight by four float-equipped Fairey IIIDs led by Wing Commander C W H Pulford. After returning to Cairo, they flew on to Lee-on-Solent, covering a total distance of 14,000 miles in a journey which ended on 21 June.

19 March: The prototype Fairey IIIF (a much improved development of the IIID) (N195) made its first flight. Production of the IIIF was to meet two basic requirements – as a two-seat general purpose type for RAF land-based squadrons and as a three-seat reconnaissance type for the Fleet Air Arm. By 1932, over 560 had been built.

17 June: The first emergency use of a parachute by an RAF pilot occurred when Pilot Officer E Pentland escaped from a doomed aircraft in an inverted spin.

26 June: It was announced in Parliament that the long established scheme for 52 RAF squadrons for home defence was 'to be created with as little delay as possible'.

August: The Fairey Fox two-seat day bomber entered service with No 12 Squadron at RAF Andover. It had a very clean aerodynamic form with a smooth pointed cowling. Not only was it 50mph faster than its predecessor, the Fairey Fawn, but it could overhaul any contemporary fighter. The Fox remained in service until replaced by the Hawker Hind in 1931. This brilliant period in the squadron's history is still commemorated by the fox emblem in its official crest. Because of the prevailing economic situation, only 28 Foxes were built. All went to No 12 Squadron.

September: The Armstrong Whitworth Siskin IIIA single-seat fighter entered service with No 111 Squadron at RAF Duxford. It featured a supercharged Armstrong Siddeley Jaguar IV of 450hp giving a maximum speed of 156mph. Eleven squadrons were eventually equipped with the type.

1 September: The crew of a DH9A bomber force landed with engine failure in Iraq and the two crew were taken as hostages.

16 September–29 September: Air Commodore C R Samson flew from Cairo to Aden and back in a Vickers Victoria troop carrier powered by two Napier Lion engines.

November: The Hawker Horsley two-seat day bomber entered RAF service with No 11 Squadron at RAF Netheravon. 112 Horsleys were built for the RAF, replacing Fairey Fawns with Nos 11 and 100 Squadrons, while the torpedo bomber version went to No 36 Squadron at RAF Donibristle in 1928. The all-metal Horsley became the first RAF land-based torpedo-armed aircraft to go overseas and was stationed in Singapore. Powered by a 665hp Rolls-Royce Condor IIIA, it had a top speed of 126mph and remained in service until 1934.

The Fairey Fox two-seat day-bomber entered service with No 12 Squadron at RAF Andover in June 1926. The only squadron to be equipped with this revolutionary aircraft, No 12 retains the fox emblem as its badge in 1993, displaying it on the engine intakes of Buccaneer S2Bs operated from RAF Lossiemouth. Eric Day's painting is reproduced by kind permission of the PMC, Officer's Mess, RAF Northolt.

Fairey Fox of No 12 Squadron by Eric Day

1927

The RAF took over responsibility for organising the British team for the Schneider Trophy Air Race following the disasters of the 1925 race at Baltimore. The Air Ministry felt that too much national prestige was at stake for it to be left in the hands of 'amateurs' with little technical, logistic and financial backing. Specifications were issued in 1926 for three specially developed racing amphibians from Supermarine, Shorts and Gloster Aircraft, while the RAF established a High Speed Flight at Felixstowe to train the crews. The three British entrants at Venice in September 1927 were two Supermarine S5s and the Gloster IVB. Unfortunately, the Short Crusader crashed soon after arriving in Italy. The race was a triumph for the RAF team, although the Gloster IVB had to retire before the finish along with all the Italian entrants. Flight Lieutenant S N Webster won in the S5 with a geared Napier Lion engine at 281.65mph from Flight Lieutenant O E Worsley in the ungeared aircraft at 273.07mph. Webster went on to take the 100 km (62.1 mile) closed-circuit record at 283.66mph.

Four metal-hulled Supermarine Southamptons of the Far East Flight based at Felixstowe, left Plymouth in October to fly to the Far East. Their course took them through Italy, Greece, Crete, Egypt, Iraq, India, Ceylon, Burma, Malaya, the Dutch East Indies, Australia, Borneo, The Philippines and Hong Kong. More than 27,000 miles were covered over the next fifteen months without major mishap, despite flying with minimal or no radio facilities and often without accurate maps. The RAF's historic flight proved to be another successful public relations coup for Trenchard in his continuing battle to stave off the aspirations of the Army and Royal Navy, both of which were still aiming to regain control of what they saw as their aircraft.

Trenchard now had a clear way forward for the RAF, provided that he could successfully counter the bitter opposition of the other two Services. Despite not being particularly articulate, he still managed to carry conviction with the Ministers of the day.

1 January: Lord Trenchard became the first Marshal of the Royal Air Force.
March: The RAF's first all-metal fighter, the Armstrong Whitworth Siskin IIIA, entered service with No 41 Squadron at RAF Northolt. Eleven squadrons, totalling some 400 aircraft, were eventually equipped with the Siskin, which served until October 1932. Powered by a 450hp Armstrong Siddeley Jaguar IV engine, the Siskin had a top speed of 156mph and was armed with twin synchronised Vickers guns.
7 March: The prototype Westland Wapiti (J8495) flew at Yeovil. It was intended as a replacement for the DH9A.
30 March–22 May: A Flight of No 47 (Bomber) Squadron of Fairey IIIFs with Napier Lion engines, commanded by Air Commodore C R Samson, flew from Cairo to Cape Town and back.
April: Headquarters RAF China formed at Hong Kong. Equipment comprised of No 2 Squadron with Bristol Fighters as the Shanghai Defence Force.
April: A High Speed Flight was formed at Felixstowe to provide aircraft and crews for the Schneider Trophy contests.
17 May: The first prototype Bristol Type 105 Bulldog, built as a private venture and powered by a Bristol Jupiter engine, made its maiden flight at Filton.

20–22 May: A distance record was set by the RAF when Flight Lieutenants C R Carr and L E M Cillman flew from RAF Cranwell to the Persian Gulf, covering a distance of 3,420 miles in 34 hr 45 min in a modified Hawker Horsley.
7 June: The first of three Supermarine S5s (N219), designed by R J Mitchell for the British entry in the Schneider Trophy Air Race, was flown by Flight Lieutenant O E Worsley of the RAF's High Speed Flight at Felixstowe.
25–29 July: The new Air Defence of Great Britain (ADGB) group held its first annual tactical air defence exercise. Staged at Andover, it produced an embarrassing result for the defenders. Thanks to an American Curtiss D-12 engine, the new Fairey Fox bomber flew 50mph faster than any interceptor aircraft.
August: The Bristol Fighter was withdrawn from Home Stations and was superseded by the Armstrong Whitworth Atlas. Overseas, they were supplanted in 1932.
12 August: A mixed flight of flying boats, comprising the Blackburn Iris II, Saunders-Roe Valkyrie and Short Singapore prototypes, plus a Supermarine Southampton, started a Baltic cruise of 9,400 miles.
26 September: Three RAF pilots competed in the Schneider Trophy Air Race at Venice, Italy, flying the Gloster IVB (N223) and two Supermarine S5s (N219 and N220). The race was won by Flight Lieutenant S N Webster in S5 N220 which

was powered by a geared Napier Lion engine.
17 October: The RAF established the Far East Flight – Group Captain H M Cave-Brown-Cave led four Southampton flying boats from Plymouth on a 27,000-mile Empire air route survey via Egypt, India, Australia and Japan before setting up a base at Singapore. It was designated as No 205 Squadron in the following February.
October: The Armstrong Whitworth Atlas two-seat biplane army co-operation aircraft entered service with No 26 Squadron at RAF Catterick. 478 Atlases were built for the RAF between 1927 and 1933, some remaining in service in this role and as trainers until 1935. Fitted with a 400hp Jaguar IVC engine, the Mark I had a maximum speed of 142mph and served with six RAF Army Co-operation squadrons.
November: The Air Ministry ordered a prototype Bristol Bulldog II to be evaluated for the Specification F.9/26 competition for a new single-seat fighter.

Alan Fearnley's painting illustrates the famous 'cruise' by four Supermarine Southampton Is (S1149–S1152) of the RAF Far East Flight that left England on 14 October 1927 to fly to Singapore and on to Hong Kong. It is reproduced by kind permission of the Royal Air Force Club.

These pages generously donated by Ernst & Young

Supermarine Southampton Is of the RAF Far East Flight by Alan Fearnley

During Trenchard's decade (1918–28) as Chief of the Air Staff he set up the RAF College at Cranwell and a Staff College for senior officers at Andover. He also established the idea of the short service commission, which saw young officers train as pilots or aircrew, serve for five years, and then be released into the Reserve. This avoided clogging the ranks with officers who wanted only to fly and had little interest in the force as a profession. He also set up the Auxiliary Air Force, the RAF's equivalent of the Territorial Army. By the late 1920s, the number of established squadrons had more than doubled to 54, 18 of them for home defence and the rest scattered around the world. Government plans envisaged 52 squadrons for home defence by the late 1920s, but economic problems prevented this.

Following the attacks by Yemeni irregulars into the Aden Protectorate and the inter-tribal conflict, the British government followed the pattern set in Iraq, when it assigned overall military command to the Royal Air Force. A detachment of armoured cars was despatched from Baghdad to become D Flight of No 8 Squadron. Together with a force of local troops, the Aden Protectorate Levies, this provided adequate ground support for the DH9As of No 8 Squadron to deal effectively with the troubles within six months.

Military aircraft in the late 1920s were more or less standardised. The classic fighter was a biplane, with either a radial or an in-line engine developing around 450hp. Engines of nearly double this horse-power were available which would have given increased speed had not the weight penalty been too great. It had a fixed undercarriage and open cockpit and carried two rifle-calibre machine guns. Aircraft performance steadily improved despite limited financial resources. The single-engined biplane fighter's top speed was between 150 and 200mph and it had a range of around 240 miles, but even the fastest light bombers were also achieving this. By 1928, the supercharger (a compressor which forced air into the carburettor, allowing the maximum power to be developed at high altitudes) had been developed. One of the first fighters to feature a supercharged engine was the Siskin IIIA, which attained 186mph at 15,000ft but only 156mph at sea level.

January: The Fairey IIIF two-seat general purpose aircraft entered service with No 47 Squadron at Khartoum, this squadron carrying out the Cairo-Cape flights of 1928 and 1929. At home, the IIIF was used as a day-bomber, going first to No 207 Squadron at RAF Eastchurch to replace DH9As. Powered by a 570hp Napier Lion XIA engine, it had a maximum speed of 120mph. A 500lb bomb could be carried, other armament being one Vickers gun and one Lewis gun.

January: Gloster Gamecocks replaced the last Woodcocks in RAF service at Upavon, with No 17 Squadron in January and No 3 Squadron by August.

1 January: The official opening of RAF Upper Heyford. In the years up to WW2, it was the home of many well-known bomber squadrons, including No 99. This was the first unit to fly the Handley Page night bomber which was named Heyford in the station's honour.

February: The defence of Aden and surrounding territory was made the responsibility of the RAF which formed the Aden Command specifically for this task.

21 February: No 8 Squadron flying de Havilland DH9As commenced air operations against recalcitrant tribesmen in the Aden Protectorate.

March: The Boulton and Paul Sidestrand bomber entered service with No 101 Squadron at RAF Bircham Newton. All 18 production Sidestrands had the servo-type rudder which was such a notable feature of the marque. No 101 Squadron operated Sidestrands until they were exchanged for Overstrands in 1935. With two 460hp Bristol Jupiter VIIIFs, it had a top speed of 140mph. It featured three Lewis guns – in the nose, mid-upper and ventral positions, and a bomb load of 1,050lb.

April: The RAF in India was reorganised into three Wings, each with two squadrons; in addition, two squadrons reported directly to the Air Headquarters.

June: Two Wapitis were introduced to fly VIP and Royal passengers from RAF Northolt. This unit later became the Royal Flight based at RAF Hendon.

June: The first prototype Hawker Hart (J9052) was flown by George Bulman at Brooklands.

28 September: The start of a 9,900-mile flight from Felixstowe to Karachi and back by a three-engined Blackburn Iris flying boat to enable the Secretary of State for Air and Director of Equipment to inspect RAF units in Malta, Egypt and Iraq. The aircraft returned to Felixstowe in November.

October: The Westland Wapiti two-seat general purpose biplane entered service with No 84 Squadron at Shaibah, Iraq. It was designed as a replacement for the long-lived DH9A, incorporating as many DH9A parts as possible. Overseas, the Wapiti was used for army co-operation, bombing and reconnaissance. Powered by a Bristol Jupiter (three versions developing between 480 and 500hp were used), it had a maximum speed of 135mph.

November: The first Hawker Tomtit all-metal, two-seat trainer was flown at Brooklands. It was designed around the 150hp Armstrong Siddeley Mongoose IIC engine as a possible replacement for the veteran Avro 504N.

23 December: The evacuation of Kabul, in which 586 civilians were airlifted from the British Legation in Afghanistan, commenced. Victoria troop-carriers of No 70 Squadron flew 28,160 miles over mountainous regions in severe weather, during the rescue operation which lasted until 25 February 1929.

Gloster Gamecocks were the last all-wooden construction biplanes to serve with the RAF. They entered service in 1926 and the aircraft in Gerald Coulson's painting joined No 17 Squadron at RAF Upavon in January 1928. Today, this squadron is a No 2 Group Panavia Tornado GR1 unit based at RAF Brüggen, Germany.

These pages generously donated by No 17 (F) Squadron

Gloster Gamecock of No 17 (F) Squadron by Gerald Coulson GAvA

Financial stringency ran through the 1920s and continued into the 1930s. Its intensity became even greater as the economic depression began to take hold in 1929. The argument was – 'no enemy in sight, money as always tight – so run the RAF on a lean budget and be ready to expand if, and when, real danger arrives'. Britain was the leader and centre of a huge Empire with responsibility for its defence – but it was being done on the cheap. For ten years, Trenchard tried to create a cohesive air force with the highest standards of training and performance, but the weaknesses arising from financial restrictions increasingly became apparent. The RAF's basic equipment when Trenchard left the post of CAS in 1929 was not so very different in performance from that of ten years earlier.

In 1929, the RAF's bomber squadrons had the Hyderabad, Virginia, Victoria, Fairey IIIF, Wapiti, DH9A and Horsley, while fighter squadrons flew Siskins and Gamecocks. Army co-operation units soldiered on with the Bristol Fighter. For a force dedicated to the offensive, the quality of its weapons was poor, being mostly of Great War pattern.

Worse still was the failure to develop the science of navigation, which, in 1929, remained very rudimentary. Defensive weaponry was no better - the fighter's guns were still of WW1 design. Trenchard's doctrine had been to put the maximum effort into offensive operations overseas to mollify the politicians and to provide a cheaper alternative to use of the Army or Navy. When Trenchard stood down in 1929, no single RAF fighter squadron was based overseas, where the service was consistently in action.

The rebellion in Afghanistan continued into 1929 and the Vickers Victorias of No 70 Squadron evacuated British and other foreign nationals out of Kabul in very poor weather conditions. This, the first major airlift in history, carried nearly 600 civilian passengers and over 24,000lb of luggage, all achieved with a handful of the twin-engined 22-seat biplanes. No 8 Squadron in Aden was re-equipped with Fairey IIIFs in January and for the first three months of 1929 was again in action against dissidents. Effectively settling the problem, the squadron spent the rest of the year on more peaceful duties in the Protectorate.

1 January: Control of the Observer Corps was transferred from the War Office (Army) to the Air Ministry (RAF).

February: The Avro Avocet (N210) underwent trials at RAF Martlesham Heath. Floats were fitted for delivery to the RAF High Speed Flight at Calshot to provide seaplane experience for Schneider Trophy Air Race pilots.

25 February: The last of 84 evacuation flights from Kabul was flown by RAF Vickers Victorias.

March: The Fairey IIIFs of No 8 Squadron were again in action against tribesmen in Aden.

24–26 April: Two RAF officers flew a Fairey Long-Range Monoplane non-stop from RAF Cranwell, Lincs to Karachi, a distance of 4,130 miles, in 50hr 48min.

26 April: The foundation stone was laid for the new permanent RAF College at Cranwell.

May: The Bristol Bulldog single-seat day and night fighter entered service with No 3 Squadron at RAF Upavon. Designed in competition with four other contenders, the Bulldog was chosen as the replacement for Siskins and Gamecocks in RAF fighter squadrons. Eventually equipping nine squadrons, the Bulldog remained the most widely used RAF fighter until 1936. The type was a popular performer at Hendon displays when Nos 3, 19 and 54 Squadrons featured coloured smoke trail formation aerobatics.

Powered by a 440hp Bristol Jupiter VIIF with a maximum speed of 174mph, 301 Bulldogs were supplied to the RAF.

July: The last Gloster Grebes in service with No 25 Squadron were finally superseded by the Siskin.

August: The Westland Wapiti entered service with No 600 Squadron Auxiliary Air Force at RAF Hendon.

7 September: The RAF High Speed Flight won the Schneider Trophy contest for the second successive time. The winning Supermarine S6 was flown by Flying Officer H R D Waghorn at a speed of 328.63mph.

7 September: Flight Lieutenant R L R Atcherley established new 50km and 100km closed-circuit records of 332mph and 331.32mph in a Supermarine S6 at Calshot.

12 September: A world speed record of 357.75mph was set by an RAF High Speed Flight Supermarine S6 flown by Squadron Leader A H Orlebar at Calshot.

October: The Handley Page Hinaidi entered service with No 99 Squadron at RAF Upper Heyford. A development of the earlier Hyderabad, this biplane heavy night bomber had a crew of four and was of metal construction. Two 440hp Bristol Jupiter VIII engines gave it a top speed of 122mph. The bomb load was 1,448lb and it was armed with three Lewis guns. The Hinaidi remained in service with No 99 Squadron until November 1933.

2 October: The 722ft long, diesel-powered Airship R101, built under state management, was unveiled at RAF Cardington, Bedfordshire.

21 November: The prototype Blackburn Iris III three-engined flying boat (N238) was flown for the first time.

5 December: The Armstrong Whitworth Starling II (J8028) made its maiden flight, powered by the new 525hp Armstrong Siddeley Panther II engine.

16 December: Two RAF officers were killed when their Fairey Long-Range monoplane (J9479) crashed in Tunisia during an attempt to set a new long-range record for a straight-line flight.

31 December: Marshal of the Royal Air Force Lord Trenchard withdrew from active duty with the RAF, having been Chief of the Air Staff for 11 years.

The Westland Wapiti IIA was used extensively for Army Co-operation on the North-West Frontier of India. It equipped Nos 11 and 39 Squadrons at Risalpur during 1929 and No 60 Squadron, illustrated here in Wilfred Hardy's painting, in the following year. This squadron continued to operate Wapitis until August 1939 by which time they had been replaced by Blenheims. Now based at RAF Benson, No 60 Squadron operates Westland Wessex HC2s in support of the Army.

These pages generously donated by Sixty Squadron

Westland Wapiti IIAs of No 60 Squadron by Wilfred Hardy

Throughout the 1920s and 1930s, the RAF was often referred to as 'the finest private flying club in the world', and that nickname was not entirely facetious. RAF light bombers, with a load of up to 550lb, followed single-seat fighter design and performance closely, the fastest in 1930 being the Hawker Hart with a speed of 184mph at 5,000ft. The principal obstacle to the advancement of the RAF's aircraft was the old rule, first established before WW1, that monoplanes were structurally dangerous and were therefore not to be procured for His Majesty's airmen. This meant that until the early 1930s almost all RAF aircraft were biplanes. Fortunately, most British aircraft companies of the period were privately owned and were pursuing other lines of aeronautical development. The RAF had flirted with the idea of transport aircraft in the shape of the Vickers Victoria, which was used as a troop carrier and for other tasks. Victorias received considerable praise at the time of the evacuation of the British Commission from Kabul in 1929, but these aircraft were gradually retired and not replaced. The failure to develop a modern transport was in part caused by Trenchard's policy, which required that the RAF should not invest in activity which could be used as an auxiliary service by the Army and Royal Navy. In fact, the Air Ministry, because of financial constraints, issued no new specification for a transport aircraft after 1920.

By 1930, Britain's economy was in dire straits and the defence estimates suffered further cuts. The Government believed that the planned disarmament conference would bring about a substantial measure of general disarmament and was thus prepared to see our forces wither away. It was also hoped that all forms of air bombardment would be outlawed – but contradicted this desire by permitting the use of light bombing in undeveloped countries. In consequence, the success of air control in Iraq and Jordan led to its extension to the Aden Protectorate, where it was equally successful. An attempt was also made to apply it to the North-West Frontier of India. However, the Army with its system of punitive columns, was too well established. Most of the experienced civil administrators were in favour of air control but the Army would have none of it. The role of the RAF in India was thus generally limited to the close support of columns of troops.

---

1 January: RAF Far East Command was formed.

1 January: Air Chief Marshal Sir John Salmond was appointed Chief of the Air Staff in succession to Lord Trenchard.

1 January: The Blackburn Iris biplane general reconnaissance flying boat entered service with No 209 Squadron at RAF Mount Batten, Plymouth. Of all-metal construction, it carried a crew of five, had three 675hp Rolls-Royce Condor IIIB engines and a maximum speed of 118mph. During its period of service from 1930 to 1934, the Iris was the largest aircraft in the RAF.

16 January: A patent for a new kind of aircraft engine was filed by a junior RAF officer – Flying Officer Frank Whittle, a flying instructor. He had been unable to arouse any interest by the RAF, the Air Ministry or the aircraft industry.

February: The Hawker Hart biplane day-bomber entered service with No 33 Squadron at RAF Eastchurch. It proved to be one of the most adaptable biplanes ever to enter service with the RAF and 415 were received. Powered by a 525hp Rolls-Royce Kestrel IB engine which gave it a maximum speed of 184mph, the Hart was faster than the contemporary fighters

then in service. It equipped seven home-based squadrons and remained in front-line service until 1938.

March: A total of 23 Bristol Bulldogs was delivered to No 54 Squadron at RAF Hornchurch and No 32 Squadron at RAF Kenley.

11 April: A survey of the Cairo–Cape Town route was completed by the RAF and Imperial Airways.

12 June: First flight of the Handley Page HP38 (J9130) prototype, later named the Heyford. This was the last bomber of biplane configuration to serve with the RAF.

28 June: The Avro 621 Tutor was shown in the New Types Park at the RAF Hendon Display. An initial batch was ordered by the Air Ministry under Specification T.3/30 for trials with No 3 Flying Training School.

July: The Handley Page Clive II (originally named the Chitral) 23-seat troop carrier version of the Hinaidi bomber entered service with the Heavy Transport Flight at Lahore, India.

29 July: The Airship R100, with a crew of 44, departed on a flight from RAF Cardington to Canada, where it arrived on 1 August. It returned to Britain during 13-16 August.

24 September: Built to Air Ministry Specification R.18/29, the Short Rangoon prototype (S1433) made its maiden flight. This was a military version of the Short Calcutta flying boat.

5 October: Airship R101 crashed near Beauvais, France en route to India, killing the Air Minister Lord Thompson and other VIPs. There were six survivors from 54 on board. This disaster ended the RAF's use of airships.

19 October: A flight of Fairey IIIDs of No 47 (B) Squadron flew from Khartoum in the Sudan to West Africa.

25 November: The prototype Fairey Hendon monoplane bomber (K1695) made its first flight at Harmondsworth. However, the first example did not enter RAF service until 1936.

Only four Blackburn Iris III flying boats entered service with the RAF, equipping No 209 Squadron at RAF Mount Batten, Plymouth from January 1930. Illustrated here by Fred Groves, the Iris was the largest aircraft flown by the RAF at the time, being used for general reconnaissance. The squadron made famous flights to Iceland and Gibraltar in July–August 1930.

These pages generously donated by Provident Mutual

Blackburn Iris IIIs of No 209 Squadron by Fred Groves

The prestigious Schneider Trophy, for which the RAF had competed successfully in 1927 and 1929, was won outright for Britain by the High Speed Flight in 1931. The winning aircraft was the Rolls-Royce powered Supermarine S6B. As with earlier contenders from Supermarine, it was designed by R J Mitchell. This advanced aircraft, which later established a record speed of 407.5mph, was the forerunner of the Supermarine Spitfire, which was also designed by Mitchell. The S6B also influenced the ideas of Sydney Camm, who conceived the contemporary Hawker Hurricane. The outright Schneider Trophy win enabled Rolls-Royce to develop a twelve-cylinder liquid cooled in-line aero-engine which developed 1,000hp. This was capable of further extensive development without major re-design and the resulting Rolls-Royce Merlin was produced in greater numbers than any other aircraft powerplant during the war years. The Schneider Trophy races, the 'Blue Riband' of air racing, made many contributions to the development of British aviation, notably in aerodynamics, aero-engines, fuels and, to some extent, propellers. The races also helped to keep aviation in the public eye at a time when there was very little money for aeronautical developments in general. However, had it not been for the generous financial support from Lady Houston, development of the S6B by Supermarine would not have been completed.

Success in overseas operations had finally secured the RAF's future as an independent air arm. At the same time, it had unfortunate consequences in other respects. The kind of aircraft needed for such work had excellent reliability, good range and could carry fairly small but varied bomb loads and other armament. They were multi-purpose aircraft, which fitted in with the government's demand for machines with long service lives, capable of enhancing their cost effectiveness by undertaking a variety of roles. Therefore, the RAF had a number of general purpose aircraft such as the Wapiti and Audax which were suitable for policing overseas, where there was no real opposition, but which were totally inadequate for aerial combat in European skies. There was a general feeling in the early 1930s that only a few first-class specialised fighters and bombers needed to be built, mainly to keep up design and production facilities – and to provide experience of high performance flight and aircraft.

March: The Hawker 'Demon' entered service with No 23 Squadron at RAF Kenley. The high performance of the Hart bomber led to the introduction of a Hart Fighter variant, thus reviving a two-seat fighter in the RAF, a class which had been absent since WW1. A 584hp Rolls-Royce Kestrel V engine was fitted which gave a maximum speed of 182mph. Two Vickers guns were fitted forward and one Lewis gun aft. Total output of Demons for the RAF was 234 and the type remained in service until 1939.

March: The first Hawker Fury (K1926) made its maiden flight at Brooklands.

3 March: Modified from a Fairey IIIF, the prototype Gordon (K1697) was flown for the first time at Harmondsworth.

April: The Short Rangoon entered service with No 203 Squadron at Basrah, the only RAF flying-boat unit in Iraq. A general reconnaissance flying boat with an all-metal hull, the Rangoon featured three 540hp Bristol Jupiter XIF engines. Only six Rangoons were built for the RAF and they served until mid-1936, when replaced by Singapores.

April: The office of Provost Marshal RAF and Chief of Air Force Police was approved by King George V.

April: The Fairey Gordon two-seat day-bomber and general purpose biplane entered service with No 40 Squadron at RAF Upper Heyford. Powered by a 525hp Armstrong Siddeley Panther IIA, the Gordon had a maximum speed of 145mph.

May: No 43 Squadron at RAF Tangmere received its first Hawker Fury Is. Designed by Sir Sydney Camm, it was powered by a 525hp Rolls-Royce Kestrel II liquid-cooled engine and armed with two synchronised machine guns. It was also the first RAF fighter in squadron service to exceed 200mph.

22 June: The pre-production Hawker Hart Fighter (re-named the Demon in 1932) made its maiden flight.

July: The final squadron to operate the Gamecock, No 23 at RAF Kenley, relinquished the type in favour of the Bristol Bulldog.

September: The first RAF instrument flying training course was established as 'E' Flight at the CFS, RAF Wittering with six Avro 504Ns.

12 September: The RAF High Speed Flight won the Schneider Trophy outright. Flight Lieutenant J N Boothman achieved 340.08mph in the Supermarine S6B and broke the 100km closed-circuit record at 342.87mph.

20 September: The prototype Hawker Nimrod naval fighter made its maiden flight. The first production Nimrod (S1577) was flown on 14 October.

29 September: Flight Lieutenant G H Stainforth of the High Speed Flight established a new World speed record at 407.5mph in the Supermarine S6B at Lee-on-Solent.

26 October: The prototype de Havilland DH82A Tiger Moth was flown for the first time. It was ordered by the RAF to meet Specification T.23/31 for an elementary trainer.

27–28 October: A non-stop flight from RAF Cranwell to Abu Sueir, Egypt, in an RAF Fairey Long-Range Monoplane with a Napier Lion engine, was made by Squadron Leader O R Gayford and Flight Lieutenant D L G Bett.

29 December: The first production Hawker Audax (K1995) army co-operation biplane built to Specification 7/31 made its maiden flight.

On 12 September 1931 at Spithead ,Flight Lieutenant J. N. Boothman, RAF flew a Supermarine S6B seaplane powered by a Rolls-Royce 'R' engine to win the Schneider Trophy outright. On 29 September 'Supermarine's Speed Machine', shown in Charles Thompson's painting, gained the World Air Speed Record at 407.5mph. S1595 and the Schneider Trophy are exhibited in the Science Museum, South Kensington. The painting is reproduced by kind permission of Mr Geoffrey Howard.

These pages generously donated by Rolls-Royce plc

Supermarine's Speed Machine by Charles J Thompson GAvA, ASAA, GMA

The League of Nations met in 1932 to study the drafting of an agreement to limit armaments. Discussions continued until 1934 but effectively fell into disarray when the developing situation in Germany rendered the exercise useless. Above all, the impossible objective of trying to define legitimate military targets precluded the working out of any practicable disarmament formula. A proposal to limit the unladen all-up weight of military aircraft to 3,000lb would have ruled out everything but the ultra-light short-range bomber, capable only of tactical support. In 1932, Britain stopped its tiny re-armament effort and it was not resumed until 1934. In November, Sir John Simon advocated the abolition of all military aircraft and the prohibition of bombing from the air, but the proposal came to nothing. During October, Prime Minister Baldwin told the House of Commons: "I think it is well also for the man in the street to realise that there is no power on earth that can prevent him from being bombed. Whatever people may tell him, the bomber will always get through. The only defence is offense, which means you have to kill more women and children more quickly than the enemy if you want to save yourself." Baldwin was expressing the standard Air Staff doctrine of the time – based largely on the views of Trenchard.

Fortunately, British aircraft and engine companies continued with independently funded projects. Hawker and Supermarine set about building what they believed to be the fighter aircraft that would be needed by the RAF. At the same time, Rolls-Royce was developing a private venture engine. Building on the success of the Kestrel (and learning from the mistakes of the steam-cooled Goshawk), they produced the Merlin, which was adopted for both the Spitfire and Hurricane prototypes.

The general deterioration in the Far East began with the Japanese invasion of China, threatening the international port and settlement at Shanghai, and all of the Pacific region where European interests were established. This was followed by Hitler's rise to power in Germany and the systematic demolition of the Versailles Treaty. After the break-up of the Disarmament Conference, the League of Nations itself began to disintegrate, and the Government then faced an alarming situation. At the end of twelve years of parsimony, with little money for anything but air control in the overseas protectorates, the RAF was hopelessly ill-equipped for a major war. In 1934, the ban on the development of bomber aircraft was lifted at last and a specification was issued for a twin-engined long-range bomber, which culminated in production contracts for the Whitley, Hampden and Wellington. In 1932, Germany left the Disarmament Conference and openly declared the intention of building up an air force. The prospective rebuilding of the Luftwaffe provoked considerable alarm in Britain.

January: The Armament and Gunnery School at RAF Eastchurch became the Air Armament School. It operated Wapitis, Fairey IIIFs and Bulldogs.

February: The DH82A Tiger Moth became the standard *ab initio* trainer in the RAF, first entering service at the Central Flying School. Over 1,000 were delivered by the outbreak of WW2. It first appeared at the Hendon display in 1932 when it gave an exhibition of inverted flying. Powered by a 130hp DH Gipsy Major, the Tiger Moth had a maximum speed of 109mph.

February: The Hawker Audax two-seat Army Co-operation biplane entered service with No 4 Squadron at RAF Farnborough. Developed from the Hart, the Audax had a message-collection hook. Built as a replacement for the Atlas, some 650 were supplied to the RAF and it remained in service with home-based squadrons until replaced by the Hector. The Audax was also used in the mid 1930s as an advanced trainer with the Flying Training Schools. Powered by a 520hp Rolls-Royce Kestrel X de-rated engine, the Audax's top speed was 170mph.

23 March: The Cabinet decided that the 'Ten Year Rule', which had been such a barrier to technical advancement by the RAF, should be abolished.

April: Sea trials with Hawker Nimrod S1577 on HMS *Eagle*. After service clearance, six Nimrods joined No 402 Flight FAA.

25–26 April: Vickers Victoria aircraft in Iraq used 'sky-shouting' equipment to warn tribesmen of Sheikh Ahmad that village in the Barzan district would be bombed.

25 April: RAF aircraft went into action in support of Iraqi forces operating against Kurdish rebels.

May: The two-seat dual-control advanced trainer variant of the Bristol Bulldog, known as the TM, entered service after evaluation by the Central Flying School. It featured a redesigned tail unit and increased sweepback on the upper wing. The Bulldog TM served with five flying training schools, until 1935.

September: Specification B.9/32 was drawn up for a medium bomber able to deliver 2.5 tons of bombs.

October: The final squadron to be equipped with the Bristol Bulldog, No 56 Squadron, replaced its Siskin IIIAs at RAF North Weald.

November: The two-seat Vickers Vildebeest torpedo bomber entered RAF service, with No 100 Squadron at RAF Donibristle; 151 Mk I to III, with 660hp Bristol Pegasus IIM3 engines, were delivered. Designed as a replacement for the Horsley, the Vildebeest served as the RAF's only torpedo bomber until the arrival of the Bristol Beaufort after the start of WW2.

The Hawker Hart, shown here in Eric Day's painting over the Royal Air Force College Cranwell, was a two-seat light day-bomber that entered service in 1930. By 1932 it had equipped seven home-based squadrons and in the following year was issued to Auxiliary Air Force squadrons. This painting is reproduced by kind permission of The Commandant, Royal Air Force College, Cranwell.

These pages generously donated by The Royal Air Force College, Cranwell

Hawker Hart over the Royal Air Force College Cranwell by Eric Day

In March 1933, in a desperate attempt to save the League of Nations, the British delegation proposed that a permanent disarmament conference should be established to work out a scheme for the abolition of military aviation and the international control of civil aviation. A numerical limit was set for military aircraft in participating states. Tentatively, the upper limit was envisaged as 500 aircraft for the major powers, but no mention was made of Germany – and Germany would have none of it. It was Britain and Germany which dispensed with the first generation of monoplane fighters. Both preferred to progress from biplanes with metal-framed fabric-covered structures, to retractable undercarriage monoplane fighters with all-metal monocoque fuselages (in which the skin forms part of the load bearing structures) and enclosed cockpits. The first two British fighters of this kind to be ordered by the RAF were the Spitfire and Hurricane.

Great strides were being made in the field of aircraft armament as well. The Armament Research Division of the Air Ministry was working to arrange the adaptation of the successful 0.3in machine gun for application to RAF aircraft. This eventually emerged in 1933 as the Browning 0.303in machine gun.

On the eve of the expansion programme, the RAF's Order of Battle was still constituted in the same formal areas as in the 1920s. Principal operational control came under the umbrella of the ADGB organisation. It comprised the Western Area with heavy bomber squadrons, all eight of them (of which three were special reserve squadrons) equipped with Vickers Virginias – except for Nos 10 and 99 Squadrons which had just converted to the new Handley Page Heyford; the Central Area with eleven squadrons of single-engined bombers (Hawker Harts, Westland Wallaces and Fairey Gordons) plus No 10 Squadron with the Boulton & Paul Sidestrand medium bomber; the Fighting Area with 14 single-engined fighter squadrons (Bristol Bulldogs, Hawker Demons, Hawker Furies and No 19 Squadron, which was the first with the Gloster Gauntlet); No 1 Air Defence Group covering the Auxiliary Air Force (seven bomber squadrons with Harts and Wapitis plus one fighter squadron with Demons). Inland Area included No 22 Group (five Army Co-operation squadrons with Hawker Audaxes) and No 23 Group which administered the flying training schools. Coastal Area looked after one torpedo-bombing squadron and four flying-boat squadrons, of which No 210 was just re-equipping with the Short Singapore four-engined flying boat.

The Fleet Air Arm was operating five carriers at this time – HMS *Courageous*, *Glorious*, *Eagle*, *Furious* and *Hermes*.

January: The Coastal Defence Training Flight was formed at Gosport with Fairey IIIFs.

January: The Westland Wallace entered service with No 501 (City of Bristol) Squadron at Filton. A Special Reserve unit formed in 1929, it subsequently became No 501 (County of Gloucester) Squadron of the Auxiliary Air Force. The Wallace, with a Bristol Pegasus engine, had been developed from the Wapiti.

January: Four Westland Wapitis of No 28 Squadron flew 6,200 miles from Ambala to Singapore and return. Wapiti J9095 was specially fitted out for the personal use of His Royal Highness the Prince of Wales.

6–8 February: Squadron Leader O R Gayford and Flight Lieutenant G E Nicholetts made the first non-stop flight from Cranwell to Walvis Bay, South Africa in 52hr 25min in a Fairey Long-Range Monoplane.

March: The Avro 504K was finally declared obsolete.

March: First flight of the Miles M2 Hawk which was eventually developed into the Magister trainer for the RAF.

April: No 23 Squadron at RAF Biggin Hill converted from the Bristol Bulldog to the Hawker Demon.

3 April: Two Westland Wallace aircraft, flown by Flight Lieutenant D F McIntyre and Squadron Leader The Marquis of Douglas and Clydesdale, made the first flight over the 29,028ft peak of Mount Everest.

22 May: Air Chief Marshal Sir Edward Ellington became the Chief of the Air Staff.

June: Deliveries of the Hawker Hart Trainer were made to the RAF College Cranwell, where they replaced Atlas Trainers.

21 June: The prototype Supermarine Seagull V (K4797) amphibian, built for the Royal Australian Air Force, made its first flight. After trials by the RAF, it was produced as the Walrus for air-sea rescue duties.

August: The first of 16 Saro Cloud flying boats entered service with 'B' Flight of the Seaplane Training Squadron at Calshot. As an amphibian, the Cloud was used for instructing flying-boat pilots. It was also used for navigation training. Fitted with two 340hp Armstrong Siddeley Serval (Double Mongoose) engines, it had a maximum speed of 118mph.

October: Hawker's chief designer, Sydney Camm, convinced that the biplane was finished, commenced design of a monoplane fighter that resulted in the Hurricane.

14 November: The last biplane heavy bomber to serve in the RAF was the Handley Page Heyford, which entered service with No 99 (Bomber) Squadron at RAF Upper Heyford. It was of unusual design, with the fuselage attached to the upper instead of the lower wings. The Heyford was issued as initial equipment to four new squadrons formed within the RAF Expansion Scheme, serving until replaced by the Whitley in 1938. Powered by two 575hp Rolls-Royce Kestrel IIIS engines, it had a top speed of 142mph and could carry a bomb load of up to 3,500lb.

The first aircraft designed specifically for service with the RAF in the Army Co-operation role was the Armstrong Whitworth Atlas. This was a sturdy single-engined biplane powered by a 450hp AS Jaguar IVC engine. As shown in Keith Woodcock's painting of a No 208 Squadron Atlas based at Heliopolis, it was equipped with a message pick-up hook. No 208 Squadron is (in 1993), based at RAF Lossiemouth with Buccaneer S2Bs for low-level maritime strike duties. This painting is in the collection of Donald C. Woodcock.

Armstrong Whitworth Atlas of No 208 Squadron by Keith Woodcock GMA, GAvA

The last disarmament proposals came in 1934, at which time Germany's Luftwaffe was rapidly increasing its strength. In January, the Foreign Secretary, Sir John Simon, proposed that if the Permanent Disarmament Commission had not decided within two years to abolish military aviation, the participating powers should be free to possess military aircraft as required to maintain numerical parity with other powers. In Britain, a Defence Requirements Committee had been established under the aegis of the Committee of Imperial Defence to review and determine the country's worst air defence deficiencies. Its report proposed that the RAF should have 40 squadrons over the next five years, with a strong emphasis on 'strengthening the position *vis-à-vis* Japan'. The first of a series of expansion schemes was announced in Parliament in July. This entailed increasing the RAF by 41 squadrons, including four squadrons already announced in the 1933 estimates. Thirty-three of the new squadrons were for Home Defence and the remainder for the Fleet Air Arm and overseas work. This programme raised the Salisbury target of 1923 (that had still not been completed) to 75 squadrons. The programme was to be accomplished over five years.

The general policy at this time was "British air power must include a Home Defence air force of sufficient strength to adequately protect against air attack by the strongest air force within striking distance of this country". By the summer of 1934, Hitler had succeeded the veteran Hindenburg as Reich Chancellor and was now firmly in control of Germany.

The British Government was determined "In no conditions to accept any position of inferiority with regard to what air force may be raised in Germany in the future". That was plain enough, though it was unfortunate that the air armament plan adopted was quite inadequate to fulfil the pledge. In November, Churchill challenged the Government's programme to strengthen the RAF. In October 1934, the MacRobertson Race was staged from RAF Mildenhall, Suffolk to Australia. It was won by the de Havilland DH88 Comet, this being a sleek, twin-engined wooden aircraft specially built for the race. This sophisticated aircraft made a deep impression on the Air Ministry. The design techniques embodied in the Comet laid the foundation for the later 'wooden wonder', the Mosquito fighter-bomber.

January: The Blackburn Perth, the largest flying boat used by the RAF in the biplane era, joined No 209 Squadron at RAF Mount Batten to succeed the Iris.

January: Failure of the Rolls-Royce Goshawk steam-cooled engine for fighter aircraft caused problems for companies putting forward contenders for Air Ministry Specification F.7/30. Rolls-Royce's new 12-litre liquid-cooled in-line engine, the PV-12, soon filled the gap.

March: The first Boulton Paul Overstrand medium bomber joined No 101 Squadron at RAF Bicester. It was the first RAF bomber to incorporate a power-operated enclosed gun turret. Twenty-four Overstrands, with two 580hp Bristol Pegasus IIM3 engines, were delivered.

17 April: The first flight of the Fairey TSR2 – subsequently known as the Swordfish.

24 May: The first Empire Air Day took place, with selected RAF stations open to the public. Proceeds went to the RAF Benevolent Fund.

15 June: The first Short Singapore III general reconnaissance flying boat (K3592), built to Air Ministry Specification R.3/33, made its maiden flight. A total of 37 was built for the RAF.

20 July: The Government made modest proposals for increasing the RAF by 41 squadrons in five years, but this was censured by the Labour party with Liberal support. Clement Attlee declared "There was no need for an increase in air armament".

27 July: Originally named the Southampton V, the prototype Supermarine Stranraer general reconnaissance flying boat was flown for the first time.

30 July: The Government instituted precautionary measures to protect the civil population and essential services against bombing.

August: The Hyderabad, of which 38 had been delivered to the RAF, was declared obsolete.

September: The prototype Gloster Gladiator (K5200), the last of the RAF's biplane fighters, first flew as the Gloster SS37.

2 September: Developed from the Audax for general purpose duties in the Middle East under Air Ministry Specification G.23/33, the first Hawker Hardy (K3013, a converted Hart) was flown for the first time.

12 September: The prototype Hawker Hind light bomber (K2915), powered by a Rolls-Royce Kestrel V engine, made its first flight. Built to Air Ministry Specification G.7/34, a total of 528 Hinds had joined the RAF by 1938.

11 October: The Prince of Wales arrived by air at Cranwell to open the new main building at the RAF College which the Air Ministry had founded on the lines of Sandhurst and Woolwich.

December: The RAF's first rotary-winged aircraft, the Cierva C30A Rota autogiro, entered service with the School of Army Co-operation at RAF Old Sarum. The Cierva was built under licence by Avro and supplied to the RAF as the Rota I. Twelve were delivered in 1934 and 1935. Powered by a 140hp Armstrong Siddeley Genet Major IA engine, the Rota had a maximum speed of 100mph. Cierva's autodynamic rotor head allowed the rotor to speed up beyond take-off revolutions with the blades at zero incidence. By suddenly applying positive pitch, sufficient excess lift was created for the machine to leap some 20ft into the air.

Twelve Avro Rota Is, licence-built Cierva C30A autogiros, were delivered to the RAF from August 1934. The first aircraft served with the Directorate of Technical Development and subsequently joined the School of Army Co-operation at RAF Old Sarum. During World War 2, the Rotas were flown by No 1448 Flight and No 529 Squadron at Duxford and Halton respectively. Colin Bradbury's painting shows the first Avro Rota I.

These pages generously donated by Jeppesen

Avro Rota I of the Directorate of Technical Development by Colin Bradbury

During the course of a visit to Germany in March to discuss a proposed Air Pact, Foreign Secretary Sir John Simon and Anthony Eden were informed by Adolf Hitler that the German Air Force had already achieved parity with the RAF and that the future intent was to achieve the same situation with France. This information was made public in April and caused great consternation in both the Cabinet and elsewhere. The Air Ministry was immediately directed to produce a new expansion programme. This was known as Scheme C and was aimed at raising the front line strength of the Home Defence air force to 1,500 aircraft by March 1937. It was estimated that this programme would match the RAF to the Luftwaffe at that date. The inadequacy of Scheme C was quickly realised – and not only by the Air Ministry. There was a general acceptance that Britain had to re-arm seriously and the necessary plans were prepared. Parity with Germany was accepted and became publicly proclaimed policy – but was unostentatiously neglected on financial and economic grounds.

When re-armament began in 1935, the bomber force was part of a unified air defence command – ADGB. Hitler then announced a formal denunciation of the Versailles Treaty's disarmament clauses, saying that since France and Russia had never disarmed, the presuppositions of the whole Treaty were invalid. The Luftwaffe then became an independent service in its own right. In October, Italy, with whom Britain was trying to promote friendly relations as a counterpoint to Germany, invaded Abyssinia.

In January, the Air Ministry established a Committee for the Scientific Survey of Air Defence under Chairman Henry Tizard, Rector of Imperial College, London and Chairman of the Aeronautical Research Committee. A demonstration of the new radio direction finding apparatus to the RAF produced an unusually quick response and a bold decision to construct a chain of stations around the coast of south-east England. This would use radar (as it was subsequently named) as a key element in what was to become the first effective system of air defence.

January: The Vickers Vincent, a modified version of the Vildebeest, entered service with No 8 Squadron at Aden and No 84 Squadron at Shaibah. A three-seat general purpose biplane, it replaced the Wapiti and Fairey IIIF with overseas squadrons. Powered by a 660hp Bristol Pegasus IIM3 engine, it had a maximum speed of 142mph.

5 January: The radio-controlled target version of the Tiger Moth, known as the Queen Bee, flew for the first time. It featured an all-wooden ply-covered fuselage, whereas the Tiger Moth had a metal, fabric-covered fuselage. 380 were built for the RAF.

March: Air Marshal Dowding, the Air Member for Research and Development, witnessed the first successful demonstration of radio direction finding (RDF), which led to an order to construct a chain of 20 air defence radar stations.

24 March: The prototype of the Avro Type 652A (K4771) flew for the first time. It was built to meet an Air Ministry requirement for a twin-engined coastal patrol landplane. This military version of the Imperial Airways' airliner later became known as the Anson.

April: The Short Singapore III flying boat entered service with No 230 Squadron at RAF Pembroke Dock.

April: The Hawker Hardy went into service with No 30 Squadron at Mosul, where it replaced the veteran Wapiti.

3 April: It was announced that the Luftwaffe had already achieved parity with the RAF.

12 April: The first flight of the Bristol 142 *Britain First* took place at Filton. This eventually became the Blenheim.

May: A new scheme of Expansion, known as Scheme C, was announced to raise the aircraft strength of the Home Defence Air Force to 1,500 by March 1937.

May: The Gloster Gauntlet, the last of the open-cockpit fighter biplanes to serve in the RAF, entered service with No 19 Squadron at RAF Duxford.

May: The Supermarine Scapa flying boat entered RAF service at Kalafrana, Malta. A modernised, re-engined version of the Southampton, it had two 525hp Rolls-Royce Kestrel IIIMS engines. Fourteen Scapas were built and operated until 1938.

May: The Air Ministry placed an initial order for Walrus amphibians for the RAF.

4 June: The Armstrong Whitworth 23 bomber-transport prototype (K3585) first flew.

19 June: Built as a private venture, the prototype Vickers Wellesley (K7556) two-seat general purpose bomber was flown for the first time.

23 June: The prototype Bristol 120 (named Bombay in April 1937) made its initial flight.

July: The first Fairey Swordfish I entered service.

6 July: King George V reviewed the RAF at Mildenhall and Duxford. 350 aircraft from 40 squadrons took part in the flypast.

23 July: A report on radio direction finding, known later as radar, was presented to the Air Defence Research Committee.

August: The last Fairey IIIF seaplanes with No 202 Squadron at Malta were retired.

September: The first Vickers Valentia troop carrier entered service with No 216 Squadron at Heliopolis. The Valentia was derived from the Victoria, which it replaced.

October: The first Short Singapores to go overseas went to No 230 Squadron at Alexandria, Egypt.

6 November: The first flight of the prototype of Hawker's monoplane fighter (later named 'Hurricane') took place at Brooklands.

18 November: British Air Forces in the Middle East were strengthened by the transfer of twelve squadrons from the UK. They were brought to a state of heightened readiness following Italian aggression in Ethiopia.

December: The Hawker Hind general purpose biplane day-bomber entered service with No 21 Squadron at RAF Bircham Newton. Developed from the Hart, a total of 452 Hinds saw service with RAF light bomber squadrons.

No 19 Squadron, a Home Defence squadron based at RAF Duxford, was the first to replace the Bristol Bulldog with the faster Gloster Gauntlet in mid-1935. Gauntlets like those shown here in Rodney Diggens' painting remained in service with the unit until 1938 when No 19 Squadron was the first to receive Spitfires. Today, No 19 (Reserve) Squadron forms part of No 7 Flying Training School at RAF Chivenor operating Hawks for advanced flying and tactical weapons training.

Gauntlets by Rodney I. Diggens GAvA

Following a general election in September 1935, Baldwin prepared a Defence White Paper in February 1936 – this gave Britain its first coherent defence policy for 20 years. For the RAF, Scheme F provided for a Home Defence Air Force of 124 squadrons by March 1939 and was the longest lived of all expansion schemes. Notable features included the substitution of medium bombers for light bombers, the provision of a full scale of reserves and the first steps towards creating a system of 'shadow' aircraft manufacturing factories.

In 1936 the decision was taken to divide ADGB into two separate echelons, forming Fighter Command under Air Marshal Sir Hugh Dowding and Bomber Command under Air Marshal Sir John Steel. Fighter Command was given the freedom to press ahead with sophisticated techniques of air defence, an opportunity of which everyone from Dowding downwards took full advantage. The disadvantages were mostly for Bomber Command which did not enjoy the benefits that might have come from the development of airborne RDF (radar) and which also lacked the training opportunities of a unified command. It did not learn as quickly as it should have done how vulnerable bombers would prove to be against modern fighters in daylight. The aircraft that equipped the new command were mostly light bombers like the Hawker Hart or night bombers such as the Handley Page Heyford biplane with its fixed undercarriage. From British bases, it could reach a few targets in France – but none in Germany.

The first bomber to be ordered in substantial numbers when re-armament began was the Fairey Battle, a single Merlin-engined monoplane which featured a retractable undercarriage, a range of 1,000 miles and a bomb load of 1,000lb. It first flew in 1936, as did the Bristol Blenheim, both types being rushed into production for the RAF. Other actions, that were to prove equally significant in due course, were taking Britain inextricably towards war - the Italians invaded Ethiopia; the Japanese were flexing their muscles in China; and Spain erupted in July into a full-scale civil war. The development of air power, kept on a short rein since 1918, was soon to be given its head once again.

---

14 February: The initial production two-seat Hawker Hector army co-operation biplane (K3719), with the 24-cylinder Napier Dagger engine, was flown for the first time.

2 March: RAF officer Frank Whittle set up Power Jets, with a capital of £10,000, to develop a turbojet aircraft engine.

5 March: The prototype Supermarine Spitfire I (K5054) made its first flight at Eastleigh. It was built to Air Ministry Specification F.37/34 for a Rolls-Royce Merlin-engined single-seat fighter aircraft with eight machine guns.

6 March: The RAF's first operational monoplane with a retractable undercarriage, the Avro Anson, entered service with No 48 Squadron at Manston. The Anson remained in production for 17 years.

10 March: The Fairey Battle prototype (K4303) made its maiden flight, this being one of the first two bomber types that was to be produced in the new 'shadow' factories.

13 March: British scientists detected an RAF aircraft flying at 15,000ft at a distance of 60 miles using an array of RDF aerials erected at the Bawdsey research station.

17 March: The prototype Armstrong Whitworth Whitley (K4586) first flew.

April: The first Saro London I flying boat (K5257) was delivered to No 201 Squadron at RAF Felixstowe as a replacement for the Southampton.

May: The first RAF unit badges were approved by HM the King.

25 May: The squadrons of the Special Reserve, Nos 500 to 504, were transferred to the Auxiliary Air Force.

15 June: The prototype Vickers Wellington long-range night bomber (K4049) was first flown. The same day also saw the maiden flight of the prototype Westland Lysander (K6127).

21 June: The prototype Handley Page Hampden bomber (K4240) first flew.

25 June: The first prototype Bristol Blenheim I (K7033) made its first flight. It was developed from the Type 142 *Britain First*.

27 June: The Hurricane and Spitfire, together with the Wellington and Lysander, made their first appearances at the RAF Display at Hendon.

July: Short Rangoons of No 210 Squadron returned from Gibraltar to RAF Pembroke Dock and were replaced by Singapores.

14 July: The RAF underwent a change of organisation when Bomber, Fighter, Coastal and Training Commands came into being.

20 July: The King's Flight was formed at RAF Hendon by King Edward VIII, later Duke of Windsor. It was created to provide air transport for the sovereign and members of the Royal family when engaged on official duties.

30 July: The formation of the RAF Volunteer Reserve was announced, designed to take 800 pilots a year.

28 September: The RAF established an aircraft altitude record when Squadron Leader F R D Swain flew the Bristol 138A to 49,944ft from Farnborough.

October: The Saro London flying boat entered service with No 204 Squadron at RAF Mount Batten.

16 October: The prototype Short Sunderland four-engined monoplane flying boat (K4774) made its maiden flight. It was built to Air Ministry Specification R.22/36 for a long-range general reconnaissance and anti-submarine patrol flying boat.

November: The Balloon Barrage Scheme was announced.

November: No 38 Squadron at RAF Mildenhall became the only unit to receive the Fairey Hendon, the first all-metal low-wing cantilever monoplane to enter RAF squadron service. 14 production models were built.

December: The Supermarine Stranraer flying boat entered service with No 228 Squadron at RAF Pembroke Dock.

3 December: The first production single-seat biplane fighter Hawker Fury II (K7263), built to Air Ministry Specification F.6/35, made its maiden flight – 112 were delivered.

Edmund Miller's painting depicts the first production Hawker Hind K4636. The Hind was first issued to No 21 Squadron at RAF Bircham Newton . At its peak period of service in April 1937, there were 452 Hinds assigned to light bomber squadrons.

These pages generously donated by British Airways PLC

Hawker Hind by Edmund Miller GAvA

In May Baldwin retired and was succeeded as Prime Minister by Neville Chamberlain. Although plans put forward for the rapid expansion of the RAF were not implemented, Fighter Command's planned strength was slowly raised from the 35 squadrons envisaged in 1935 to the final peacetime plan for 49 squadrons. A new generation of twin-engined, long-range 'heavy' bombers was heralded by the first flight of the Armstrong Whitworth Whitley. Other important technological developments were taking place.

The first airborne radar was tested in a Handley Page Heyford in 1937. Utilising a substantially higher frequency than the Chain Home sets, the airborne radar was developed for both Air Interception (AI) and Air-to-Surface Vessel (ASV) use. At the end of the year, the Air Ministry agreed that the primary role of Coastal Command in a war should be "trade protection, reconnaissance and co-operation with the Royal Navy". ASV, which made it possible to detect ships and surfaced submarines, had not yet reached the squadrons, but was under development.

With the expansion programme finally well under way, 1937 was to see the entry into service of several new aircraft types. Fighter Command started to receive what was destined to be its last biplane fighter, the Gloster Gladiator, with initial deliveries going to No 3 Squadron at RAF Kenley and No 72 Squadron at RAF Tangmere.

The Bristol Blenheim medium bomber joined Bomber Command with No 114 Squadron at RAF Wyton. In March, the Fairey Battle light bomber was delivered to Nos 52 and 63 Squadrons at RAF Upwood and the Armstrong Whitworth Whitley heavy bomber went to No 10 Squadron at RAF Dishforth. The Handley Page Harrow, an 'interim' heavy bomber, joined No 214 Squadron at RAF Feltwell and the Vickers Wellesley went to No 76 Squadron at RAF Finningley. Finally, at the end of the year, No 111 Squadron at RAF Northolt became the first unit anywhere in the world to operate an eight-gun monoplane fighter when the Hawker Hurricane entered front-line service.

January: The first Handley Page Harrow bombers to enter service went to No 214 Squadron at RAF Feltwell.

January: The RAF's last biplane fighter, the Gloster Gladiator, entered service with No 3 Squadron at RAF Kenley and No 72 Squadron at RAF Tangmere.

February: The Hawker Hector army co-operation biplane entered service with No 4 Squadron at RAF Odiham as a replacement for the Audax.

9 February: The first flight of the Blackburn Type B-24 prototype (K5178) was made at Brough. Later known as the Skua, it was the first monoplane to enter FAA service, and the first dive-bomber of British construction.

March: The Bristol Blenheim I medium bomber entered service with No 114 Squadron at RAF Wyton.

March: The Vickers Vildebeest IV entered service with No 42 Squadron at RAF Donibristle, becoming the RAF's first sleeve-valve engined aircraft.

March: The Armstrong Whitworth Whitley I bomber entered RAF service with No 10 Squadron at RAF Dishforth, where it replaced the Heyford.

10 March: The prototype Hawker Henley (K5115) first flew at Brooklands.

April: The first production aircraft to embody geodetic criss-cross lattice construction was the Vickers Wellesley, which entered service with No 76 Squadron at RAF Finningley.

12 April: Frank Whittle's first gas turbine was ground tested.

May: The Fairey Battle light bomber entered service with No 63 Squadron at RAF Upwood. Within a year, it equipped 15 squadrons in Bomber Command.

19 June: The prototype Airspeed Oxford twin-engined trainer aircraft (L4534) was flown.

30 June: The RAF established a new altitude record when Flight Lieutenant M J Adam flew a Bristol Type 138A to 53,937ft from Farnborough.

July: Reserve Flying Schools were opened at Castle Bromwich, Redhill and Shoreham to increase the number of RAF pilots under training.

30 July: After battling since 1918, the Royal Navy took control of the Fleet Air Arm from the RAF.

August: An experimental airborne RDF transmitter was fitted to an Avro Anson. This led to the development of airborne interception (AI) radar sets for operational use.

11 August: The prototype Boulton Paul Defiant fighter (K8310), the first with a four-gun power-operated turret, made its maiden flight.

September: The first Miles Magister trainer (L5913) was delivered to the Central Flying School.

September: The Bristol Bulldog was declared obsolete.

1 September: Air Chief Marshal Sir Cyril Newall became Chief of the Air Staff.

October: The first deployment of the Saro London flying boat to Malta, where it replaced the Scapas of No 202 Squadron.

November: Three Gloster Gauntlets of No 32 Squadron were directed by ground radar to intercept a civil airliner flying over the River Thames. This was the world's first successful radar-controlled fighter interception.

November: The Airspeed Oxford, the RAF's first twin-engined monoplane advanced trainer, entered service with the Central Flying School at RAF Upavon.

December: The Hawker Hurricane I, the RAF's first eight-gun monoplane fighter with a fully enclosed cockpit and fully retractable undercarriage, entered service with No 111 Squadron at RAF Northolt, replacing the Gauntlet. Powered by a 1,030hp Rolls-Royce Merlin II engine, it was the first RAF fighter aircraft to exceed 300mph, having a maximum speed of 316mph. This signalled the end of the twin-gun fighter biplane in front-line service with the RAF.

23 December: Ordered to Specification 29/36, the first of 180 production Vickers Wellington Is (L4212) was flown for the first time.

In 'Gloster Gladiators', Keith Woodcock has captured the colourful markings of the last of the RAF's biplane fighters operating from a pre-war grass airfield. A Gladiator of No 87 Squadron at RAF Debden prepares for take-off whilst Gladiator K7985 of No 73 Squadron at RAF Digby flies overhead. This painting is in the collection of Owen Thetford Esq.

These pages generously donated by Music for Pleasure

Gloster Gladiator Is of Nos 87 and 73 Squadrons by Keith Woodcock GMA, GAvA

The problem of manning all the new squadrons and providing enough crews for the expanding service was a challenge. To meet this, the RAF Volunteer Reserve was created, drawing upon a new field of entrants. Instead of looking for university material, the new organisation drew mainly on grammar school boys who would join and receive non-commissioned rank. The idea was to train 800 pilots a year and to do this new flying schools were set up near the main centres of population. Called Elementary and Reserve Flying Schools, they took over the elementary pilot training for the RAF on weekdays and provided the same facility for Volunteer Reservists at weekends. So successful was this organisation that, in three years, 5,000 men were trained as part of the RAFVR. Balloon squadrons were formed, originally under the Auxiliary Air Force, but this expanded in November 1938 into a separate Balloon Command, to provide barrages around the major British cities and high-priority targets.

In the material sense, Britain's inferiority to Germany in the air decreased during the period September 1938–September 1939. Aircraft production had nearly caught up with Germany's output. In March, the Services were freed from the requirements that their orders must not upset civilian trade. 'Shadow' factories were set up throughout the country. Mostly run by motor manufacturers, production from these factories was initially slow, so Britain placed orders in the USA. These included 200 North American Harvard single-engined trainers and 200 Lockheed Hudsons. In June 1938, the Supermarine Spitfire joined No 19 Squadron at Duxford.

Germany's intentions were quite clear since she had already seized Austria and Czechoslovakia. In August, when Czechoslovakia was invaded, the RAF brought its emergency plans into play and moved all its squadrons to war stations. RAF stations were camouflaged so as to cut down the ease with which they could be identified from the air. RAF aircraft were also camouflaged and squadron identity markings were either removed or scaled down in size. A new squadron identity code system consisting of two letters painted on the fuselage sides was introduced – this standard system was used in the European theatre throughout WW2.

---

20 January: The Air Ministry announced that the RAF display at Hendon was to be discontinued – the reason given was that Hendon airfield was too small for modern aircraft.

10 February: Squadron Leader J W Gillan flew a Hawker Hurricane from Edinburgh to Northolt in 48 minutes, covering the 327 miles at an average speed of 408.75mph.

2 March: A White Paper on rearmament was issued by the Government. RAF flying training schools were to be increased from four to eleven. Over 1,000 men had joined the RAF as pilots in the previous twelve months.

20 April: Led by Air Commodore A T Harris, a purchasing mission visited the USA and contracts were subsequently placed for the Harvard and the Hudson, a decision that was criticised by all British political parties. The object was to find suitable types of American aircraft which the RAF could rapidly obtain.

21 April: Conditions under which British firms had agreed to run 'shadow' factories to produce aircraft and aero-engines for the RAF were disclosed.

26 April: The UK Government announced plans for compulsory military service.

May: The Short Sunderland flying boat entered service with No 230 Squadron at Seletar, Singapore.

25 May: The British Air Minister, Lord Swanton, was sacked in response to public criticism of Britain's failure to achieve parity with Luftwaffe air strength.

June: The Westland Lysander entered service with No 16 Squadron at RAF Old Sarum.

June: The Supermarine Spitfire fighter entered service with No 19 Squadron at RAF Duxford.

14 June: First flight of the prototype Hawker Hotspur (K8309).

7–8 July: Four Vickers Wellesleys of the RAF Long Range Development Flight flew non-stop from Cranwell to Ismailia, Egypt and back. The total distance of 4,300 miles was covered in 32 hours.

23 July: The formation of the Civil Air Guard was announced.

September: The prototype Supermarine Sea Otter (K8854) made its maiden flight. It was the last biplane of any category to enter RAF service and 290 were eventually delivered for air-sea rescue service tasks with Coastal Command.

24 September: The Munich Crisis. RAF emergency procedures brought into force. Formation of Mobilisation Pools ordered on 27 September.

11 October: The prototype single-seat Westland Whirlwind twin-engined, long-range fighter (L6844) was first flown at Yeovil.

15 October: The prototype Bristol Beaufort (L4441), which became Coastal Command's standard torpedo bomber from 1940–1943, made its maiden flight.

31 October: The Vickers Wellington bomber entered service with No 99 Squadron at RAF Mildenhall.

1 November: RAF announced a boost to fighter aircraft production – up to April, bombers had been given priority in aircraft procurement.

1 November: The Hawker Henley target tug entered service with No 1 AACU.

1 November: Home Defence of the UK was strengthened by the formation of RAF Balloon Command.

5–7 November: Squadron Leader R Kellett and Flight Lieutenant A N Combe set up a World distance record in Vickers Wellesley aircraft, by flying 7,158 miles from Ismailia, Egypt to Darwin, Australia.

December: The Bristol Blenheim IF night fighter entered service with No 25 Squadron at RAF Hawkinge.

28 December: The prototype Blackburn Botha (L6014) made its first flight.

The two Vickers Wellesleys in Rex Flood's painting are from No 14 Squadron whilst based at Ramleh, Palestine and Amman, Transjordan. It clearly shows the difficult terrain over which these RAF aircraft had to operate. No 14 Squadron currently operates the Panavia Tornado GR1 at RAF Brüggen, Germany. The painting is reproduced by kind permission of The Commandant, RAF Staff College, Bracknell.

These pages generously donated by No 14 Squadron

Vickers Wellesley Is of No 14 Squadron by Rex Flood

By the beginning of 1939, there were 135 front-line units, one more than the target of 134 squadrons set in 1936. The last of the key new types of aircraft, the Vickers Wellington bomber, had entered service in reasonable numbers, while front-line strength of the Home Defence Air Force (stretched well beyond what the Air Staff believed to be wise) stood at some 1,400. However, these figures still fell far short of Germany's Luftwaffe which had 3,500 aircraft plus 500 transports. In March, Kingsley Wood, Secretary of State for Air, announced that Scheme F would shortly be completed as planned. By 1939, barely in time, the RAF was completing the chain of RDF (radar) stations that could give advance warning of approaching enemy aircraft. It also had IFF (Identification Friend or Foe) – this indicated which of the returns on the radar screens were British/friendly aircraft and which were hostile. Equally importantly, it had integrated the system in a communications net that provided RAF fighter controllers with information from a number of sources and allowed them to direct air defence aircraft towards the incoming threat. By the spring, an improved form of magnetron valve was developed, which was to prove essential in the development of night air defence.

At the outbreak of war (3 September) there were 35 squadrons in Fighter Command. 16 had Hurricanes and 10 had Spitfires, the remainder comprising Blenheims, Gladiators, Gauntlets and Hinds. In the five years since the beginning of RAF expansion in 1934, 142 new sites for airfields had been acquired and most of these new RAF stations had been completed.

January: The Vickers Wellington entered service with No 9 Squadron at RAF Stradishall and the North American Harvard trainer was assigned to No 12 FTS at RAF Spittlegate.

17 January: The Air Ministry announced that an Auxiliary Air Force Reserve had been formed to enable ex-aircrew of the Auxiliary Air Force to serve with Auxiliary flying squadrons in an emergency.

March: The Bristol Blenheim IV entered service with No 90 Squadron at RAF Bicester.

May: The Lockheed Hudson entered service with No 224 Squadron at RAF Leuchars.

14 May: The first flight of the Short Stirling four-engined bomber prototype (L7600) took place, but it crashed on landing and was destroyed.

June: The first Consolidated Catalina flying boat (P9630) arrived for experimental testing at the Marine Aircraft Experimental Establishment at Felixstowe.

26 June: The Air Minister announced that British civil aircraft would be taken over by the RAF for transport and other purposes in the event of war.

1 July: The foundation of the Womens' Auxiliary Air Force (WAAF), for duty with the RAF in wartime, was announced.

11–25 July: Over 240 RAF aircraft took part in training flights over France.

17 July: The first prototype Bristol Beaufighter (R2052) made its maiden flight at Filton.

25 July: The prototype Avro Manchester bomber (L7246) was flown for the first time.

13 August: Designed to Specification B.1/35, the prototype Vickers Warwick I (K8178), a heavier version of the Wellington for service with Coastal Command, made its first flight.

24 August: The general mobilisation of the RAF. Coastal Command began regular North Sea reconnaissance patrols with Ansons and Hudsons.

1 September: All RAF reservists ordered to report for duty and all RAF squadrons put on a state of readiness. Foundation of the Air Transport Auxiliary (ATA) was announced.

2 September: The Advanced Air Striking Force formed with ten squadrons of Fairey Battles and two squadrons of Hawker Hurricanes. The air component of the British Expeditionary Force (BEF) was also formed. It comprised four squadrons each of Westland Lysanders and Bristol Blenheims plus two squadrons each of Gloster Gladiators and Hawker Hurricanes. Both forces flew to France.

3 September: War was declared against Germany. Blenheim IVs of No 139 Squadron made a photo-reconnaissance of the German fleet leaving Wilhelmshaven.

4 September: 15 Blenheims and 14 Wellingtons attacked enemy warships off Brunsbuttel, Schillig Roads, and entering Wilhelmshaven.

5 September: An Anson of No 500 Squadron made the first attack on an enemy U-boat.

October: The prototype Hawker Tornado (P5219) made its maiden flight.

1/2 October: The first British bombers to fly over Berlin in WW2 were Armstrong Whitworth Whitleys of No 10 Squadron, which dropped propaganda leaflets.

8 October: A Hudson of No 224 Squadron, Coastal Command, was the first aircraft to attack an enemy aircraft – a Dornier Do 18 over the North Sea.

16 October: Fighter Command's first action; two Heinkel He 111s were shot down by Spitfires of Nos 602 and 603 Squadrons over the Firth of Forth.

25 October: The first prototype Handley Page Halifax four-engined heavy bomber (L7244) made its first flight at RAF Bicester.

30 October: Service operational trials of VHF radio commenced at Duxford.

30 October: The first enemy aircraft to be shot down by RAF fighters on the Western Front in WW2 was a Dornier Do 17 destroyed by a Hurricane of No 1 Squadron.

November: The Bristol Beaufort entered service with No 22 Squadron at RAF Thorney Island.

November: The prototype Miles Master II (with a Pratt & Whitney radial engine) trainer (N7422) made its first flight. 1,747 were built.

December: The first operational squadron, No 209 at RAF Oban, formed with the Saro Lerwick flying boat. The Lerwick was replaced by Catalinas within 18 months.

December: The Boulton Paul Defiant turret fighter entered service with No 264 Squadron at RAF Martlesham Heath.

8 December: The Secretary of State for Air disclosed that certain Polish squadrons were to be re-formed and attached to the RAF.

Four Supermarine Spitfire Is of No 65 Squadron at RAF Hornchurch during a formation take-off from this Fighter Command airfield. This painting, 'The Gathering Storm' by Brian Withams, shows Spitfires, newly received in March 1939, rehearsing a scramble prior to the outbreak of hostilities on 3 September 1939.

These pages generously donated by Aviation Leathercraft

The Gathering Storm by Brian Withams GAvA

The severe winter of 1939–40 was accompanied by early and prolonged fog, frost and snow which effectively restricted air operations over most of north-west Europe. It brought atrocious conditions to the ill-prepared airfields of France. The war began in earnest in April with the German attack on Denmark and Norway. Bomber Command tried to stem the German advance but distance was a barrier. Some Gladiators and Hurricanes also made heroic attempts to intervene, by operating from frozen lakes, but this was short-lived. The German assault on France and the Low Countries on 10 May put an end to the 'phoney war'. The RAF gave maximum support against the advancing German columns but, in the face of overwhelming odds, its efforts achieved little. By the end of June, the remaining aircraft and personnel in France had been withdrawn to Britain. Spitfires and Hurricanes, operating from airfields in Kent and Sussex, covered the evacuation from Dunkirk, which enabled the bulk of the British Army to be evacuated from the beaches, but 959 RAF aircraft were lost in the Battle for France, including 477 fighters – mainly Hurricanes. Fortunately, Sir Hugh Dowding had been successful in refusing to send further fighter squadrons to France; these reserves proved essential in the forthcoming Battle of Britain.

During the aerial battle, which lasted from 10 July to 30 October, the German intention was to destroy the Royal Air Force, as other air forces in Europe had been destroyed by *blitzkriegs* from September 1939 to May 1940. Then, with air superiority assured, the Luftwaffe's bomber force would have been used to support a cross-Channel invasion of southern England. The large aerial battles showed the Germans that the air superiority they needed for the invasion was far from won and caused its postponement. The price of victory in the Battle of Britain was high – 375 pilots were killed and 358 wounded. Fighter Command lost 915 aircraft against 1,733 bombers and fighters lost by the Luftwaffe, but the aircraft factories continued to function day and night and managed to keep pace with losses. New versions of the Spitfire (Mark II) and Hurricane (Mark IIA) began to appear in the autumn. The Defiant was redeployed as a night fighter and the Blenheim night fighter was replaced by the Beaufighter with Airborne Interception radar.

Italy entered the war in May, thus involving the RAF in the Mediterranean. Malta faced heavy air attacks and squadrons were sent to Egypt and the Middle East to resist the initial Italian advance. Defeat in France and Norway left Britain without any foothold on the mainland of Northern Europe, and it faced an enemy from the North Cape to the Spanish border. The Luftwaffe failed to appreciate the importance of the RDF chain, which was seldom attacked. At the critical moment, the Germans switched their attacks on RAF airfields to the bombing of London, thus giving Fighter Command desperately needed relief. Fighter Command had won the Battle of Britain, but Bomber Command still had the task of taking the war to the enemy's homeland.

January: The Photographic Development Unit formed at RAF Heston to capitalise on Sidney Cotton's Heston Flight.

14 February: The German prison ship *Altmark* was found in a Norwegian fjord by Lockheed Hudson aircraft of No 220 Squadron.

24 February: The prototype Hawker Typhoon (P5212) made its first flight.

11 March: The first U-boat to be sunk by the RAF was claimed by a Blenheim of No 82 Squadron.

20 March: The prototype Armstrong Whitworth Albemarle (P1360) was flown for the first time.

11 April: Bomber Command's first raid on a European mainland target was carried out when Wellingtons of No 115 Squadron struck at Stavanger airfield.

29 April: The Empire Air Training Scheme was initiated in Canada, Australia and New Zealand.

7 May: The first 2,000lb bomb was dropped by a Coastal Command Beaufort on an enemy cruiser near Nordeney.

12 May: The first RAF VCs of WW2 were awarded posthumously to Flying Officer D E Garland and Sergeant T Gray of No 12 Squadron, for a Fairey Battle daylight attack on Maastricht Bridge.

15/16 May: The first strategic bombing of German industry took place when 99 Bomber Command Wellingtons, Hampdens and Whitleys attacked targets in the Ruhr.

27 May: RAF Training Command was divided into Flying Training and Technical Training Commands.

11 June: War began in the Middle East and Blenheims of Nos 45, 55 and 113 Squadrons bombed El Adem in Libya.

11/12 June: Wellingtons of No 3 Group made the first raids on Italy, operating from the UK and refuelling in the Channel Islands.

16 June: The Ground Radio Interception Unit began work with specialised aircraft to investigate German navigation aids with a view to Radio Countermeasures.

22 June: The Parachute Training School was formed at Ringway.

10 July: The first phase of the Battle of Britain began with German attacks on shipping and coastal towns.

25/26 August: The first night attack by the RAF on Berlin was carried out by 81 aircraft.

15 September: This was the peak day of the Battle of Britain when 'the tide was turned'.

24 October: Air Chief Marshal Sir Cyril Newall was replaced as Chief of the Air Staff by Air Chief Marshal Sir Charles Portal.

25 November: The first prototype de Havilland Mosquito (W4050) made its first flight at Hatfield, having been completed in just ten months.

1 December: Army Co-operation Command was formed.

20 December: Two Spitfires of No 66 Squadron inaugurated *Rhubarb* offensive sweeps over France.

26 December: Blind Approach equipment was introduced for use in operational aircraft.

Chris Stothard's painting illustrates three Handley Page Hampdens from No 44 Squadron at Waddington making a low-level night attack on German invasion barges in one of the Channel ports. At the time of this action, in early autumn 1940, a seaborne invasion was a real threat. The painting is reproduced by kind permission of the PMC, Officers' Mess, RAF Waddington.

These pages generously donated by DTZ Debenham Thorpe

The Other Battle of Britain by C. J. Stothard

During the winter of 1940–41, the offensive against military targets in Germany and Italy built up steadily. By the middle of 1941, it had become clear that only a small proportion of aircraft were accurately locating and bombing their targets. More effective aircraft such as the Stirling and Halifax, together with the Mosquito, were beginning to roll off the production lines. New navigational aids such as *Gee,* to be followed by *Oboe* and H$_2$S, were coming into use. Better bombs and bomb aiming techniques were also being introduced. There was actually an aircrew surplus in 1941, due to a shortage of aircraft stemming from production failures and a reduction of training time in OTUs. A total of 2,451 front-line aircraft at the outbreak of WW2 had increased only slightly by August 1941 and RAF strength was still substantially below that of the Luftwaffe, although production was now well ahead of that of Germany. The first operation by a four-engined bomber (the Short Stirling) took place in February, but it was giving problems in service. Its short wing span (designed to the requirement that it should fit in pre-war hangars) meant that it had difficulty in climbing above 10,000ft when fully laden. The Halifax was more successful – after a series of modifications, it became an effective heavy bomber. Twenty Boeing B-17C Fortress Is were obtained from the USA in the spring of 1941, but they were a disappointment for daylight missions and were transferred to a maritime role with Coastal Command after 51 sorties. The Avro Manchester, with its troublesome Rolls-Royce Vulture engines, was also a failure.

In June, Germany invaded Russia, taking pressure off Britain. Target Force E was inaugurated in June 1941 to expand Bomber Command to 250 standard-size squadrons, under eight operational groups, by the spring of 1943. By early 1941, Fighter Command had grown to eight groups comprising 72 squadrons. These mainly used Hurricane IIAs and IIBs, but the four-cannon IIC was also being received, as was the Spitfire V. By June, Yugoslavia, Greece and Crete had been overrun by the Axis and RAF units were withdrawn to the Canal Zone. In August, two Hurricane squadrons were sent to Northern Russia and daylight operations were undertaken over Northern France during the year by the Biggin Hill, Kenley and Hornchurch Wings. In the second half of 1941, Fighter Command discovered that German fighters had vastly improved – the Messerschmitt Bf 109F displayed superiority over the Spitfire V and in October the Focke Wulf FW 190 entered the fray. In December, the Japanese attacked Pearl Harbor which brought the USA into the War.

9 January: The first Avro Lancaster (BT308) made its first flight.

10 January: The first *Circus* operation (bomber sweep with fighter escort) flown by Blenheim IVs of No 114 Squadron. Escorted by nine fighter squadrons, they hit targets in Fôret de Guines.

February: The Curtiss P-40 Tomahawk entered service with No 26 Squadron at RAF Gatwick.

February: Douglas Boston III day bombers entered service with No 85 Squadron at RAF Debden for intruder duties.

10 February: The first British airborne operation involved Whitleys of Nos 51 and 78 Squadrons which dropped paratroops to destroy an aqueduct at Tragino in Italy (Operation *Colossus*).

10/11 February: The first operational use of the Short Stirling heavy bomber was made by No 7 Squadron in a raid on Rotterdam.

24/25 February: The first operational use of the Avro Manchester was made by No 207 Squadron in a raid on warships at Brest.

10/11 March: The first operational use of the Handley Page Halifax heavy bomber was made by No 35 Squadron in a raid on Le Havre.

1 April: The first 4,000lb bombs were dropped by Wellington IIs of Nos 9 and 149 Squadrons on Emden.

1 April: The Consolidated Catalina entered service with Coastal Command's No 209 Squadron at RAF Castle Archdale.

6 April: The German pocket-battleship *Gneisenau* was torpedoed in Brest harbour by a Beaufort of No 22 Squadron. The pilot, Flying Officer Kenneth Campbell, was awarded a posthumous VC.

May: The Boeing Fortress I entered service at RAF West Raynham.

1 May: The first production North American P-51 Mustang I (AG345) made its first flight.

15 May: Gloster's first jet aircraft, the experimental E28/39 (W4041), made its initial flight at Cranwell.

24–27 May: The German battleship *Bismarck* was sunk after Catalinas of Nos 209 and 240 Squadrons spotted and shadowed it in mid-Atlantic.

June: The Consolidated Liberator entered service with No 120 Squadron Coastal Command at RAF Nutts Corner, Belfast.

22 June: The first *Gee* (navigation aid) chain of three ground stations was completed – Daventry, Ventnor and Stenigot.

20 July: Ferry Command was formed, taking over the work of the ATFERO (Atlantic Ferry Organisation).

August: The de Havilland Mosquito entered service with the Photographic Development Unit at RAF Benson.

11/12 August: The first use of *Gee* involved Wellingtons of No 405 Squadron in a raid on München Gladbach.

27 August: A Lockheed Hudson of No 269 Squadron caused submarine U-510 to surrender. This was the first U-boat captured in a solely RAF operation.

September: The Hawker Typhoon, the first RAF fighter to exceed 400mph, entered service with No 56 Squadron at RAF Duxford.

20 September: The first mission by Hurricanes operating as fighter-bombers was staged from Malta.

29 November: The first German U-boat sunk in the Bay of Biscay by Coastal Command using ASV was claimed by a Whitley VII (Z9190) of No 502 Squadron.

December: The Avro Lancaster entered service with No 44 Squadron at RAF Waddington.

A Hawker Hurricane II, landing at sunset after a demanding sortie searching for Luftwaffe attackers, is captured by Geoffrey Lea in this evocative painting 'Evensong'. More Hurricanes were on strength with Fighter Command in 1940 than Spitfires. During 1941, the Hurricane IIC with four 20mm guns entered service with Nos 3 and 257 Squadrons.

These pages generously donated by The Aircrew Association

Evensong – Hurricane Landing at Sunset by Geoffrey E. Lea

By 1942 Coastal Command was struggling to protect the ocean approaches to Britain's ports from enemy aircraft and submarines in the 'Battle of the Atlantic'. Air Chief Marshal Sir Arthur Harris was appointed Commander-in-Chief of Bomber Command in February. When Harris arrived, more than two-thirds of the night bomber force still comprised Wellingtons, Whitleys and Hampdens. The Blenheim gave way to the Boston, Ventura and, most important of all, the Mosquito. Bomber Command dropped parachutists on Bruneval on the French coast to capture a German early warning *Wurzburg* radar. In April, 20 Lancasters of Nos 44 and 97 Squadrons carried out a low-level daylight raid on the MAN factory at Augsburg. Harris unleashed his first 1,000-bomber raid on Cologne (Operation *Millennium*) on the night of 30/31 May. In addition to night bombing, Bomber Command was also devoted to supporting the Battle of the Atlantic by mounting attacks on U-boat factories and ports and by minelaying. On 11/12 February, the German warships *Prinz Eugen, Scharnhorst* and *Gneisenau* made a dash through the Channel from Brest. Because of bad weather, they were not spotted by the RAF until they were two-thirds through. In the Dieppe raid, the RAF was unable to provide adequate close support, with the result that numerous enemy aircraft succeeded in penetrating the massive air umbrella. The RAF lost 106 aircraft, including six Typhoons.

The enemy continued heavy attacks on Malta. In early 1942, an average of 50 aircraft struck the island each day. By April, Spitfires had arrived in Malta, and these helped to turn the tide. Beauforts of No 217 Squadron at Malta continued attacks on Axis shipping. In the Western Desert, prior to the battle of El Alamein in October, the RAF was able to field 1,200 serviceable front-line aircraft. Operation *Torch*, the American invasion of North Africa, was supported by RAF aircraft operating from Gibraltar. Later in 1942, Fighter Command started to receive the Rolls-Royce Griffon-engined Spitfire XII, which was used to counter German bomb-carrying fighters attacking southern England in daylight. In the Far East, the RAF was often outnumbered twenty to one in action by the Japanese. Eventually, combat-ready aircraft had to withdraw to India to defend Calcutta. The loss of Burma gave rise to fears that the Japanese might attempt to take Ceylon or even India from the sea. The RAF was strengthened in Ceylon, the Maldives, the Cocos Islands, Mauritius and the Seychelles.

January: Mosquito night fighters entered service with No 157 Squadron at RAF Castle Camps, Cambridgeshire.

January: The Martin Baltimore bomber entered RAF service with No 223 Squadron at Shandur, Egypt.

11/12 February: The German warships *Scharnhorst, Prinz Eugen* and *Gneisenau* escaped up the English Channel.

12 February: Formation of the RAF Regiment.

15 February: Singapore surrendered and the RAF elements in the Far East were flown to the Dutch East Indies.

16 February: The first operational use of the Boston III came when Nos 88 and 226 Squadrons made anti-shipping strikes off the Dutch coast.

22 February: Air Chief Marshal Sir Arthur Harris became AOC Bomber Command.

27/28 February: Paratroops involved in the raid on Bruneval were dropped from Whitleys of No 57 Squadron.

3–4 March: The first operational use of the Lancaster came when No 44 Squadron carried out mine-laying sorties; a night bombing attack against Essen followed on 10/11 March.

12 March: The Empire Central Flying School was formed at RAF Hullavington from elements of the CFS.

April: The North American Mustang entered service with No 2 Squadron at RAF Sawbridge. The first Curtiss Kittyhawks arrived in the Middle East. The Douglas Dakota entered service with No 31 Squadron at Dum Dum, Calcutta.

17 April: Twelve Lancasters from Nos 44 and 97 Squadrons made a daylight flight to Augsburg to bomb the MAN diesel-engine factory. Squadron Leader J D Nettleton was awarded the VC.

30/31 May: The first 'Thousand Bomber Raid' was made by the RAF on Cologne. 1,045 aircraft dropped over 2,000 tons of bombs in 90 minutes.

3/4 June: The first sortie and attack on a U-boat using a Leigh Light was made by a Wellington of No 172 Squadron.

4 June: The Spitfire IX entered service with No 64 Squadron at RAF Hornchurch.

July: The Martin Marauder entered service with No 14 Squadron at LG224 in Egypt.

6 August: *Moonshine* radio counter-measures were first used operationally to confuse enemy early warning radar.

15 August: The Pathfinder Force was formed by Group Captain Don Bennett.

September: The North American Mitchell bomber entered service with Nos 98 and 180 Squadrons at RAF West Raynham.

10/11 September: The first 4,000lb incendiary bomb was dropped by Bomber Command on Dusseldorf.

29 September: The RAF's American 'Eagle' squadrons – Nos 71, 121 and 133 – were transferred to the US Eighth Air Force.

October: The Armstrong Whitworth Albemarle glider tug and transport entered service with No 13 OTU at RAF Finmere.

October: The Mustang became the first RAF single-engined fighter to fly over Germany, in a raid on the Dortmund–Ems Canal.

2 November: Eastern Air Command was set up at Gibraltar to provide air cover for Operation *Torch* – the invasion of North Africa.

17 November: Liberators of No 159 Squadron, based at Salbani, India made their first raids on Japanese targets in Burma.

20/21 December: The first operational use of *Oboe*, a blind-bombing device, was made by Mosquitoes of No 109 Squadron in a raid on a Dutch power station.

David Wright's painting 'Winter Warm-up' shows three Westland Lysanders of No 277 Squadron on detachment to a snow-covered temporary location. This squadron operated as an air-sea-rescue unit based at Stapleford Tawney, Essex. Its Lysanders covered the busy area between south-east England and northern France over which large numbers of RAF fighters and bombers operated. They gave excellent service to downed aircrew.

These pages kindly donated by Arkell's Brewery Ltd

Winter Warm-up by David Wright

The new and effective Avro Lancaster and de Havilland Mosquito bombers became established in service. At the same time, new aiming and marking techniques did much to eradicate haphazard and wasteful bombing. The short-range *Gee* navigational aid was introduced for raids on the Ruhr. In August, Bomber Command sanctioned a major new bombing procedure. This entailed the use of 'pathfinder' aircraft, with the creation of a special force composed of experienced aircrews under the command of Group Captain D C T Bennett. In a raid on Hamburg, Bomber Command introduced a new navigation/bombing aid – H_2S. This centimetric radar was self-contained within the aircraft and 'painted' a basic picture of the ground below on a radar display screen. In due course, H_2S enabled bombers to carry out their attacks when the ground was wholly obscured by cloud. Mosquitoes were the first aircraft to use *Oboe* – an exceptionally accurate navigation/bombing aid which employed a ground-distance measuring station. The famous dams raid by Lancasters of No 617 Squadron, led by Wing Commander Guy Gibson VC, took place on 16/17 May.

A new device, codenamed 'Window', was used on a large scale for the first time. This comprised clouds of aluminium foil dropped by bomber aircraft which seriously disrupted Germany's radar network. Bomber Command continued to face heavy losses after a substantial increase in the number of Luftwaffe night fighters. Indeed, German defences destroyed 1,047 RAF bombers during a seven-month period in 1943. Aware that enemy 'revenge' weapon development was centred at Peenemünde, Harris ordered a heavy raid in August. Subsequently, Harris turned his attention to the Battle of Berlin and losses were again heavy. The Airspeed Horsa glider was first used in July for the invasion of Sicily. In September, Italy was invaded, but the Italian campaign slowed in the winter of 1943–44 as many of the forward airfields were transformed into acres of mud.

The improved Spitfire V arrived in the desert, together with the Curtiss Kittyhawk. The first four-engined bombers (Halifaxes, Liberators and Fortresses) had also been received in that theatre. The new Martin Baltimore was flying sorties against enemy troop concentrations and supply depots. The final phase of the Tunisian campaign started at the end of March and on 13 May the Axis forces in North Africa capitulated. At the end of 1943, South East Asia Command (SEAC) came into being as a unified organisation embracing all British Commonwealth and American forces under Admiral Lord Louis Mountbatten. The RAF element comprised 48 squadrons. The first Arakan campaign in Burma was fought between December 1942 and May 1943. The Chindits (jungle-trained troops) under Brigadier Orde Wingate were entirely supplied by RAF airdrops.

8 January: The Pathfinder Force became No 8 Group, Bomber Command.

16/17 January: Target Indicator bombers first used by No 8 Group in a raid on Berlin.

22 January: The first operational use of the Mitchell medium bomber by Nos 98 and 180 Squadrons in a raid on Ghent.

30/31 January: First use of H_2S by Stirlings and Halifaxes of Nos 7 and 35 Squadrons for navigation during a raid on Hamburg.

2 February: Mediterranean Air Command formed under Air Chief Marshal Sir Arthur Tedder, to control all air forces in north-west Africa and operating in the Mediterranean theatre.

March: The first Douglas Dakota transport in Europe, supplied under Lend-Lease, was delivered to No 24 Squadron at Gibraltar.

25 March: Ferry Command became Transport Command.

1 April: Squadron standards were introduced by HM The King to mark the RAF's 25th Anniversary. The first presentation was made to No 1 Squadron on 20 April.

18 April: The first successful shipping strike was made by Coastal Command's Strike Wing at RAF North Coates, comprising Nos 143 (Fighter), 236 (Bomber) and 254 (Torpedo-bomber) Squadrons.

May: Avro York LV633 *Ascalon* was delivered to No 24 Squadron at RAF Northolt for use as a VIP transport.

16/17 May: The Mohne and Eder Dams were breached by specially equipped Lancasters of No 617 Squadron.

1 June: Army Co-operation Command disbanded. Second Tactical Air Force (2 TAF) formed.

28 June: The prototype Hawker Tempest (LA602) made its maiden flight.

9/10 July: Mediterranean Air Command provided cover for the Allied landings in Sicily.

24/25 July: The first use of 'Window' (metal foil strips dropped to fool radar) was made by Bomber Command aircraft and first use of H_2S blind bombing radar system.

27/28 July: 787 bombers dropped more than 2,300 tons of bombs on Hamburg. The resulting fire-storm burnt everything combustible within three hours.

17/18 August: The first attack was made by Bomber Command on Peenemünde, where V-weapons were being developed.

15 September: RAF Regiment units were air-transported with their weapons to Cos and Southern Italy.

15/16 September: The first use of 12,000lb bombs on the Dortmund–Ems Canal by Lancasters of No 617 Squadron.

22/23 September: 'Spoof' raid techniques were employed by Bomber Command for the first time.

10 October: No 38 Group (RAF Airborne Forces) formed.

23 October: Mediterranean Allied Strategic Air Force formed.

7 November: Mosquitoes of No 248 Squadron, Coastal Command, made the first attack on a U-boat with the 57mm Molins gun.

15 November: Allied Expeditionary Air Force formed.

16 November: Air Command South-East Asia formed.

19/20 November: The first use of a *FIDO* (Fog Intensive Dispersal Operations) fuel-burning installation at RAF Graveley.

30 November/1 December: The first operational use of No 100 (Bomber Support) Group came when Wellingtons of No 192 Squadron carried out radio countermeasures flights over Germany.

December: The first Mustang IIIs joined No 65 Squadron at RAF Gravesend.

Edmund Miller's painting 'Diving for Home' depicts five Lancasters of No 166 Squadron based at RAF Kirmington, Lincs encountering flak whilst flying in cloud over the enemy coast. The pilot of the aircraft shown in the foreground was Pilot Officer Alec Gibson DFM, RNZAF and the navigator was Pilot Officer C. Martin DFC.

These pages generously donated by Ercol Furniture

Avro Lancaster B1s of No 166 Squadron by Edmund Miller GAvA

The long and arduous campaign continued in Italy. While the Allied Tactical Air Forces were able to dominate the skies, the land forces faced stiff resistance. There was bitter fighting on the main front throughout the winter of 1943–44 at the Anzio beachhead, prior to the capture of Rome in June. Throughout this period, the RAF had over 5,000 aircraft in the Italian theatre.

The Mediterranean Air Force was involved in supporting the landings in the South of France in August and the Balkan Air Force, based in Italy, provided assistance to partisan forces led by Marshal Tito in Yugoslavia. The success of the Allied invasion of Normandy owed much to the effective application of the lessons learnt in the Desert and Italy. The D-Day landings saw RAF aircraft of all types in action. They managed to virtually eliminate the Luftwaffe from the area during the Normandy landings – and barred the enemy's ability to move in reinforcements rapidly thereafter. The Tactical Air Force quickly began to deploy across the Channel and give close air support to the ground forces. The Allies continued to maintain air superiority and kept the ground battle isolated. When the break-out came in August, the RAF was ready to assist the rapid advance across France with reconnaissance and attacks on retreating formations. In September, an attempt was made to hasten the end of the war with the Rhine crossing which opened up the route into Germany. The airborne assault on Arnhem, though gallantly supported by Transport Command aircrew, was not the success that had been expected. The RAF was at its peak strength in June 1944, when it possessed over 8,000 front-line aircraft and 1,175,000 servicemen and women.

By early 1944, Coastal Command possessed some 430 operational aircraft at home, including many Mosquitoes equipped with rockets or heavy guns. Their main task was to prevent U-boats from the Biscay bases interfering with the invasion. The attacks by Bomber Command on Berlin continued into the Spring of 1944. The Nuremberg raid in late March brought disastrous losses to Bomber Command when 108 aircraft and 545 aircrew did not return. From April, Bomber Command was directed almost exclusively against targets whose destruction would have a direct effect upon the coming invasion of Europe. It was a diversion that was prolonged by a campaign against the V1 flying bomb industry and launching sites. The Polish partisan uprising in Warsaw in August required RAF aircraft from the Mediterranean theatre to drop supplies, but this was a hazardous operation and many Liberators were lost. Elsewhere, the besieged defenders of Kohima and Imphal were supplied by air for three months, this being a landmark in the history of air transport. It paved the way for the campaign in 1945 when the 14th Army reconquered Burma, throughout relying almost entirely on air power as a source of supply and reinforcement.

January: The Hawker Tempest entered service with No 486 Squadron.

11 January: The strategic offensive that preceded Operation *Overlord* began.

19 March: Operation *Strangle* road/rail interdiction operations in Central Italy began. They continued until 11 May.

11 April: Six Mosquitoes of No 613 Squadron bombed an art gallery at The Hague where Dutch resistance movement records were kept.

14 April: The strategic bombing of Europe was placed under the control of SCAEF.

May: The Republic Thunderbolt fighter entered service with No 135 Squadron at Minneriya and No 14 Squadron at St Thomas' Mount.

1 June: RAF Balkan Air Force formed.

5–6 June: Allied airborne troops were flown from England by No 38 Group aircraft and dropped on Normandy.

6 June: Operation *Overlord* – D-Day. Allied landings took place on the coast of NW France at Normandy. The RAF flew 5,656 sorties.

8/9 June: The first Tallboy deep penetration bombs were dropped by No 617 Squadron Lancasters on the Samur tunnel.

9 June: The prototype Avro Lincoln (PW925) first flew.

18 July: The first use of VHF R/T was made to call up direct support from rocket-firing Typhoons, known as the 'cab-rank'.

27 July: Operational sorties by the RAF's first jet squadron began. No 616 (South Yorkshire) Squadron Aux AF at RAF Manston used Meteor F1s to intercept V1 flying bombs.

28 July: The prototype de Havilland Hornet (RR915) made its first flight.

August: The Vickers Warwick III transport entered service with No 525 Squadron at RAF Lyneham.

August: Liberators from No 178 Squadron fought their way into Poland to drop supplies from low level to the Polish Home Army.

8 September: The first V2 rockets fell on Paris and London.

12 September: The first use of Loran (long-range navigation and bombing aid). This gave up to 1,200 miles range.

17 September: Operation *Market Garden* saw the First Allied Airborne Army land in Holland at Arnhem and Nijmegen.

14/15 October: The largest ever Bomber Command raid on German territory took place when 1,576 aircraft dropped 5,453 tons of bombs. In addition, the largest tonnage (4,547 tons) to be directed at a single target at night fell on Duisburg.

18 October: The Combat Cargo Task Force, Air Command South-East Asia, was established.

27 October: The prototype Bristol Buckmaster (TJ714) made its maiden flight.

28 October: The RAF Central Navigation School was renamed the Empire Air Navigation School.

12 November: The German battleship *Tirpitz* was destroyed when Tallboy bombs dropped from Lancasters of Nos 9 and 617 Squadrons scored direct hits in a fjord near Tromsö.

14 December: The largest military flying boat to be built in Great Britain, the Short Shetland (DX166), made its first flight.

No 98 Squadron at West Raynham was the first RAF squadron to receive the Mitchell I. In May 1944, No 98, by then part of the 2nd Tactical Air Force, received the Mitchell III. Initially operating from RAF Dunsfold, it moved to airfield B58 at Melsbroek, Belgium in October. Edmund Miller's painting shows a daylight formation of Mitchell IIIs led by Wing Commander (now Air Commodore, retd) Chris Paul, CB, DFC, MA, CEng, FRAeS, Belgian Croix de Guerre and Czech MC, encountering heavy flak over Colombelles.

These pages generously donated by Kodak Limited

North American Mitchell IIIs of No 98 Squadron by Edmund Miller GAvA

1945

In December 1944/January 1945, as the leading Allied troops moved into Germany, enemy resistance stiffened and the Germans mounted a desperate counter-offensive in the Ardennes, supported by a temporary come-back from the Luftwaffe. Every form of close air support by the RAF was still needed by the ground forces, but the heavy bombers had to return to the direct assault on the German homeland, with oil the primary objective. The way was prepared for the final offensive across the Rhine in March, assisted by a further airborne operation. Between June 1944 and March 1945, some 1,847 flying bombs were destroyed by RAF aircraft and ground defences. As the Luftwaffe struggled to eke out its dwindling fuel reserves, priority was afforded to those units defending the Reich against the day and night raids of the RAF and USAAF. In February, over 62,800 tons of bombs were dropped on the oil industry alone, which by March was virtually at a standstill. Two raids on Dresden on the night of 13/14 February by 773 Lancasters, evoked considerable and bitter controversy. These were carried out in accordance with a plan to assist advancing Russian forces by attacking centres of transport and munitions. The fact that the town was packed with refugees from the Eastern Front was not considered significant in the general conduct of the war at that stage.

At sea, flying-boat and other coastal squadrons ranged far and wide over the Bay of Bengal and Indian Ocean, covering an area twice that of the North Atlantic. In early 1945, Beaufighters played havoc with Japanese shipping. Victory in Burma was completed by the end of July and no campaign in WW2 had made such demands on an air force – nowhere else were the demands so desperate and nowhere else were they so completely satisfied. As the war in Europe drew to a close, the RAF turned to humanitarian missions, such as dropping food to the starving people of the Low Countries and bringing home thousands of prisoners of war, many of whom were aircrew. VE Day came on 8 May, with Germany's unconditional surrender. The RAF, with the formation of the *Tiger Force*, was planning for the forthcoming invasion of Malaya and Singapore scheduled for September. Bomber Command was also tasked for the conventional bombing of the Japanese homeland. However, the use of nuclear weapons by USAAF B-29s on Hiroshima and Nagasaki in August brought the war in South-East Asia to an end.

January: The Short Stirling V transport entered service with No 46 Squadron at RAF Stoney Cross.

January: The RAF Helicopter Training School, equipped with Sikorsky R-4s, was formed at RAF Andover.

13/14 February: Firestorm raids were made on Dresden by RAF Bomber Command and the US Eighth Air Force.

13 March: The first 22,000lb Grand Slam bomb was dropped from a Lancaster B1(Special) (PD112) of No 617 Squadron on the Bielefeld viaduct.

24 March: Operation *Varsity* airborne operations in support of the Rhine crossing began.

31 March: The end of the British Commonwealth Air Training Plan. It had trained 137,739 aircrew, of which 54,098 were pilots.

9/10 April: The German battleship *Admiral Scheer* was hit and capsized, and the *Admiral Hipper* and *Emden* were badly damaged in a raid on Kiel.

16 April: The first operational use of RAF jet aircraft based on mainland Europe involved Meteors at Nijmegen airfield.

20 April: The first production de Havilland Vampire F1 (TG274) made its maiden flight.

26 April: The first prisoners of war were repatriated by air. This continued until 1 June when Bomber Command alone had carried 75,000 POWs.

29 April: Food-dropping operations began over Holland by 250 RAF bombers and continued until 8 May.

May: The strength of the RAF, including Dominion and Allied officers and airmen, amounted to 1,080,000, of whom 190,000 were aircrew.

2 May: Italian fighting ended. In Burma, a Mosquito crew landed at Mingaladon and became the first Allied personnel to enter Rangoon.

7 May: The 196th and last U-boat to be destroyed by Coastal Command was claimed by a No 210 Squadron Catalina.

8 May: The Royal Observer Corps stood down. At the time, it comprised 32,000 observers in 1,420 posts.

26 May: Lancaster *Aries* of the Empire Air Navigation School returned to RAF Shawbury after a flight over the true North and magnetic North Poles.

16 June: It was announced that special operations to 19 countries had been flown during the war from RAF Tempsford, Beds. They included the transportation of supplies to resistance movements in countries occupied by the enemy.

July: The 2nd Tactical Air Force in Germany was renamed British Air Forces of Occupation.

August: The Avro Lincoln entered RAF service with No 57 Squadron at RAF East Kirkby.

August: The Hawker Tempest II entered service with No 183 Squadron at RAF Chilbolton.

6 August: The first atomic bomb was dropped on Hiroshima.

9 August: The second atomic bomb was dropped on Nagasaki.

14/15 August: The unconditional surrender of Japan was announced.

6 September: A twin-engined photographic reconnaissance Mosquito flew from RAF St Mawgan to Newfoundland, covering the 2,350 miles in 7hr 2min.

20 September: The first aircraft powered by propeller-turbine engines made its maiden flight. It was a Meteor with Rolls-Royce Trent engines driving four-bladed propellers.

7 November: A world speed record of 606.25mph was set by Group Captain H J Wilson flying a Meteor F4 over Herne Bay.

Michael Turner's painting, commissioned for the 50th Anniversary of the RAF Regiment, commemorates the historic defence of Meiktila in March 1945. This valuable airfield complex in Burma, from which the RAF undertook close support of the 14th Army, had been captured by No 1307 Wing, RAF Regiment. The painting illustrates a dawn counter-attack by RAF Regiment forces to retake the airstrip from the Japanese before the start of flying operations. The painting is reproduced by kind permission of the PMC, Officers' Mess, RAF Regiment Depot, Catterick.

The Defence of Meiktila by Michael Turner PGAvA

The immediate post-war years were faced by a very large RAF, equipped mainly with aircraft that had been developed during WW2. It inherited responsibilities that spread across the world from Germany to the Mediterranean, the Middle East, India, Hong Kong and Singapore. There was pressure to reduce the size of the force and allow many of its wartime members to return to civilian life. In the Far East, the sudden surrender of Japan presented enormous problems. Throughout South-East Asia, POWs and internees had to be freed and repatriated. The Japanese had to be rounded up and law and order re-established. RAF squadrons were heavily committed throughout 1946 in the Dutch East Indies – this was an onerous task carried out in the face of local suspicion and, at times, hostility. In the British Zone of Germany, the RAF took over many former Luftwaffe bases. In the context of Britain's financial and industrial weakness in the aftermath of WW2, the decision to limit defence expenditure and establish priorities was inevitable. What made it acceptable, even to the Services, was the assumption – endorsed by the Government – that a major war was unlikely in the next five years, and hardly more likely within ten years. For the RAF, Government policy inevitably meant a concentration on essentials – including developing the resources of Fighter and Bomber Commands, and, to a lesser extent, those of Coastal Command. This would be detrimental to other elements, particularly Transport Command.

The Defence Statement published in February announced that the total strength of the armed forces was expected to fall from 5 million at the end of WW2 to 1,100,000 by December. The decline of RAF manpower was rapid. The maximum number of personnel permitted in Fiscal Year 1946/47 was 750,000, including 142,000 on terminal leave – falling by the following year to less than 375,000. A problem which affected all operational commands of the RAF was the provision of aircraft and other equipment. Many of the aircraft being operated at the end of WW2 had been provided by the United States under the Lend-Lease Act of 1941. With the exception of the Dakota transports, all Lend-Lease aircraft were to be given up and replaced by British types. The Government also announced a very considerable reduction in the provision of new weapons and equipment. This was primarily to limit the burden on the frail national economy and assist industrial recovery, but also to avoid the accumulation of equipment which would quickly become obsolete as research led to new and more advanced weapons. Inevitably, a number of promising designs were lost in the process. The 1946 Defence Statement stated that existing stocks would be used wherever possible and modern replacements made available to only a limited degree. An Air Ministry specification was issued in December for a turbojet-powered bomber capable of a speed of 600mph and able to reach 45,000ft over the target. It was to have a five-man crew, but no defensive armament.

---

1 January: Marshal of the Royal Air Force Sir Arthur Tedder succeeded Lord Portal as Chief of the Air Staff.

January: The French were able to resume control in French Indo-China. The RAF had been represented by Spitfires of No 273 Squadron and the main body of No 684 (Photographic Reconnaissance) Squadron.

12 March: The Secretary of State for Air said that 742,000 members of the RAF's strength of 1,100,000 at the end of WW2 would be released by 30 June.

27 March: The re-establishment of RAF Reserve Command was announced for the maintenance and training of reserve organisations.

28 March: Transport squadrons based overseas transferred from Transport Command to overseas Commands. Transport Command retained home-based transport units and was responsible for the operation of trunk routes.

31 March: The first flight of the prototype Percival Prentice.

April: The de Havilland Vampire jet fighter entered service with No 247 Squadron at RAF Chilbolton.

May: The de Havilland Hornet twin-engined fighter, the fastest twin piston-engined combat aircraft to reach operational status, entered service with No 64 Squadron at RAF Horsham St Faith.

1 May: The last English-based Mustangs were withdrawn by No 64 Squadron at RAF Linton-on-Ouse. They served in Cyprus until 1947.

1 May: The Accident Investigation Branch was transferred from the Air Ministry to the Ministry of Civil Aviation.

7 May: The Central Flying School re-formed at RAF Little Rissington.

22 May: The first flight of the de Havilland Chipmunk.

2 June: The Auxiliary Air Force re-formed with 13 day fighter, three night fighter and four light bomber squadrons.

8 June: Victory Day observed in Britain. There was a flypast by 300 RAF aircraft.

10 July: The Air Ministry announced that the RAF Regiment would remain an integral part of the peacetime RAF, maintaining rifle, armed and light AA squadrons. In addition, units would be trained as airborne and parachute troops.

12 July: It was announced that an RAF High Speed Flight had been formed at RAF Tangmere with the objective of increasing the performance of aircraft.

7 September: A new world speed record was set by the RAF High Speed Flight when Group Captain E M Donaldson flew at 616.81mph over Littlehampton in a Meteor F4 (EE549).

October: Coastal Command front-line strength was reduced to two squadrons of flying boats, four land-based squadrons of general reconnaissance aircraft and two medium-range strike squadrons.

December: The last P-47 Thunderbolt squadrons in India, Nos 5 and 30, re-equipped with the Tempest F6.

30 December: The prototype Handley Page Hastings (TE580) made its first flight at RAF Wittering.

Successor to the Lancaster, the Avro Lincoln was just too late to see action in WW2, becoming the mainstay of Bomber Command in the post-war period until replaced by the Canberra. Chris Stothard's painting is of Lincoln B1 RF578 QR-R flown by Flight Lieutenant Joe Waddington of No 61 Squadron based at RAF Waddington portrayed over Lincoln Cathedral. The painting is reproduced here by kind permission of the PMC, Officers' Mess, RAF Waddington.

These pages generously donated by the Officers of Royal Air Force Waddington

Waddington's Lincoln by C. J. Stothard

The Air Staff plan for a broadly-based air force emerged from detailed discussions undertaken four years earlier, in September 1943. Over the intervening period, a number of plans had been produced, but none had been given official sanction and none was based on any clear indication of what resources would be available and what responsibilities the post-war RAF would be allocated. Plan E, which emerged in mid-1947, just before the Government's pronouncement on defence expenditure, was believed by the Air Staff to be adequate for immediate needs. At the same time, it would provide the structure upon which the permanent peacetime RAF could be built and from which it could expand when the necessary resources became available. Plan E proposed a front-line target of 165 squadrons of some 1,500 aircraft, which included 51 fighter squadrons (536 aircraft), 41 bomber squadrons (328 aircraft), 13 maritime squadrons (84 aircraft) and 42 transport squadrons (341 aircraft). Most of this front-line squadron strength would be retained in the UK, but 24 squadrons would be based in Germany, 18 in the Middle East and a further 18 in the Far East. A strategic reserve, with a high mobility factor, would be available to reinforce overseas theatres at short notice. The defence statements of the immediate post-war years stressed the need to keep a balance between the requirements of industry in helping to rebuild the national economy and those of the services in carrying out essential tasks in the aftermath of war. The memoranda accompanying the air estimates explained the consequences to the RAF of rapid demobilisation. In February, the Air Ministry pointed out that in normal times the flow of officers and airmen into and out of the air force was small, compared with its overall size.

Since VE-Day, a high proportion of wartime entrants had been released, the most experienced being the first to leave. Consequently, an abnormally large part of the RAF was engaged either in training or in the routine administrative work involved in the process of demobilisation and reorganisation. The 1947 Defence Statement referred to the progressive rearmament of Fighter Command with the most modern types of jet fighters, and of Transport Command with small numbers of British designed and built transport and airborne forces aircraft. To make this easier, some of the squadrons which made up the RAF were given two number plates, while others existed only in cadre form. By the end of 1947, a plan to replace the piston-engined heavy bombers with jet bombers got under way. Handley Page was to proceed with what became the Victor, and Avro with the Vulcan. As insurance against undue development and production delays with these advanced types, prototypes of two more conventional bomber aircraft were ordered – the Short Sperrin, which did not proceed beyond the prototype stage, and the Vickers Valiant. The Valiant was an 'interim' V-bomber, the last to be ordered but the first to enter squadron service. 1947 saw the end of the RAF's deep involvement with the Indian sub-continent, following the granting of independence. Henceforth, the focus of the RAF's Far East activities lay in Singapore – with subordinate formations in Malaya, Ceylon (until 1957) and Hong Kong.

---

3 January: The Air Ministry announced that the King had approved the reconstitution of the King's Flight. Based at RAF Benson, it received four Vickers Viking aircraft.

6 January: Announcement of agreement for exchange postings of RAF/USAF officers.

February: Mustangs of No 213 Squadron in Cyprus were replaced by Tempest F6s.

4 March: The Air Estimates provided for a maximum of 370,000 officers and airmen to be maintained in the RAF during 1947–48.

April: The RAF College Cranwell absorbed the resident No 19 Flying Training School to re-form its flying training element, which it had lost towards the end of the war.

30 April: The London–Cape Town record was broken by a Mosquito PR34, which covered the distance of 6,717 miles in 21hr 31min.

30 May: A prototype of the proposed advanced trainer, the Boulton Paul Balliol (VL892), was flown for the first time.

30 June: The prototype Vickers Valetta C1 made its maiden flight.

10 July: The Battle of Britain Memorial in Westminster Abbey was dedicated in the presence of HM King George VI.

17 July: The prototype Vickers Varsity T1 made its first flight.

27 July: The Bristol Sycamore, the first British designed production helicopter, made its first flight at Filton.

28 July: Sixteen RAF Lancasters landed at Andrews Field, Maryland on a goodwill mission and to take part in the celebrations of the USAAF's 40th anniversary on 1 August.

August: A number of Coastal Command Lancasters deployed to Ein Shemer in Palestine to reinforce their counterparts in the Mediterranean and to locate ships carrying illegal immigrants to Palestine.

November: The first Percival Prentice T1 entered service with the RAF at the Central Flying School Basic Training Squadron, RAF South Cerney.

December: The two remaining RAF Air Gunnery Schools closed down, their functions being absorbed into the Central Gunnery School at Leconfield. Several Air Navigation Schools remained, equipped mainly with Wellingtons and Ansons.

December: Hostility to the British presence in Burma was increasing. With independence and the decision to leave the Commonwealth, the Air Headquarters in Rangoon was disbanded.

16 December: The RAF's Auxiliary Air Force was retitled Royal Auxiliary Air Force.

Short Sunderland V PP164 in Keith Woodcock's painting carries the markings of No 201 Squadron over its base at RAF Pembroke Dock. The Sunderland V was the final version of this flying boat and 150 were built for Coastal Command. No 201 Squadron was the last of two home-based Sunderland squadrons of the RAF and operated them until February 1957. The painting is in the collection of Flight Lieutenant I. D. E. de Hamel RAFVR, the pilot of PP164. No 201 Squadron currently operates the Nimrod MR2P maritime patrol aircraft from RAF Kinloss.

These pages generously donated by No 201 Squadron

Short Sunderland V of No 201 Squadron over Pembroke Dock by Keith Woodcock GMA, GAvA

In 1948, the Air Staff acknowledged that the RAF was under severe strain, with a low average level of experience, frequent postings and a very considerable dilution of manpower. Demobilisation had combined with the very different periods of training required by the various RAF trades to produce not only an overall shortage of trained men, but also a lack of balance between trades, which was seriously disrupting the work of many units. In June, when Britain was simultaneously faced with crises in Europe and the Far East, the RAF was considerably smaller than the target proposed in Plan E, or even the revised version produced after Government cuts in defence expenditure. At home, the front-line force comprised 80 squadrons, with a further 20 squadrons in the Royal Auxiliary Air Force, while overseas there were 33 more full squadrons and six cadre squadrons. Shortages of manpower, equipment and spares were affecting all operational commands and causing a rise in unserviceability, a reduction in flying hours and an overall loss of efficiency. Whereas Fighter Command had been progressively rearmed with the best jet fighters then available, Bomber Command's weakness was that it did not have aircraft with the radius of action needed to strike against targets as far afield as the USSR. Similarly, Coastal Command had yet to obtain replacement aircraft of adequate range, and an effective anti-submarine weapon such as the American torpedo used during the war (American stocks having been returned). In Transport Command, replacements had yet to arrive for the York and Dakota. Although the British Air Force of Occupation in Germany had received a substantial number of Vampires, Middle East and Far East commands had still to acquire any modern jet aircraft. By mid-1948, the front-line establishment of Bomber Command had been cut from 1,560 aircraft at the end of the war to just 160 – specifically, 48 Lancasters, 96 Lincolns and 16 Mosquitoes.

All operational Commands were working to the limit of their resources, reorganising and retraining their front-line units and extending their tasking. Coastal Command had continuing meteorological and survey commitments. Transport Command established new trunk routes to the Middle East and Far East. In the Far East, the RAF was involved, with the army, in fighting a long and bitter campaign on the Indonesian island of Java. In June, all surface communications between the West and Berlin came to a halt in defiance of international agreements. Both the RAF and USAF were adequately prepared to mount a limited airlift to keep their Berlin garrisons supplied., but the requirement to supply the needs of two million inhabitants entirely by air was a different matter. Such a massive airlift had never been contemplated before. The problem for the RAF was that the rundown in the immediate post-war years had left its transport force without the resources to sustain such an intense level of operation. By the end of the year, however, two squadrons of Hastings had arrived to help the Dakotas and Yorks.

---

16 February: RAF fighters took part in exercises over southern England with USAF B-29 Superfortresses which had flown from the US to Germany on a training mission.

23 March: An altitude record of 59,446ft was established by Group Captain John Cunningham in a de Havilland Vampire.

24 March: A Boulton Paul Balliol powered by an Armstrong Siddeley Mamba turboprop made its maiden flight. It was the world's first aircraft to fly with a single propeller gas turbine engine.

May: As part of the withdrawal of British forces from Palestine, Nos 37 and 38 Squadrons were sent to Malta and No 32 Squadron to Nicosia, Cyprus.

June: The beginning of Operation *Firedog* – RAF operations against terrorists in Malaya. The first sorties were strikes by Spitfires of No 60 Squadron in support of security forces.

28 June: The RAF joined the USAF in supplementing the Berlin Airlift (Operation *Plainfare*) by flying between Wunstorf (West Germany) and Gatow (Berlin).

July: A task force was created in Kuala Lumpur, Malaya with detachments of Spitfires from Nos 28 and 60 Squadrons, Beaufighters from No 45 Squadron based in Ceylon and Dakotas from No 110 Squadron.

5 July: The first crossing of the North Atlantic by jet fighters was made by six Vampire F3s of No 54 Squadron, which flew from RAF Stornoway via Iceland and Greenland to Goose Bay, Labrador.

6 August: The Air Ministry announced that the first Royal Auxiliary Air Force squadrons to be rearmed with jet fighters would be No 500 (County of Kent) and No 605 (County of Warwick) Squadrons, using Meteors and Vampires respectively.

September: The Handley Page Hastings transport entered service with No 47 Squadron at RAF Dishforth.

3–7 September: RAF aircraft and USAF B-29s took part in Exercise *Dagger*, designed to test the air defences of Britain.

12 October: The first flight of a prototype Meteor F8 (VT150).

15 October: It was announced that RAF and USAF elements involved in the Berlin Airlift had been merged in a Combined Air Lift Task Force. All of the RAF's front-line transport aircraft were then in Germany, this force comprising 64 Dakotas, 56 Yorks and ten Sunderlands.

26 October: The first Meteor T7 (VW410) two-seat jet trainer made its maiden flight.

1 November: The RAF's first Hastings squadron, No 47, joined the Berlin Airlift.

December: The Meteor T7 became the first jet trainer to enter into service with the RAF.

December: In the Far East, Beaufighters replaced Mosquitoes whose wooden construction had proved unable to withstand the high humidity.

Developed from the Avro Lancaster bomber, the Avro York equipped eight RAF Transport Command squadrons in 1948, all of which took part in the Berlin Airlift. Charles J. Thompson's painting, specially commissioned by the Royal Air Force Benevolent Fund, depicts a trio of Yorks on final approach to land at RAF Gatow, Berlin in deteriorating weather conditions. Yorks made 29,000 flights to Berlin and carried some 230,000 tons of supplies to the city, almost half the RAF's total contribution.

These pages generously donated by FlyPast Magazine

Finals at Gatow by Charles J. Thompson GAvA

The Air Estimates of 1949 took the initial steps needed to produce the aircraft and equipment that would ensure the effectiveness of the RAF well into the next decade and beyond. In this respect, the immediate post-war years were a particularly successful period from which emerged not only the English Electric Canberra twin-jet bomber and the trio of heavy bombers, the Vickers Valiant, Handley Page Victor and Avro Vulcan, but also the de Havilland Venom, Hawker Hunter, Gloster Javelin and Avro Shackleton. Events in the Middle East and Far East were alarming enough – of more immediate concern was the conduct of the USSR towards occupied Germany and the overthrow of democratic governments in a succession of East European countries and their replacement by Communist regimes allied closely to Moscow. The blockade of Berlin was lifted in May but the airlift continued for another four months. This was to build up a stockpile of supplies in case of any further Russian interference with surface communications.

The emphasis was then to restore RAF resources that had been lost in the previous four years. During 1949, the remaining Lancaster squadrons were re-equipped with Lincolns – but Bomber Command still did not possess an aircraft with a radius of action that would enable it to attack targets in Russia in the event of war. The British Government requested the United States to supply B-29 Superfortresses under the Mutual Defense Assistance Program (MDAP) as an interim measure and the first squadrons of Washingtons, as the B-29 was known in RAF service, were equipped during the following year. Bomber Command raised objections to the acquisition of the B-29 on the grounds that it would be expensive to operate and maintain. They required a crew of eight compared, with the Lincoln's six, further exacerbating the RAF's acute manpower problem. A new directive to Fighter Command in April underlined changes in priorities– the main task was to defend the UK against air attack, and in the following two years a number of important steps were taken. The Command's readiness state was increased when day fighters were put on amber alert, codenamed *Fabulous*, to intercept any unidentified aircraft approaching British airspace.

The presence of forces in the Far East was to defend Britain's colonial territories and trading interests. The RAF provided air defence as a contribution to the overall stability of the area. Britain's Far East forces were to be involved in fighting of one kind or another for the next 18 years. The *Amethyst* incident in April was an indication of a new factor in Far Eastern affairs – the approaching victory of the Communists in China and their hostility to the West. In April, a Sunderland flying boat of No 88 Squadron was damaged when it landed alongside HMS *Amethyst* in the Yangtse River to deliver medical supplies.

January: The Bristol Brigand strike aircraft entered service with No 84 Squadron at Habbaniya.

7 January: The Israeli Air Force attacked RAF reconnaissance patrols over the Egyptian frontier and shot down four Spitfires and one Tempest. Two RAF pilots were killed.

1 February: The Womens' Auxiliary Air Force was re-named the Womens' Royal Air Force.

9 March: The prototype Avro Shackleton MR1 made its first flight.

4 April: The North Atlantic Treaty was signed, to come into effect on 24 August 1949.

21 April: An RAF Sunderland flying boat reached HMS *Amethyst* with doctors and medical aid. The *Amethyst* was stranded in the Yangtse River in China when it was a target for Communist gunfire.

May: The Vickers Valetta C1 transport entered service with No 204 Squadron at Kabrit in Egypt.

11 May: Spitfires of No 28 Squadron left Malaya for a 2,300-mile flight to reinforce the defences of Hong Kong.

11/12 May: The Berlin Blockade was officially lifted – at which time the RAF had 40 Yorks, 40 Dakotas and 14 Hastings employed on the Airlift. The RAF had flown 18,205,284 miles on 49,733 flights, lifting 251,542 tons of freight in and 26,368 tons out of Berlin. It also carried 67,373 passengers.

13 May: The prototype Canberra B2 twin-engined jet bomber (VX165) made its first flight at Warton.

June: The Empire Radio School at Debden became the Signals Division of the RAF Technical College.

1 June: The Far East Air Force was formed.

1 June: The RAF Flying College was formed at RAF Manby by combining the Empire Air Navigation School, the Empire Air Armament School and the Empire Flying School.

28 August: The de Havilland DH113 Vampire NF10 night fighter first flew.

2 September: The prototype Venom FB1 (VV612) made its first flight.

4 September: The first British delta-wing aircraft, the Avro 707, made its maiden flight. It was a small size research representation of the projected Avro 698 Vulcan bomber.

1 October: The guided-missile range at Cape Canaveral in Florida was established, following agreement by Britain, the USA and the Bahamas. It was controlled by the USAF.

10 December: The first production Meteor F8 (VZ438) was delivered to the RAF.

14 December: An agreement on air training between Britain and Southern Rhodesia was signed. This provided for the continuation of the wartime training scheme in Rhodesia on a permanent basis.

The Percival Prentice replaced the biplane Tiger Moth with Flying Training Command and remained the standard basic trainer until the arrival of the Provost. Most RAF pilots who trained in the late 1940s and early 1950s went through their basic flying instruction on the Prentice, which was the RAF's first basic trainer with side-by-side seating. Eric Day's painting illustrates a gathering of student pilots and instructors in front of a line-up of Prentices at the RAF College, Cranwell. The painting is reproduced by kind permission of The Commandant, RAF College, Cranwell.

These pages generously donated by Morgan Grenfell Asset Management

Percival Prentices at the Royal Air Force College by Eric Day

The Korean War erupted in 1950 and lasted for three years. The RAF's contribution was, of necessity, severely limited, as the air arm was already heavily involved in Malaya. Sunderlands of Nos 88, 205 and 209 Squadrons were made available to help in Korea, where, working in conjunction with the USAF, they flew over 1,600 sorties, totalling some 13,000 flying hours. Seventeen RAF pilots served with the Royal Australian Air Force and United States Air Force fighter squadrons in Korea. In Malaya, the light bomber element of FEAF's strike force was re-equipped with the Bristol Brigand. Serving with Nos 45 and 84 Squadrons, the type was plagued with reliability problems. The first of a number of Bomber Command Lincoln squadrons arrived in March, together with Lincolns from No 1 Squadron, RAAF. In April, the RAF's first operational Westland-Sikorsky Dragonfly helicopters were received for the Casualty Evacuation Flight. Although severely underpowered and untested in the hot and humid Malayan conditions, they proved their worth, and their pilots began to develop new operating procedures for that theatre to meet the urgent requirement for a casevac helicopter. The establishment of the Federal Republic in the Western Zone of Germany brought further changes in that country.

The RAF investigated the possibility of introducing the four-jet North American B-45 Tornado bomber into squadron service and a small number of aircrew undertook operational evaluation of the aircraft both in the USA and the UK. The Hawker Hunter and Supermarine Swift swept-wing, single-seat fighter aircraft were ordered off the drawing board to replace the Meteor, Vampire and Venom, after lengthy indecision by the Ministry of Supply and the Air Staff. Coastal Command's meteorological reconnaissance flights over the North Atlantic were carried out by Handley Page Hastings in place of the ageing Halifaxes. These flights provided data on the weather systems approaching the British Isles which were important for forecasting conditions over the UK, Europe and the civil air routes across the North Atlantic. In 1950, it became evident that Russia was engaged in a rapid expansion of its naval forces and was planning to have 1,000 submarines in service within a short time. The RAF urgently required a replacement for the Sunderland and Lancaster with a larger radius of action and a British version of the homing torpedo. By 1950, the Percival Prentice had replaced the Tiger Moth and the Boulton Paul Balliol was partially adopted in place of the Harvard. The Meteor T7 had entered service with Advanced Flying Schools as the sole jet trainer for the RAF.

January: The RAF's first British manufactured helicopter, Westland Dragonfly HC2 (WF308) powered by an Alvis Leonides engine, was delivered.

27 January: An Anglo-American agreement, covering the lease of 70 Boeing B-29 Superfortresses to the RAF, was signed in Washington.

February: The first RAF Chipmunks were delivered to the Oxford UAS, where they replaced Tiger Moths at Kidlington. The Chipmunk was adopted for all of the University Air Squadrons and other initial flying training units.

24 February: The first prototype Hunting Percival Provost (WE522) made its initial flight.

20 March: Lincoln bombers of No 57 Squadron arrived at Singapore to support operations against terrorists in Malaya.

22 March: The first Boeing Washington (ex-USAF B-29 Superfortress) arrived in England for the RAF. No 149 Squadron at RAF Marham was the first to re-equip. A total of 88 Washingtons entered RAF service.

22 March: The prototype Gloster Meteor FR9 was flown.

29 March: The English Electric Canberra PR3 prototype (VX181) made its maiden flight.

1 April: Personnel on strength of the RAF was 202,400, some 10,000 below the planned figure.

31 May: The first Armstrong-Whitworth designed and built Meteor NF11 (WA546) made its maiden flight at Baginton.

20 June: The prototype of the four-engined Universal Freighter (subsequently named the Beverley), built by Blackburn and General Aviation at Brough, made its first flight.

July: The first unit to be equipped with the Meteor FR9 was No 208 Squadron at Fayid in the Canal Zone.

22 July: Reserve Command was renamed Home Command.

22 August: General Douglas MacArthur's Headquarters announced that RAF Sunderlands from Hong Kong were engaged in blockade operations on the west coast of Korea.

22 August: The prototype de Havilland Venom NF2 (WP227) made its first flight.

28 August: A plan was announced for the training of 200 RAF aircrew in Canada during 1951.

31 August: The Vickers Valetta T3 prototype made its first flight. 40 were built for five Air Navigation Schools and the RAF College, Cranwell.

September: First flight of the Avro 707B, a second scale delta research aircraft for the Avro 698 bomber.

14 September: It was announced that British troops would be flown to Japan to augment forces already in Korea.

12 November: Vampires were despatched by air to reinforce FEAF squadrons – the longest jet delivery flight by any air force up to that date (8,500 miles).

15 November: The prototype Vampire T11 two-seat jet trainer (WW456), built by Airspeed at Christchurch, flew for the first time.

December: No 2 Squadron became the first squadron in Germany to be equipped with the Meteor PR9.

December: The Valetta was issued to No 622 Squadron. This was the only transport squadron in the Royal Auxiliary Air Force.

The de Havilland Hornet was designed as a long-range fighter for wartime use in the South Pacific but came too late to see action. Hornets were delivered to Fighter Command and were the fastest piston-engined fighters ever used by the RAF. Michael Turner's painting shows two Hornet F3s in the colours of No 41 Squadron at Church Fenton which operated them until converted to the Meteor in early 1951. No 41 Squadron currently operates the SEPECAT Jaguar GR1A at RAF Coltishall.

These pages generously donated by Adwest Group plc

Hornets of No 41 Squadron by Michael Turner PGAvA

The English Electric Canberra, which was to constitute the second phase of Bomber Command's post-war expansion programme and provide the main strength of its front-line forces until the arrival of the V-bombers, began to enter service in May. With the RAF's small force of Lincolns and Washingtons already obsolete, and relations with the Soviet Union becoming more tense, it was imperative to have as many Canberras in squadron service as quickly as possible. Consequently, considerable effort was made to get the Canberra B2 operational, with No 101 Squadron at RAF Binbrook being the first to receive this twin-jet bomber. By early 1951, Fighter Command's front-line day fighter strength had been doubled and all squadrons were equipped with new jet aircraft. By December, Fighter Command possessed 25 front-line squadrons with a total of 402 aircraft, including 276 Meteor F8s, 48 Vampire FB5s, 38 Meteor NF11s and 35 Vampire NF10s. In addition, there was the RCAF Sabre Wing plus 160 Meteors and Vampires of the Royal Auxiliary Air Force squadrons.

A specification for a new long-range Coastal Command land-based aircraft based on the Avro Lincoln had been issued in 1946 and the resulting Avro Shackleton MR1 was introduced into service in 1951. This became the RAF's mainstay for the following two decades. It was to be some time before sufficient Shackletons would be available to meet Coastal Command's increasing commitments and new responsibilities within NATO. A stop-gap solution was found under MDAP with the procurement of 52 Lockheed P2V-5 Neptunes to equip four squadrons. These remained in service until 1956. For medium transport duties, the Vickers Valetta started to replace the Dakota. In Germany, the RAF's front-line strength grew to 16 squadrons – 13 with the Vampire FB5 in the day fighter and ground attack roles, two in the fighter reconnaissance role with Meteor FR9s and one photographic reconnaissance squadron with Meteor PR10s. No 2 Group was re-formed to take control of BAFO squadrons, but No 85 Wing, which had been raised to Group status during the Berlin Airlift, was disbanded. Simultaneously, all 16 squadrons were assigned to the operational control of NATO's newly-established Supreme Allied Commander Europe (SACEUR). In September, to emphasise that Britain was no longer an occupying power and would serve alongside Germany in a new military alliance, BAFO was renamed the 2nd Tactical Air Force (2 TAF). The Mosquito T3 and FB6 continued to serve as trainers for night-fighter pilots at the advanced flying schools and operational conversion units but the Wellington was giving way to the Vickers Varsity at bomber training and conversion units.

January: The first turbojet-powered night fighter to enter service with the RAF, the Armstrong Whitworth Meteor NF11, joined No 29 Squadron at RAF Tangmere.

21 January: The first jet aircraft to fly the Atlantic non-stop and unrefuelled was an RAF Canberra B2, which flew from Britain to Baltimore. It was subsequently used to develop the Martin B-57 version for the USAF.

29 January: The Prime Minister announced plans to speed up the British rearmament programme, to call up reservists and institute refresher training for the Royal Auxiliary Air Force.

February: The Shackleton MR1 entered service with the Coastal Command OCU at RAF Kinloss – followed by No 120 Squadron in April.

March: No 1 Basic Flying Training School was formed at RAF Booker. Although civilian operated, it was equipped with Chipmunk T10s as were four other BFTSs that formed subsequently.

April: No 8 Advanced Flying Training School formed at RAF Dalcross with Airspeed Oxfords, to provide advanced training for National Service pilots that had received initial instruction at a BFTS. Three more schools were established later in the year.

May: The English Electric Canberra B2 entered service with No 101 Squadron at RAF Binbrook. The Canberra became the RAF's principal light bomber.

May: Four Flying Refresher Schools were formed to cater for aircrew returning to flying duties after ground tours.

18 May: The Vickers Valiant swept-wing jet bomber prototype (WB210) – the first of the trio of four turbojet-powered heavy bombers – made its maiden flight.

26 May: The first Royal Colour was presented to the RAF at a ceremony in Hyde Park by Princess Elizabeth.

June: The Vickers Varsity trainer entered service with No 201 AFS at RAF Swinderby, replacing the Wellington T10.

July: No 25 Squadron at RAF West Malling became the first RAF front-line unit to receive the Vampire NF10.

20 July: The prototype Hawker P1067 (WB188), later to be named the Hunter, made its first flight.

5 August: The prototype Vickers Supermarine Swift (WJ960) made its maiden flight.

1 September: British Air Forces of Occupation (BAFO) in West Germany was renamed the 2nd Tactical Air Force.

17 October: Following anti-British rioting and disturbances in Egypt, RAF transports flew army parachutists from Cyprus to Fayid in the Suez Canal Zone.

15 November: RAF North Luffenham was occupied by No 1 Fighter Wing, Royal Canadian Air Force.

26 November: The prototype Gloster Javelin delta-wing all-weather fighter (WD804) made its first flight at Moreton Valence.

Bristol Brigand B1s in this painting by Michael Turner served with No 84 Squadron at RAF Tengah, Singapore during the Malaysian campaign and are depicted in action attacking terrorists with rockets. The Brigand was conceived as a torpedo bomber but its role was switched to that of a light bomber for overseas squadrons. No 84 Squadron currently operates the Westland Wessex in the search and rescue and support helicopter roles from RAF Akrotiri, Cyprus.

These pages generously donated by No 84 Squadron, RAF

Brigands of No 84 Squadron in Malaya by Michael Turner PGAvA

Seven new Canberra squadrons were formed during the year – Nos 9, 12, 50, 105, 109, 139 and 617. Preparations for the introduction of the new V-bombers included the development of ten Class I airfields at Coningsby, Cottesmore, Finningley, Gaydon, Honington, Marham, Scampton, Waddington, Wittering, and Wyton. Runways were to be 9,000ft long together with a 1,000ft overrun. They had to be 200ft wide and capable of withstanding aircraft weights of 200,000lb. In addition, taxi-ways and hard-standings had to be provided for at least 16 V-bombers at each station. Dispersal airfields were also developed to ensure that aircraft would not be destroyed at their home bases by a pre-emptive strike. The bomb which the V-force was to carry was the *Blue Danube*, a free-fall plutonium device developed for the RAF and tested in October in the Monte Bello Islands.

The major problem of the early 1950s was that the RAF still relied on 'stop-gap' fighters to counter the growing power of the formidable Soviet air force. The RAF aircraft in service were only slightly better than their predecessors – the Venom, for example, was an improvement on the Vampire, but was no match for the Soviet MiGs. Deliveries of Canadian-built F-86E Sabres, under the US Mutual Defense Assistance Program (MDAP), began at the end of the year. The fighters were ferried across the Atlantic by RAF pilots under Operation *Beecher's Brook*. World tension, sparked by the Korean War, had highlighted the degree to which the RAF's air defence coverage of the air space surrounding the United Kingdom was falling behind, as well as its inadequate equipment overall. A sixth sector – the Western – became operational in January and at the same time No 81 Fighter Group had re-formed to control Fighter Command's training units.

Britain had been faced with labour unrest amongst African workers in Kenya since 1948. This was fomented by the Kikuyu tribe, which was beginning to claim back land that it had previously sold to European settlers. In 1952, the violence escalated and a state of emergency was declared in October. Handley Page Hastings of Transport Command began supplying reinforcements to RAF Eastleigh in Nairobi. Britain signed a treaty of friendship with Oman in 1951, to confirm close ties which went back more than 150 years. The boundary with Saudi Arabia was disputed and there was a long standing problem of exercising authority over tribes in the interior. Vampire FB5s of No 6 Squadron deployed from Habbaniya to Sharjah to fly low-level sorties over the disputed Buraimi Oasis. The overall trend in MEAF was to move RAF squadrons out of the Canal Zone. Nos 6 and 683 Squadrons moved to Habbaniya in 1952. Two Allied Tactical Air Forces were formed as part of the NATO structure in Central Europe – 2 ATAF operating in the North and 4 ATAF in the South – with the RAF assuming the leading role in the North and the USAF in the South. However, NATO's resources remained inadequate and an urgent expansion of 2 ATAF's front line force was authorised.

January: The first of 52 Lockheed Neptune patrol bombers for Coastal Command began arriving in the UK. They entered service with No 217 Squadron at RAF St Eval.

3 January: The prototype Bristol Type 173 made its first flight at Filton. It combined two sets of Sycamore powerplants in tandem and was the RAF's first twin-rotor helicopter. It was developed into the Type 192 Belvedere.

February: The first British-designed helicopter, the Bristol Sycamore, entered service with the Coastal Command Development Unit at RAF St Mawgan.

17 March: The last sortie of a Halifax in front-line service was flown by GRVI RG841 of No 224 Squadron from Gibraltar.

7 June: Air Vice-Marshal D F W Atcherley, AOC No 205 Group, RAF Middle East disappeared on a flight in a single-seat Meteor from Fayid in Egypt to Nicosia, Cyprus.

July: The RAF's postwar peak strength was reached with 6,338 aircraft on charge.

July: The Vampire T11 entered service with Advanced Flying Schools at RAF Valley and RAF Weston Zoyland.

August: The first de Havilland Venom FB4 fighter-bomber entered service with No 11 Squadron at Wunstorf.

16 August: The Bristol Britannia made its first flight at Filton.

26 August: A Belfast-Gander-Belfast point-to-point record was set by a Canberra. This was the first two-way crossing of the Atlantic in one day by any aircraft.

29 August: XA249, the first of 28 Miles Marathon navigation trainers for the RAF, made its first flight.

30 August: The prototype Avro 698 Vulcan (VX770) delta-wing strategic bomber flew for the first time.

October: The Bomber Command Bombing School was formed at RAF Lindholme with Lincolns and Varsities.

3 October: The first British atomic weapon was detonated at Monte Bello.

1 November: The prototype Percival Pembroke C1 light transport (WV698) made its maiden flight.

2 November: The Air Ministry announced that the RAF was to receive between 300 and 400 F-86 Sabres to serve with 2TAF. The airframes were to be built in Canada.

December: The Canberra PR3 entered service with No 540 Squadron at RAF Benson.

24 December: The prototype of the Handley Page Victor crescent-wing, four jet bomber (WB771) made its first flight.

The Rolls-Royce Merlin-engined Boulton Paul Balliol T2 in Keith Woodcock's painting served as a two-seat trainer at the RAF College Cranwell until superseded by the Vampire T11 in 1956. The painting depicts a student and instructor leaving an aircraft after the final flight of the day. This painting is reproduced by kind permission of The Commandant, RAF College, Cranwell.

Boulton Paul Balliol T2 of the Royal Air Force College, Cranwell by Keith Woodcock GAvA

The first allocation of the newly delivered F-86 Sabres went to No 66 Squadron at RAF Linton-on-Ouse and Nos 3, 67 and 71 Squadrons in Germany. The fixed-wing element of the short-range transport force in Malaya was significantly improved in September when the first of the short take-off and landing Scottish Aviation Pioneers arrived to form No 1311 Transport Flight. This later became part of the newly established No 267 Squadron at Kuala Lumpur, with Pembrokes and Dakotas as well as the Pioneers. Because of substantial reinforcements, the RAF was able to offer the Malayan ground forces much improved support as they drove the terrorists further back into the jungle. The troubles in Oman continued and a blockade was instituted to prevent Saudi Arabian supplies reaching the Buraimi Oasis. Meteor FR9s from No 208 Squadron in the Canal Zone were tried but their short endurance made it impossible to cover the blockade area with the few aircraft available. Lancaster GR3s from Nos 37 and 38 Squadrons at Malta were deployed to Sharjah, but they had to return to Malta to fulfil NATO commitments and the role was taken over by Valettas and Ansons.

By early 1953, the RAF's 2nd Tactical Air Force in Germany had grown to 25 squadrons and a second group Headquarters, No 38, was established. Its Vampires were replaced by Venom FB1s and by the Canadian Sabres supplied under MDAP. In the night fighter role, 2TAF squadrons acquired the Meteor NF11. Additional airfields at Jever and Oldenburg were brought into service. Four new airfields, well to the west of the Rhine, were also developed. Wildenrath was the first, followed by Geilenkirchen, Brüggen and Laarbruch. At the same time, 2TAF moved its headquarters back from Bad Eilsen (less than 100 miles from the East German border) to Rheindahlen, west of Dusseldorf. Canberra B2s started deploying to Germany, partly as a result of a shortage of suitable airfields for the operation of these jet bombers in the UK.

The Boulton Paul Balliol T2, originally planned as a turboprop-powered advanced trainer but now fitted with a Rolls-Royce Merlin piston engine, was overtaken by events as jet trainers (Vampire T11s) were introduced as a preliminary step to all-through jet training. The Prentice started to be phased out of the basic flying training schools, being replaced by the Percival Provost T1. This Alvis Leonides-powered side-by-side aircraft was used as the RAF's basic trainer until 1959 when it began to give way to its jet-powered counterpart, the Jet Provost. By the early 1950s, it was becoming increasingly obvious that Britain, as a power with world-wide colonial responsibilities and an interest in maintaining stability wherever it might be threatened, would more than ever need to deploy ground and air forces appropriate to the situation. Speed of deployment was more essential than hitherto and had become a prerequisite of success. The airlifting of troops was becoming a more widely accepted practice and air transport assumed greater significance in planning the RAF's equipment for the second half of the fifties.

---

27 January: A point-to-point record was set by a Canberra for the 3,921 miles between London-Heathrow and Mauripur, Karachi in 8hr 52min. Continuing its flight, the aircraft set a new London–Australia (Darwin) record of 22hr 21min.

1 February: The Far East Air Force's Casualty Evacuation Flight was re-formed as No 194 Squadron, the first RAF helicopter squadron with Westland Dragonfly HC2s and HC4s.

4 February: Aircraft from RAF Transport Command in Britain and 2TAF in Germany were sent to assist in the rescue operations after disastrous floods in Holland.

12 March: An RAF Flying Training Command Lincoln was shot down by Russian jet fighters after straying into the Russian Zone in Germany.

April: Harvards became operational in Kenya against the Mau Mau uprising.

14 June: The first British transport aircraft specifically designed for the air-dropping of heavy loads, the Blackburn Beverley (WZ889), flew for the first time. It entered service with No 47 Squadron in March 1956.

15 July: The Coronation Review of the RAF by HM The Queen at RAF Odiham. The flypast included 640 aircraft, of which 440 were jets.

27 July: Hostilities ended in Kenya.

August: The Scottish Aviation Pioneer STOL light transport aircraft entered service with the RAF.

27 August: The first production model of the Comet II made its maiden flight at Hatfield.

8–10 October: The London–New Zealand Air Race was won by RAF Canberra PR3 (WE139) covering the 11,792 miles in a total time of 23hr 50min at an average speed of 494.5mph. It also established a London–Shaibah record of 5hr 11min at an average speed of 544.3mph. Another Canberra set a London–Colombo record of 10hr 25min at 591.5mph.

17 October: HM The Queen opened, and the Archbishop of Canterbury dedicated, the Commonwealth Air Forces Memorial at Runnymede. This commemorates 20,455 airmen who lost their lives during World War 2 whilst flying from bases in the UK and who have no known grave.

November: The first Venom NF2 two-seat night fighter was issued to No 23 Squadron at RAF Coltishall.

December: The last Vampire FB9 single-seat fighter variant for the RAF (WX260) was delivered.

21 December: The first production Vickers Valiant (WP199) made its first flight.

Anthony Cowland's painting 'Auxiliary Rivals' shows a Gloster Meteor F8 of No 610 Squadron based at RAF Hooton Park overflying de Havilland Vampire FB5s of Thornaby-based No 608 Squadron. Both units were Royal Auxiliary Air Force Squadrons.

Auxiliary Rivals by Anthony R. H. Cowland GAvA

No 92 Squadron at RAF Linton-on-Ouse replaced its Meteor F8s with MDAP supplied Canadair Sabre F4s in February, being the second Fighter Command squadron to receive the interim type. The long awaited Hawker Hunter and Supermarine Swift were pushed into service with the RAF but development work was still continuing to overcome a number of shortfalls in performance as well as quite major technical problems. The Swift required considerable modifications to its powerplant and armament, as well as aerodynamic improvements which caused it to become a very complex aircraft. Although it was issued to No 56 Squadron at RAF Waterbeach in February 1954, it was withdrawn 15 months later because of a large number of accidents. The Hunter also had its share of problems but these were overcome and it went on to become the RAF's standard single-seat fighter, replacing the Meteor and Sabre. By 1954, Coastal Command's expansion was complete and it possessed nine Shackleton squadrons, four with Neptunes, two flying Sunderlands and a Hastings MET squadron. The Shackletons and Sunderlands were based on the Western seaboard to cover the eastern Atlantic, and the Neptunes at RAF Kinloss and RAF Topcliffe for the North Sea. The squadrons began to receive the Mark 30 homing torpedo. This, together with a new directional sonobuoy, gave maritime aircraft a much improved tracking and attack capability. The Bristol Sycamore helicopter joined No 194 Squadron in Malaya. With its larger cabin, better performance and more positive handling characteristics, it was a significant improvement on the Dragonfly. The RAF developed a new technique using Lincolns to mount a main bombing attack, while de Havilland Hornets struck simultaneously at nearby targets which were pinpointed by Austers flying forward air control missions.

The Omani conflict ended in July when both sides agreed to withdraw their forces while arbitration took place. Nevertheless, problems continued and Lincolns from No 7 Squadron were eventually deployed to form No 1426 Flight at Bahrain to patrol the disputed frontier. No 249 Squadron was withdrawn from Egypt to Amman, Jordan. All too quickly, it was appreciated that the Soviet threat could not be effectively countered by conventional forces alone. While the USA already possessed nuclear weapons, it seemed to the British Government that the security of the UK could be guaranteed only if such weapons and a means of delivery were available on this side of the Atlantic. Consequently, the development of British nuclear weapons resulted in an operational bomb that could be delivered by the new generation of 'medium' bombers. As a result, what quickly became known as the V-Force, entered service in the mid-1950s. The Vickers Valiant, the first of the three new types of aircraft, was used for the main atomic bomb trials – and subsequently both as a bomber and tanker for air-to-air refuelling. The Vulcan, the next into front-line service, formed the core of the deterrent force along with the Victor.

January: The Canberra T4 entered service with No 231 OCU at RAF Bassingbourn.

February: No 267 Squadron, FEAF, at Kuala Lumpur, was the first to receive the Scottish Aviation Pioneer short take-off and landing light transport.

February: The last Lancaster (RF273) was retired from Bomber Command service.

February: Venoms were introduced in the Middle East Air Force, replacing Vampires with No 6 Squadron.

13 February: The Supermarine Swift single-seat, swept-wing fighter entered service with No 56 Squadron at RAF Waterbeach.

19 March: The Auster AOP9 (WZ662) made its first flight.

1 April: The last operational sortie by an RAF Spitfire, operating from Seletar, was carried out by a PR19 aircraft of No 81 Squadron over the Malayan jungle.

May: Canberra PR3s joined No 69 Squadron in Germany.

18 May: Swift F1s were grounded pending the result of an investigation into a number of accidents.

23 June: An RAF order for an unspecified number of Vickers 1000 transport aircraft with Rolls-Royce engines was announced by the Secretary of State for Air.

July: The Hawker Hunter F1 fighter entered service with No 43 Squadron at RAF Leuchars.

22 July: The first production Gloster Javelin FAW1 (XA544) made its maiden flight.

4 August: The English Electric P1 (subsequently developed into the Lightning fighter) made its first flight at Boscombe Down. It was the first British fighter able to exceed the speed of sound in level flight.

11 August: The Folland Midge (the precursor of the Gnat) made its maiden flight at Boscombe Down.

23 August: The Air Ministry announced that a squadron of Canberra bombers was to be stationed at Ahlhorn, Germany.

October: Bombing operations were conducted by Lincolns of Nos 61 and 214 Squadrons against the Mau Mau in Kenya.

October: Canberra B2 *Aries IV* of the RAF Flying College made the first jet flight over the North Pole.

31 October: Northolt airport was closed to civil flying and handed back to the RAF for use as the London terminal for RAF transport aircraft.

5 November: The Air Ministry revealed that radar-controlled bombing operations were being carried out against Mau Mau hideouts in Kenya.

December: The Sector Operations Centres and the GCI stations were moved into underground shelters. The vintage Chain Home Type 7 radars were replaced at key sites by Type 80 radars. These gave much improved coverage of up to 200nm against targets flying at heights up to 40,000ft.

Eric Day's painting illustrates Meteor NF12 WS697 of No 25 Squadron based at West Malling flying over Gloucester Cathedral. The night fighter versions of the Meteor were designed by Armstrong Whitworth at Baginton, Coventry. No 25 Squadron is currently an air defence squadron flying Panavia Tornado F3s from RAF Leeming. The painting is reproduced by kind permission of the PMC, Officers' Mess, RAF Innsworth.

Meteor NF12 of No 25 Squadron over Gloucester Cathedral by Eric Day

In February, No 22 Squadron at RAF Thorney Island received its first helicopters for search and rescue (SAR) duties, when six Westland Whirlwind HAR2s were delivered. The squadron pioneered the effective use of helicopters for SAR around the UK coast, both for military and civilian emergencies. Air transport operations in Malaya had become increasingly important as the number of troops active in the jungle approached its peak in 1955. The Valetta's tasks were supply dropping, troop-carrying and resupply of forward airfields. Alongside these medium transports, the small Auster's value lay in its forward air control duties of target marking and visual reconnaissance. As a communications aircraft, its use was limited, for it was only able to carry one passenger safely in Malayan conditions. However, the newly delivered Pioneers could carry up to four passengers and 800lb of freight. Another role undertaken by the RAF transport squadron, and one that increased in importance as the anti-terrorist campaign gained momentum, was the use of aircraft to wage psychological warfare. Leaflet dropping, which had begun in the first months of the Emergency, increased steadily to a peak of 141 million leaflets dropped in 1955 by Dakotas, Austers and Valettas. Broadcasting from the air was also adopted, using loudspeakers fitted to Dakotas and Austers of No 267 Squadron.

There was a further withdrawal by the RAF from Egypt when Nos 32 and 39 Squadrons moved to Malta and No 70 Squadron was transferred to Nicosia, Cyprus. This Mediterranean island, used as a major British base, was attracting substantial local hostility and the Greek Cypriot community was demanding an end to the Crown Colony status. From April 1955 until February 1959, British forces were engaged in a struggle with Greek Cypriot EOKA guerrillas. Once again, the RAF was closely involved in anti-terrorist activities. Shackletons of Nos 37 and 38 Squadrons mounted surveillance patrols from Malta to monitor shipments of arm being smuggled from Greece. In December, an Internal Flight of Ansons was formed to counter the airdrops of arms which the guerrillas were receiving.

During 1955, the RAF began to withdraw from Iraq, including the major base that had been built up over many years at Habbaniya, although a staging post was retained there until 1959.By the middle of 1955, a total of 29 Canberra squadrons had been established, of which 26 were engaged in the light bomber role, including four deployed to RAF Germany. A further three squadrons operated in the PR role and total Canberra strength stood at 259.

---

14 January: It was announced that the Woomera rocket range and its associated establishments and laboratories were to be amalgamated under the title of Weapon Research Establishment.

February: The Westland Whirlwind HAR2 entered service with No 22 Squadron at Thorney Island for SAR duties.

9 February: The Vickers Valiant B1, the RAF's first V-bomber, entered service with No 138 Squadron at RAF Gaydon.

17 February: The personnel strength of the RAF was 259,300.

17 February: It was stated that Britain would proceed with the development and production of thermo-nuclear weapons (Hydrogen bombs).

23 February: The RAF revealed that the Swift Mks F1 to F4 could not be brought up to a safe operational standard. After further tests on the F4, it was decided that further production should be severely limited and that orders should be switched to the Hunter. Development work on other marks of Swift, intended for fighter reconnaissance, continued.

23 March: The last RAF pilots to qualify for their 'wings' on Harvards completed their course at No 3 FTS at RAF Feltwell. However, the Harvard continued in service with UASs of Home Command and it was also used in an operational role against the Mau Mau in Kenya and terrorists in Aden.

24 March: The Ministry of Supply announced an order for six Folland Gnat light fighters for development purposes.

30 May: It was announced that a new fighter group had been added to Fighter Command – No 13 Group with headquarters at Ouston, Northumberland. The other two Groups were No 11 at Uxbridge and No 12 at Newton.

June: The last Venom variant, the NF3 two-seat night fighter, entered service with No 141 Squadron.

7 July: Middle East Air Force re-organised. Northern Group, under Air Headquarters, Levant at Nicosia, was established to control units in Iraq, Jordan, Cyprus and Libya; Southern Group, under Headquarters British Forces, Aden, was responsible for units in Aden, South Arabian Coast, Kenya and staging posts.

8 July: The Hawker Hunter T7 two-seat fighter trainer prototype (XJ615) was flown for the first time.

18 July: The first Folland Gnat lightweight fighter powered by a Bristol Orpheus engine made its maiden flight.

August: The first RAF 'all-jet' training programme began at No 2 FTS, RAF Hullavington using an initial batch of Jet Provost T1s. The first pilot with no previous experience flew solo on 17 October after 8hr 20min tuition.

3 August: Flying Officer Hedley Molland was the first RAF pilot to survive a supersonic ejection when he abandoned a Hunter at 40,000ft.

2 September: The first Avro Shackleton MR3 (WR970) made its maiden flight.

3 September: Squadron Leader J S Fifield made the first ejection from a moving aircraft (a Gloster Meteor) before it became airborne.

December: The last Avro Lincolns were retired from Bomber Command, which it became an all-jet force with Canberras and Valiants.

December: The Air Ministry announced that flying was due to commence from the RAF airfield at Akrotiri in the Sovereign Base Area of Cyprus. The airfield, constructed on a flat rock peninsula on the south coast of the island, would cater for the fastest and largest types of military jet.

The Gloster Meteor T7 was used extensively as an advanced trainer by the RAF. Air Vice-Marshal Norman Hoad's painting depicts two Meteor T7s banking over a hangar at the RAF Flying College airfield at Strubby. A T7 is being towed out of the hangar by a David Brown fluid-flywheel tractor, whilst another is being refuelled from a 2500 gal AEC Matador bowser.

These pages generously donated by Bombardier Services

Gloster Meteor T7s at Royal Air Force Strubby by Air Vice-Marshal Norman Hoad CVO, CBE, AFC*, GAvA

Abu Sueir, the last airfield to be evacuated by the RAF in the Canal Zone, was formally handed over to the Egyptians in April 1956. Three months after this withdrawal, the Egyptian Government, in breach of treaty, announced the nationalisation of the Suez Canal. In case armed intervention should be necessary to protect British interests, RAF units were concentrated in the Eastern Mediterranean at Malta and Cyprus. After a period of tension on the Israeli/Egyptian border, Israel mobilised her forces and moved against Egypt on 29 October, with the declared intention of forestalling aggression. The British and French governments then issued an ultimatum calling on both sides to cease hostilities. Egypt rejected the ultimatum and on 31 October Valiants and Canberras began a series of attacks to neutralise Egyptian airfields. A large number of Egyptian aircraft were destroyed or damaged on the ground in these attacks. The Egyptian Air Force had been supplied with Russian aircraft and equipment in the previous months. Although the RAF did all that was asked of it, the task force as a whole was not geared to exploit the situation fully in the time available before a ceasefire, leaving the British and French governments to make an embarrassing withdrawal. The Kenyan Government had declared an amnesty in 1955 and in 1956 the police and civil administration assumed responsibility for the maintenance of law and order – but the state of emergency was destined not to end for another five years.

In 1956, the RAF introduced the de Havilland Comet C2 into service with No 216 Squadron at RAF Lyneham. This was the first military squadron in the world to be entirely equipped with a jet transport. The Comets had originally been ordered by BOAC, but cancelled after the disasters that befell the earlier Comet 1s. The Gloster Javelin, a twin-engined, two-seat, delta-winged night/all-weather fighter, came into use with No 46 Squadron in February to complement the Hawker Hunter day fighter. The Swift FR5, a much modified fighter reconnaissance version of the troubled aircraft, went to Germany where it replaced the Meteor FR9 with Nos 2 and 79 Squadrons. From the inception of the Hendon Air Pageants, the RAF had presented formation aerobatics by current front-line or training aircraft. The RAF's first major aerobatic team following WW2 comprised the all-black Hunter F6s of No 111 (Treble-One) Squadron, which formed in 1956. After a performance in France, they were applauded as *Les Fleches Noir* and were thereafter known at home and throughout the Continent as the *Black Arrows*. Bomber Command introduced a programme to improve the readiness state of its bombers. Two categories of warning were devised. The *strategic* warning gave 24 hours notice, during which 20% of the force would be at readiness within two hours, 40% in four hours, 60% in eight hours and 75% within 24 hours.

January: De Havilland Vampire T11 jet trainers replaced Balliols at RAF Cranwell, becoming the first jet trainers to serve at the RAF College.

11 January: The formation of an air task force to take part in British atomic tests at Monte Bello Island, off the northern coast of Australia, was announced.

10 February: Death of Marshal of the Royal Air Force, Lord Trenchard, aged 83.

22 February: The Air Ministry disclosed the duties of the new aircrew category of Air Electronics Officer (AEO).

24 February: The Gloster Javelin FAW1 all-weather jet fighter entered service with No 46 Squadron at RAF Odiham.

March: The Blackburn Beverley C1 transport entered service with No 47 Squadron at RAF Abingdon.

6 March: It was disclosed that the de Havilland Comet 2 transport aircraft was to serve with the RAF.

12 April: Canberra bombers deployed to Luqa, Malta for Exercise *Medflex Dragon*, and exercises with US and Italian aircraft.

30 April: No 215 Squadron, the only UK-based Scottish Aviation Pioneer CC1 squadron, was formed at RAF Dishforth for army support duties.

May: The Avro Vulcan B1 entered service with No 230 OCU at RAF Waddington.

May: The last Sabres in Germany were replaced by Hunters with Nos 71 and 234 Squadrons.

7 June: The de Havilland Comet C2 entered service with No 216 Squadron at RAF Lyneham.

August: The RAF started to withdraw its Lockheed Neptunes from Coastal Command after only four years in service. Four squadrons had been equipped by the US under MDAP, pending delivery of Avro Shackletons.

2 September: The first non-stop transatlantic flight by a British V-bomber was completed by a Valiant. It flew from Loring, Maine to RAF Marham in 6hr 15min.

11 October: The first British nuclear bomb to be dropped from an aircraft was released by Valiant WZ366 of No 49 Squadron at Maralinga, Southern Australia.

15 October: The RAF retired its last Lancaster, an aircraft of the School of Maritime Reconnaissance at RAF St Mawgan.

30 October/6 November: The Suez Campaign.

26 November: A production order for an unspecified number of English Electric P1 fighters was announced.

December: Fighter Command reached a peak strength of some 600 front-line aircraft in 35 squadrons – including 16 with Hunters.

6 December: It was announced that 13 Bristol Britannia turboprop long-range transport aircraft had been ordered for the RAF.

Frank Wootton's painting shows HM The Queen and the Duke of Edinburgh on a visit to RAF Marham reviewing a line-up of Vickers Valiant B1s and their crews from Nos 148, 207 and 214 Squadrons. The Valiant was the first of the 'V' bombers to enter RAF service.

These pages generously donated by VICKERS P.L.C.

Royal Review by Frank Wootton FPGAvA

The introduction of the Avro Vulcan B1 into RAF squadron service coincided with a Defence White Paper which looked forward to the replacement of the manned bomber force by long-range missiles. In spite of this, the V-force was steadily built up until it became the central feature of British defence policy – with the focus on its readiness, flexibility and mobility. A high state of alert was introduced in the V-force squadrons, with crews manning the aircraft on the operational readiness platforms (ORPs) that had been specially constructed adjacent to the runways, ready to scramble at the first warning of an attack from the Warsaw Pact countries. Government policy, under the influence of Duncan Sandys as Minister of Defence, placed greater emphasis on missile forces for future defence planning. The V-bombers were to be 'supplemented by ballistic rockets' and agreement was reached with the US Government 'for the supply of some medium-range missiles of this type'. For defence of bomber bases, fighters would 'in due course be replaced by a ground-to-air guided-missile system'. As a corollary, the RAF was 'unlikely to have a requirement for fighters more advanced than the Lightning' and 'work on other such projects would stop'. The Government also decided, 'having regard to the high performance and potentialities of the Vulcan and Victor bombers and the likely progress of ballistic rockets and missile defence' not to go on with the development of a supersonic bomber. Having enunciated these radical changes in defence policy, the 1957 White Paper, *Defence – Outline of Future Policy*, admitted that the new plan it set out involved 'the biggest change in military policy ever made in normal times'. It also conceded that 'in carrying it through a certain amount of disturbance' was inevitable – including a large reduction in the size of the armed forces.

In 1957, as well as the usual outbreaks of tribal unrest and the continuing threat of armed incursions from the Yemen, a rebellion broke out in Muscat and Oman territory to the north-east. To meet treaty obligations to the Sultan of Oman, troops were flown into Sharjah, to build up the legitimate forces in the area. Meteors reconnoitred the Jebel, Venoms attacked strong-points and all available support was given to the Special Air Service in its campaign to defeat the rebels. The first British hydrogen bomb was dropped at Christmas Island, in the Pacific, in May. The RAF aerobatic team, the *Black Arrows*, became the first to fly with five Hunters. The team also performed a formation landing. At the 1957 SBAC display at Farnborough, team numbers had been increased to nine aircraft. Something of a sensation was caused by a formation loop and roll by nine aircraft, which had not been seen since the biplane days. Coastal Command's final two Sunderland squadrons were disbanded in 1957.

March: All Royal Auxiliary Air Force squadrons were disbanded, thus reducing Fighter Command's strength by 20 squadrons at a stroke.

April: The Air Signallers' School operating Ansons and Varsities at RAF Swanton Morley was re-titled the Air Electronics School.

April: The Meteor F8 finally disappeared from front-line service when No 245 Squadron converted to Hunters.

4 April: The Conservative Government's Defence White Paper foreshadowed far-reaching changes in the RAF's strength and role. It carried the implication that the RAF's long-range striking force would re-equip with ballistic missiles and that the days of the manned bomber were numbered.

May: The remaining RAF element in Jordan was withdrawn.

15 May: The first British hydrogen (thermo-nuclear) bomb was dropped over Christmas Island by a Valiant of No 49 Squadron.

21 May: The first Vulcan to enter squadron service joined No 83 Squadron at RAF Waddington.

11 July: Although the RAF's last operational mission by Spitfires took place in 1954, it was not until 1957 that the remaining Spitfires were struck-off charge. The last three (PR19s) went to RAF Biggin Hill to join the newly formed Battle of Britain Memorial Flight.

August: No 220 Squadron was the first to be equipped with the Avro Shackleton MR3 at RAF St Eval – but was only allocated six aircraft.

1 September: The Army Air Corps came into existence. It brought together and rationalised the Army's air observation post, forward air control and communications light aircraft which were previously under the control of the RAF.

October: The second Vulcan squadron – No 101 (previously the first of the Canberra squadrons) – was formed at RAF Finningley.

4 October: The Soviet Union launched the first Sputnik satellite. This resulted in a US decision to deploy Thor intermediate range ballistic missiles to European NATO forces. Britain reached an agreement to station a number of these missiles in the UK.

November: The last Venom NF3 night fighters in service – with No 89 Squadron at RAF Stradishall – were replaced by Javelin FAW2s.

November: The third and last of the V-bombers, the Handley Page Victor B1, entered service with No 232 Operational Conversion Unit at RAF Gaydon.

December: No 45 Squadron, which had been operating Venom FB1s at Butterworth, Malaya, was re-equipped with Canberra B2s.

The Bristol Sycamore was the first British-designed helicopter to go into service with the RAF at home and overseas. In this painting, Wilfred Hardy shows Sycamore HAR14 XJ918 of No 194 Squadron hovering over a clearing in the Malayan jungle. In 1959, the Squadron merged with No 155 to re-form No 110 Squadron at Seletar. It operated Sycamores until 1964 when they were replaced by Whirlwinds.

These pages generously donated by Imperial Tobacco Limited

Bristol Sycamore HR14 of No 194 Squadron in Malaya by Wilfred Hardy GAvA

The Bristol Bloodhound, a surface-to-air missile complete with supporting radars and effective against aircraft up to normal operating heights, entered service with Fighter Command in 1958. Following the 1957 Defence cuts, there had been a reduction in fighter strength as the perceived threat from a potential enemy switched from manned bombers to missiles. However, forecasts that the manned fighter was becoming obsolete proved somewhat premature. Manned fighters armed with air-to-air missiles were required for a number of defence purposes – notably to deter and prevent reconnaissance and other forms of air intrusion, such as attempts to investigate and jam our early warning systems. The first fighter/missile combination was the Javelin/Firestreak which went into service in October. The delta-winged fighter carried four under-wing missiles in addition to its two 30mm cannon.

The Air Council organised a conference in London in May (code-named *Prospect*) at which its views, particularly on manned aircraft, were put across to a respective cross-section of the British public. The V-bombers were to be supplemented by Thor ballistic missiles, supplied by the US Government, rather than by the British Blue Streak. These American IBRMs, capable of delivering a nuclear warhead over a distance of more than 1,500 miles, were positioned on East Anglian sites from 1958 to 1963 to strengthen the Western strategic nuclear deterrent forces. The 60 missiles loaned for this period under a US-UK agreement were kept under American control but manned by Bomber Command personnel. Their static, above-ground, locations did not commend them to the Air Staff as deterrent weapons. As fixed targets, they were more likely to draw enemy attacks, whereas the V-bombers were mobile and would operate from dispersed bases.

St Clement Danes Church in the Strand was reconsecrated on 19 October 1958 and became the Central Church of the Royal Air Force. It had been largely destroyed by enemy action on 10 May 1941, but the walls and steeple were left standing and it was rebuilt from this shell. Over 700 squadron and unit badges are embedded in the floor. At the West door is an impressive rosette of Commonwealth Air Force badges surrounding the badge of the RAF. At the base of each window are the Books of Remembrance, recording the names of those who have died while serving in the RAF.

January: A photographic survey of Aden Colony and Protectorate (112,000 square miles) was completed for the Colonial Office and Directorate of Military Survey by RAF Meteors, Canberras and Valiants.

January: The second Shackleton MR3 squadron – No 206 – was formed at RAF St Mawgan.

February: After months of negotiations, the US agreed to provide Thor IRBMs to be operated by RAF units. The warheads were to be kept in US custody, and launching was to take place only after a joint positive decision by both Governments.

February: Canberras and V-bombers of Bomber Command were given nuclear capability and V-bombers successfully accomplished flight-refuelling trials.

29 March: The first of 13 Canberra T11s (WJ734) made its first flight. These modified B2s were used to train AI radar operators.

9 April: The Handley-Page Victor B1 entered service with No 10 Squadron at RAF Cottesmore.

6 May: Exercise *Prospect II*, the Air Council conference, was attended by 300 guests at which present and future roles and organisation of the RAF was clarified.

June: Miles Marathon navigation trainers were retired.

20 June: The prototype Westland Wessex made its first flight at Yeovil.

22 June: The Hunting Jet Provost T3 made its maiden flight. This jet trainer served with the RAF's Basic Flying Schools until 1993.

July: Bristol Bloodhound Mk 1 surface-to-air missiles entered service with No 264 Squadron at RAF North Coates.

July: The King of Iraq was assassinated and a revolutionary government installed. The RAF was banned from overflying Iraq and using the important staging post at Habbaniya.

August: Bomber Command's first IRBM squadron, No 77, was formed at RAF Feltwell. The first Douglas Thor missile for the squadron was received on 19 September.

August: Hawker Hunter T7s entered service with No 229 OCU at RAF Chivenor for weapons training.

September: The RAF aerobatic team, the *Black Arrows*, displayed its famous 22-Hunter loop during the SBAC Show at Farnborough. It was the greatest number of aircraft ever looped in formation.

October: Firestreak, the first RAF air-to-air guided missile, was fitted to Javelins of Fighter Command.

19 October: St Clement Danes, Strand, London, was reconsecrated as the Church of the Royal Air Force in the presence of HM The Queen.

November: The Scottish Aviation Twin Pioneer STOL aircraft entered service with No 78 Squadron in Aden.

November: No 2 Group in Germany was disbanded. With the exception of RAF Gütersloh, the 2TAF forward airfields were relinquished and the displaced squadrons moved to the four new 'Clutch' airfields near the Dutch border.

3 November: Signals Command was formed at RAF Medmenham from No 90 (Signals) Group.

7 November: First flight of the Hawker Hunter FR10 (XF429). Production FR10s replaced the troubled Swift FR5 with fighter reconnaissance squadrons.

17 December: The Secretary of State for Air announced that "It has been decided to develop a new tactical strike/reconnaissance aircraft as a Canberra replacement. It will be capable of operating from small airfields with rudimentary surfaces and have a very high performance at all levels" – this was to be the ill-fated BAC TSR2.

Air Vice-Marshal Norman Hoad's painting illustrates four Avro Vulcan B1s at a Quick Reaction Alert (QRA) dispersal of No 83 Squadron at RAF Waddington – No 83 was the first squadron to operate Vulcan B1s in July 1957. It handed over its aircraft to No 44 Squadron in August 1960 and moved to Scampton to become the first RAF squadron to receive the B2 version in October 1960. No 83, a pathfinder squadron in WW2, was disbanded in August 1969. The painting is reproduced by kind permission of The Commandant, RAF Staff College, Bracknell.

These pages generously donated by Haynes & Cann Limited

Avro Vulcan B1s of No 83 Squadron by Air Vice-Marshal Norman Hoad CVO, CBE, AFC*, GAvA

With defence experts calculating that three minutes was the maximum warning time available for V-bombers to fly clear before their bases would be devastated by an incoming missile attack, urgent steps were taken to reduce reaction time below four minutes. Operational Readiness Platforms (ORPs) were improved and better equipped near to the runway threshold and a modification programme was introduced to provide simultaneous starting of all four engines. As a result, the reaction time was cut to two minutes. Bomber Command's first megaton weapon, the *Yellow Sun* free-fall bomb, was delivered on a limited-approval basis for use by Vulcans operating from airfields in the UK. The second generation of Vulcan and Victor bombers was being developed for delivery within two years. Some redesign work was required to accommodate longer and more powerful engines to give a better take-off performance, especially at dispersal airfields where the runways were usually shorter than at the main bases. The radius of action would also be substantially increased, with the result that more targets in the Soviet Union lay within range. The installation of new and improved countermeasures equipment would give the Vulcans and Victors a better chance of survival in the presence of surface-to-air missiles and interceptors. Maximum speeds would be increased to Mach 0.98 for the Vulcan and Mach 0.92 for the Victor. There would be an increased operating height over the target – a matter of particular importance as long as manned fighters remained the enemy's main defence.

Although terrorist activity by the Imam of Oman's followers continued, the main resistance was broken. This prompted the Imam and his brother to flee and in 1959 the operation was brought to a successful conclusion. Attempts in early years to lead the Western Protectorate Emirates into some form of union resulted in 1959 in six states joining together in a Federation. The backbone of the Middle East Air Force in 1959 was the Canberra. Four squadrons had been sent to Akrotiri in 1957 in fulfilment of Britain's pledge to support what was then known as the Baghdad Pact but which became the Central Treaty Organisation (CENTO) in 1959 after one of the signatories, Iraq, had withdrawn. None of the other members, except Pakistan, had a bomber capability and the British contribution, along with No 13 (PR) Squadron, was an essential element in achieving CENTO's main objectives, namely the maintenance of peace and stability in the area and the frustration of any Soviet ambitions. The Canberra force acted also as a buttress to NATO's southern flank.

---

8 January: The Armstrong Whitworth Argosy C1 turboprop tactical support, medium range transport made its first flight at Bitteswell.

11 February: It was announced that the Short Britannic (later renamed Belfast) strategic freighter was to be built for the RAF.

28 February: The prototype Westland Whirlwind HAR10 (XJ398) made its maiden flight, being the first version for the RAF with a Rolls-Royce Gnome turbine engine in place of a piston engine. A total of 67 was built for the RAF's search and rescue squadrons and for Army support pending delivery of the larger Wessex.

March: No 99 Squadron at RAF Lyneham, formerly equipped with the Hastings, was the first unit to receive the Bristol Britannia transport.

March: The last of 45 Avro Vulcan B1s was delivered to the RAF.

4 April: RAF Home Command disbanded. Control of the Air Training Corps passed to Flying Training Command and, later, to the Air Ministry.

18 April: The first live firing of a Thor missile was made by a No 98 Squadron crew at Vandenberg AFB, California.

May: The third Vulcan squadron, No 617 (The Dambusters), re-formed at RAF Scampton.

6 May: The prototype two-seat Lightning T4 (XL628) made its first flight at Warton. It was lost over the Irish Sea on 1 October.

15 May: The last operational flight was made by a Short Sunderland GR5 of No 205 Squadron at Seletar, Singapore.

June: The Jet Provost T3 entered service with No 2 FTS at RAF Syerston to start *ab initio* jet flying courses in the RAF's all-through jet flying training programme.

9 July: The first non-stop flight from the UK to Cape Town, South Africa was made by a Valiant B1 of No 214 Squadron. Air-refuelled twice en route, it covered 6,060 miles in 11hr 28min.

12–23 July: The RAF won the London to Paris air race – using a Hunter T7, a Sycamore helicopter and two bicycles to cover the distance between the capital city centres in 40min 44sec.

August: A total of 2,000 test flights had been made by pre-production Lightnings by this time.

31 August: The first pre-production Hawker Siddeley (Folland) Gnat T1 advanced jet trainer (XM691) made its first flight.

1 October: Establishment of the first major inter-Service overseas command since WW2 took place, with the British Forces Arabian Peninsula having an Air Chief Marshal as its commander.

29 October: The first production Lightning F1 (XM134) made its maiden flight at Warton

1 November: Formation of the first Maritime Headquarters Unit, Royal Auxiliary Air Force at Edinburgh. Others were later established at Northwood, Plymouth and Belfast.

December: The RAF's Canberra force was further reduced as more V-bomber squadrons appeared. By the end of the year, only 21 squadrons were still operating Canberras.

The Gloster Javelin was the world's first twin-jet delta-winged fighter. Electronic and radar devices enabled it to operate in all weathers, night and day. Tony Harold's painting shows Javelin FAW7 XH715 of No 33 Squadron based at RAF Middleton St George, Co Durham in 1959. It carries four de Havilland Firestreak air-to-air missiles. No 33 Squadron currently operates Westland Puma HC1s at RAF Odiham. The painting is reproduced by kind permission of the PMC, Officers' Mess, RAF Strike Command, High Wycombe.

Gloster Javelin FAW7 of No 33 Squadron by A. C. Harold

In July, the persistence of the Security Forces and their air support was rewarded when the twelve-year state of emergency in Malaya was declared to be at an end. RAF fighter, bomber, transport, helicopter and photo-reconnaissance squadrons had operated throughout the emergency. Some were based permanently in the Far East, while others participated on a rotational basis,. Together with units of the Royal Australian and Royal New Zealand Air Forces, they had played a decisive part in the long struggle to stabilise internal conditions in Malaya. In addition to halting the advance of Communism, it contributed at the same time to the overall defence plans of the area under the South East Asia Treaty Organisation (SEATO). The RAF alone flew 350,000 hours in direct and indirect support of anti-terrorist operations in Malaya. The British presence in Cyprus stemmed from the 1960 treaty under which the former colony became a republic, but with the British Government retaining two small areas (Sovereign Base Areas or SBAs) for British defence purposes. These totalled 99 square miles and remained British territory, with the AOC-in-C as their Administrator. Another right given by the 1960 treaty was the use of several 'retained sites' outside the SBAs such as the Mount Olympus radar and the military side of Nicosia airfield – plus freedom of movement and overflying throughout the island. The HQ of NEAF was at Episkopi in the Western SBA, while the main operational base was RAF Akrotiri, some 14 miles away.

In 1960, the first supersonic RAF fighter, the Mach 2 English Electric Lightning, entered service. Initially armed with the Firestreak, it subsequently employed Red Top air-to-air missiles. The United States decided in the late 1950s to fund the development of an air-launched bomb with a 1,000 mile range. Named Skybolt, it was to be used by the improved Mk 2 Vulcans and Victors and give them greater protection as the weapon would be launched at a considerable distance from the target. The Ministry of Defence announced that the British Blue Steel air-launched bomb with a range of just 100 miles was to be replaced by Skybolt, which would enable the RAF nuclear bombers to stay well outside Soviet missile belts. In this way, operational viability of the V-force would be retained well into the 1970s.

---

1 January: The Joint Experimental Helicopter Unit at RAF Andover with Sycamore HR14s and Whirlwind HC2s became No 225 Squadron for the continued development of Army helicopter support.

1 January: The RAF introduced a new system of pilot training whereby those who had successfully completed the basic flying training course on the Jet Provost then went on to one of three forms of advanced flying (fast jet, multi-engine or helicopter) before being awarded their wings.

1 January: No 38 Group re-formed as a specialised tactical group in RAF Transport Command.

February: Scottish Aviation Twin Pioneers joined Pioneers of No 230 Squadron at RAF Upavon. This was the only Transport Command unit to operate the type for Army support in the UK.

17 February: The Air Ministry announced that the first Ballistic Missile Early Warning Station (BMEWS) in the UK would be at RAF Fylingdales, North Yorkshire. It would be commanded and operated by the RAF and would become operational in 1963.

March: Exercise *Starlight*, the largest strategic exercise to be held outside the UK, took place in North Africa, with 4,000 troops and 130 vehicles carried by Transport Command aircraft.

2 March: RAF interest in the Skybolt air-launched missile was announced. It would be carried by improved Vulcans and Victors.

2 March: It was revealed that four V-bombers could be scrambled within less than four minutes from warning.

2/3 March: The longest non-stop flight ever made by an RAF aircraft involved a Valiant of No 214 Squadron which flew 8,500 miles around the UK in 18hr 5min, twice being refuelled in the air.

25–26 May: The first non-stop flight from Britain to Singapore was made by a Valiant of No 214 Squadron. It was refuelled in the air over Cyprus and Karachi.

29 June: The Lightning F1 single-seat all-weather supersonic fighter entered service with No 74 Squadron at RAF Coltishall.

July: RAF Transport Command aircraft were made available to the Government of Ghana to airlift troops, police and stores between Accra and Leopoldville as part of the United Nations requirement in the Congo. Aircraft of MEAF and BFAP were also engaged in freighting and evacuation tasks.

July: The first Vulcan B2s were delivered to No 230 OCU at RAF Waddington.

31 July: The end of Operation *Firedog* – the emergency campaign against terrorists in Malaya. From the beginning of operations in 1948, FEAF aircraft flew approximately 48 million miles in 361,442 flying hours.

2 August: It was announced that the RAF's order for Victor B2s was to be reduced because, the proposed introduction of Blue Steel and Skybolt meant that the deterrent could be maintained with fewer aircraft.

16 August: Cyprus became a Republic and administration of the Sovereign Base Areas of Akrotiri and Dhekelia passed to the AOC-in-C MEAF.

13 October: The RAF's first twin-engined twin-rotor helicopter, the Bristol Belvedere, was delivered to the Trials Unit which later became No 66 Squadron, at RAF Odiham.

December: Ministry of Defence announced that the United Kingdom would be one of four NATO air-defence regions and that RAF Fighter Command would operate under SACEUR (Supreme Allied Commander Europe) direction.

December: Vulcan B2s entered front-line service with No 83 Squadron at RAF Scampton.

The Hawker Hunter F4 introduced additional fuel capacity in the wings as well as provision for a wide range of external stores. Air Vice-Marshal Norman Hoad's painting depicts an F4 being directed to its parking spot at the RAF Flying College, Manby, Lincolnshire. The painting is reproduced here by kind permission of The Commandant, RAF Staff College, Bracknell.

Hawker Hunter F4s of the Royal Air Force Flying College Manby by Air Vice-Marshal Norman Hoad CVO, CBE, AFC*, GAvA

This was the peak year for the RAF's V-bomber force, with 17 squadrons fully operational. Aircraft were kept at almost instant readiness and were able to deploy quickly to 36 dispersed sites should the need arise. The V-force also operated in close co-operation with the USAF's Strategic Air Command.

It was Iraq which precipitated the next major operation in the Middle East when it threatened to seize Kuwait. To forestall the anticipated attack, the RAF quickly flew in two squadrons of Hunters to Bahrain and mounted a major air transport operation to convey ground forces from Cyprus and Aden and keep them supplied. Canberra squadrons from Cyprus were concentrated at airfields in the Gulf, and V-bombers were flown from the UK and held at readiness in Malta. In five days, 7,000 men and 720 tons of equipment and stores were moved into the Persian Gulf area, mostly from Aden, a quick reaction which fulfilled its purpose of preventing an attack on Kuwait. In 1961, following the establishment of the Republic of Cyprus, and the restriction of the British there to two Sovereign Base Areas, the command structure in the Near and Middle East was again reorganised. The regional air force based on Cyprus and Malta, guarding the southern flank of NATO and providing the striking power to support the Central Treaty Organisation, was renamed the Near East Air Force (NEAF). In addition, Air Forces Middle East was established at Aden to provide the air power for Middle East Command's area of responsibility, which extended from the east coast of Africa to Bahrain.

In 1961, the air defence squadrons of Fighter Command were assigned to NATO. The development of in-flight refuelling techniques and the creation, within Bomber Command, of a tanker force, greatly enhanced the ability of fighters and other combat aircraft rapidly to reinforce overseas theatres. Mobility became the central strategy of military planners, with the RAF playing a key role. This involved holding units of a Strategic Reserve at home, to be flown rapidly to potential trouble spots overseas by Transport Command, which had been re-equipped with Britannias, Comets and Argosies. This 'fire brigade' role was subsequently practised in large-scale exercises in the Mediterranean area, in which a large part was played by No 38 Group, re-formed the previous year as a specialised tactical force working closely with the Army.

Treble-One Squadron held the premier aerobatic position until 1961 when No 92 Squadron's *Blue Diamonds* Hunter F6s continued the tradition of the *Black Arrows*, introducing some new formations and flying 16 blue-painted Hunters. The ultimate version of the Javelin – the FAW9 – entered service with No 25 Squadron at RAF Leuchars. Javelins served in Germany, Cyprus, Malaya, Singapore and Zambia as well as with home-based night/all-weather squadrons. A total of 385 production Javelins was built.

February: MFEF renamed Near East Air Force (NEAF) and BFAP renamed Air Forces Middle East (AFME).

March: No 2 Squadron became the first unit to be equipped with the Hunter FR10 with the 2nd Tactical Air Force in Germany.

March/April: Transport Command and AFME aircraft dropped food to famine-stricken Africans in Kenya.

4 March: The first production Armstrong Whitworth Argosy (XN814) made its first flight.

13 March: The Hawker Siddeley P1127 experimental V/STOL aircraft made its first conventional flight.

1 May: Fighter Command squadrons were assigned to SACEUR. The AOC-in-C assumed the additional title of Commander, UK Air Defence Region.

20/21 June: The first non-stop UK-Australia flight was made by a Vulcan B1A (XH481), covering 11,500 miles in 20hr 3min.

July: The final Meteor PR10 was retired when No 81 Squadron at Tengah completed its re-equipment with Canberra PR7s.

1 July: Following a request from the ruler of Kuwait for British assistance, RAF Hunter ground attack fighters and transport aircraft with troops were sent to Kuwait. Canberra squadrons were concentrated in the Persian Gulf area and V-bombers held at readiness in Malta. The build up of forces was virtually completed by 6 July. By then, 7,000 men and 720 tons of stores had been moved to Persian Gulf area.

19 July: The British and US Governments decided to establish a MIDAS (Missile Defence Alarm System) ground read-out station at Kirkbride.

15 August: The Beagle B206 light communications aircraft, which eventually became the Basset CC1 in RAF service, was first flown.

September: The Hunter FGA9 entered service with FEAF, where it equipped No 20 Squadron at Tengah.

October: RAF Vulcans took part for the first time in Exercise *Skyshield*, a US national air-defence exercise.

October: The first Victor B2 was delivered to No 232 Operational Conversion Unit at RAF Gaydon.

1 October: Operation *Tana Flood* – aircraft of Transport Command and AFME dropped food to Kenyans cut-off by floods. Large-scale operations were later extended to Somalia and continued until January 1962. Four Twin Pioneers of No 21 Squadron flew 146 sorties, dropping 254,000lb of food.

November: The Jet Provost T4 entered service with Flying Training Schools.

2 November: Operation *Sky Help* in which Transport and Coastal Command aircraft flew supplies to Belize, British Honduras following devastation by Hurricane *Hattie*.

4 November: The Westland Whirlwind HAR10 entered service with No 225 Squadron at RAF Odiham.

18 November: The Armstrong-Whitworth Argosy transport aircraft entered service with No 242 OCU at RAF Benson.

Mark Postlethwaite's painting illustrates Blackburn Beverley C1s XH152/A and XH124/G of No 30 Squadron from RAF Eastleigh, Kenya flying over Mount Kilimanjaro. At the time of its introduction, the Beverley was the largest aircraft to enter service with the RAF. It was also the first British aircraft specially designed for the dropping of heavy Army equipment through rear loading doors. No 30 Squadron currently operates the Lockheed Hercules at RAF Lyneham.

Blackburn Beverley C1 of No 30 Squadron over Mount Kilimanjaro by Mark Postlethwaite GAvA

By now, the RAF presence in the Middle East was concentrated very much on Aden, with aircraft for almost every role operating from the major airfield at Khormaksar. A coup in neighbouring Yemen in 1962 led to increasing disturbances in the South Arabian Federation. The need for rapid reinforcement was demonstrated in December, when Indonesian opposition to the incorporation of the Borneo territories in the Malayan Federation caused a rebellion in Brunei. Though quickly put down by British forces airlifted from Singapore, the revolt was soon followed by the start of guerrilla infiltration across the borders from Indonesian Borneo, heralding a three-year undeclared war that became known as the 'Confrontation'. There were attempts at infiltration in Singapore and Malaya and a very real Indonesian air threat. Consequently, the RAF had to provide not only air defence of the Singapore base but also a bombing force, including V-bombers and Canberras, able to act as a deterrent in the conventional role. A continuous air transport operation had to be mounted between Singapore and Borneo as well as over the 8,000-mile route from the UK. By December, the rebellion in Sarawak had been countered but tension continued in Brunei. Reinforcements were flown in by Shackletons of No 205 Squadron, an RNZAF Bristol Freighter and an RAAF Hercules. Troops and supplies were then moved to their destinations by Beverleys and Pioneers, as well as by the Belvederes of No 66 Squadron, that had arrived in the Far East in May.

In December, President Kennedy cancelled the Skybolt missile project, just 18 months after the RAF had been deprived of another major nuclear weapon, with the cancellation of Blue Streak. The V-force was left with the Blue Steel Mk 1 missile as its only stand-off weapon. One of the alternatives which the President offered the UK was the submarine-launched Polaris. Its acceptance would mean that Britain's nuclear deterrent would pass from the RAF's V-bombers to the Royal Navy's submarines before the end of the decade. Although the original plan to have 120 Vulcan B2s and Victor B2s in 12 squadrons was not fulfilled, by 1962 the RAF had six squadrons (Nos 9, 12, 27, 35, 83 and 617) with Vulcan B2s and two (Nos 100 and 139) with Victor B2s. In addition, the front-line force included one Canberra tactical reconnaissance squadron and six Valiant squadrons (No 543 in the strategic reconnaissance role, Nos 49, 148 and 207 then assigned to NATO as a tactical bombing force, and Nos 90 and 214 undertaking in-flight refuelling). The remaining Valiant squadrons had been disbanded.

In 1962, the trade of Air Quartermaster was awarded aircrew status and ten airwomen were among members of the first course to qualify for the new flying brevet. The first women to be trained as Air Traffic Controllers took up their duties in 1962, some of them having gained previous experience as Fighter Controllers.

January: The Secretary of State for Air announced that the first British unit had arrived at Eglin AFB, Florida for operational testing of the Skybolt ALBM.

31 January: The Air Minister announced that Nord AS30 air-to-surface missiles were to equip RAF Canberras and help extend the life of these aircraft until the TSR2 entered service.

February: The Hawker Siddeley Gnat T1 entered service with the Central Flying School at RAF Little Rissington/Kemble, replacing the Vampire T11 as the standard advanced trainer.

12 March: The Air Minister announced that the Hawker P1127 was to be used by the RAF to gain V/STOL experience.

12 March: It was announced that arrangements had been made for No 38 Group, Transport Command, to operate with Canberras and reconnaissance aircraft. Two squadrons of Hunter ground-attack fighters were transferred from Fighter Command to No 38 Group in January 1962.

26 April: A Belvedere helicopter placed the 80ft spire on top of the new Coventry Cathedral.

May: The HQ Near East Command was disbanded. The AOC-in-C became AOC-in-C NEAF and British Forces Cyprus.

12 May: A total of 600 former RFC/RNAS members attended an Air Council/Admiralty reception at Lancaster House to mark the 50th year of British military aviation.

16 June: A special anniversary flying and static display was held at RAF Upavon to mark the Golden Jubilee of military aviation.

July: The last Venoms in service with the RAF were the FB4s of No 28 Squadron at Kai Tak, Hong Kong (FEAF). They were replaced with Hunter FGA9s.

July: The RAF Flying College at Manby became the College of Air Warfare.

July: The Lightning Conversion Unit was formed at RAF Middleton St George.

July: No 2 Field Squadron, RAF Regiment converted to the parachute role, as part of the Regiment's Strategic Reserve.

5 August: A nuclear test-ban treaty (US/UK/USSR) was signed in Moscow. The RAF testing base at Christmas Island had closed on 3 June 1960.

27 September: Exercise *Fall Trap*, in Northern Greece – the largest RAF peace-time exercise involved fighters, helicopters and No 38 Group transport aircraft.

November: The RAF's last Mosquitoes (TT35s operated by No 3 Civilian Anti-Aircraft Co-operation Unit at Exeter) were withdrawn from service and replaced by Vampire T11s.

November: Gnat T1s re-equipped the advanced fast jet pilot training school (No 4 FTS) at RAF Valley.

14 November: Three Vulcans (from Nos 27, 83 and 617 Squadrons) set out on a round-the-world flight in which they covered 30,000 miles in 50 hours flying time.

December: The total front-line establishment in Fighter Command had fallen to 140 aircraft.

8 December: FEAF fighter and transport aircraft began operations to quell the Brunei Revolt.

A Handley Page Victor B1A of No 55 Squadron landing with braking parachute deployed on a wet runway at RAF Honington is illustrated by David Shepherd. The Victor was the last of the three V-bombers to enter RAF service and the aircraft of this period were operated in the nuclear deterrent role. No 55 Squadron received its first aircraft in October 1960. The painting is reproduced by kind permission of the PMC, Officers' Mess, RAF Wittering.

These pages generously donated by Motorola

Handley Page Victor B1A by David Shepherd OBE, FRSA, FRGS, VPGAvA

The opening of the new radar station at RAF Fylingdales completed the supporting infrastructure for the RAF's nuclear deterrent posture. The station's function was to provide early warning of a Soviet missile attack so that the V-bomber force could be alerted and scrambled to hit targets in the USSR. Increased flexibility was provided with the introduction of the Blue Steel stand-off bomb which was carried by both the Victor and Vulcan. Released outside the enemy defence zone, it had an inertial navigation system which directed it to its target. Mobility was further enhanced by increased numbers of in-flight refuelling Valiants to support the V-bombers. The last National Service entrants left the RAF in 1963, and it became a fully professional air arm, with all the advantages that this carried.

No 74 Squadron, equipped with Lightning F1s at RAF Coltishall had become fully operational, and been presented to the public as a unique fast-jet formation display team. The *Tigers,* as they were known, performed wing-overs and rolls with nine aircraft in tight formation and gave co-ordinated displays with the *Blue Diamonds* Hunter F6s of No 92 Squadron. Another Lightning squadron – No 56 with the F1A at RAF Wattisham provided the *Firebirds* team of nine red and silver aircraft to display at the 1963 Farnborough Air Show. This was the last year that the RAF's aerobatic display team came from a front-line fighter squadron.

Although the Thor missiles based in the UK were far more reliable than had been anticipated, the US government decided to concentrate on strategic missiles, and had announced that logistic support for the RAF Thor squadrons would be withdrawn in 1964. As a result, they were phased out of RAF service in 1963, and returned to the United States. By then, Britain was facing a crisis over the deterrent. It had long been appreciated that what was needed in the face of the extensive Russian surface-to-air missile point defence systems was unmanned invulnerability to maintain bomber effectiveness throughout the decade, or at least until the new Polaris missiles were in service. There were two alternatives: a surface-to-surface medium to long-range missile; or an air-launched weapon, of medium range which flew to the target after being dropped by a manned bomber from a position outside the effective range of the Soviet or Eastern Bloc SAMs. The RAF knew what it wanted, but obtaining it seemed doubtful, since it had lost its leading role to the Royal Navy which was destined to deploy missile-equipped submarines.

The RAF's commitment in Borneo grew rapidly, with a consequent increase in FEAF's army-support transport force. In August, two squadrons were re-formed – No 215 with Armstrong Whitworth Argosies and No 103 with the greatly improved Westland Whirlwind HAR10, powered by a Gnome turboshaft engine.

February: No 617 Squadron, the RAF's first Vulcan B2 squadron to be equipped with the Blue Steel stand-off bomb, was declared fully operational at RAF Scampton.

March: Valiant tankers air-refuelled a Vulcan on a non-stop UK-Aden flight of 3,673 miles in 6hr 13min. Valiants also refuelled Javelins and Lightnings flying non-stop to Cyprus.

31 March: Nos 11 and 12 Groups were disbanded and replaced by Sectors in a re-organisation of Fighter Command (Sectors were themselves disbanded on 31 December 1965).

1 April: The Air Ministry Directorate-General of Works (AMDGW), formed as AMWD in 1919, became part of the Ministry of Public Building and Works.

May: The Avro Lincoln was finally withdrawn from service with Bomber Command.

May: Singapore-based (RAF Tengah) Hunter FGA9s of No 20 Squadron and Javelin FAW9s of No 60 Squadron began patrols in support of counter-insurgency operations in Borneo.

6 May: Valiants of Bomber Command were assigned to NATO for the first time in the tactical 'low-level' bombing role.

6 June: Three Standards – a record for one occasion – were presented at Ballykelly to Nos 203, 204 and 210 Squadrons by HRH The Princess Margaret. All three squadrons operated Avro Shackleton MR2s.

31 July: RAF Netheravon, opened in 1913 as a Royal Flying Corps military airfield, was closed.

August: To maintain the RAF's commitment in Borneo, two transport squadrons were added to the strength of the Far East Air Force in Singapore. No 215 Squadron, that had been re-formed at RAF Benson on 1 May 1963, moved to RAF Changi with Argosy C1s, and No 103 Squadron was formed from B Flight of No 110 Squadron at RAF Seletar to operate Whirlwind HAR10s for SAR and Army support tasks.

15 August: The last of the RAF's Thor IRBM bases was declared non-operational and closed.

September: The Fylingdales ballistic missile early warning system (BMEWS), part of the radar chain designed to give warning of a ballistic missile attack in time for V-bombers to disperse, became operational.

November: The first RAF element withdrew from Aden.

15 November 1963: No 225 Squadron deployed to RAF Seletar, Singapore with its Whirlwind HAR10s from RAF Odiham, for operations against Indonesian terrorists infiltrating into Malaysia and Borneo.

December: The RAF base at Bahrain was re-named RAF Muharraq.

21 December: The prototype Hawker Siddeley HS748MF twin Rolls-Royce Dart-powered tactical military transport made its maiden flight. It was later named Andover by the RAF.

31 December: By the end of the year, Coastal Command helicopters had been involved in 389 civilian and military rescue incidents since 1 March.

Bristol Britannia C1 XM491 Procyon *is illustrated here by Air Vice-Marshal Norman Hoad, having an engine changed in the servicing dock at RAF Lyneham. An AEC Matador Coles crane is lifting a Bristol Siddeley Proteus 255 engine on to its mountings. Twenty Britannia C1s were delivered to RAF Transport Command and served until January 1976 with Nos 99 and 511 Squadrons.*

Bristol Britannia in the Servicing Dock by Air Vice-Marshal Norman Hoad CVO, CBE, AFC*, GAvA

With the establishment of the unified Ministry of Defence (MoD) on 1 April the Air Ministry ceased to exist as a separate entity and became the Air Force Department of the new Ministry. The Air Council became the Air Force Board. The first sign of a structural fault in the Vickers Valiant was detected during a routine inspection of wing-spars of some aircraft in August. Some Valiants had been used for low-flying training for their new tactical bombing role and it was first thought that the weakness was confined to these aircraft. However, signs of metal fatigue were subsequently diagnosed on Valiants in all roles and in December they were grounded, and placed in reserve for use solely in a national emergency. Because of the high cost, the spars were not replaced and the Valiants were finally scrapped in 1965, by which time conversion of Victor B1s had commenced for air-to-air refuelling work. A decision was made to replace the offensive support Hunters with a combination of McDonnell Douglas Phantoms and the V/STOL Harrier. The former would be purchased from the USA, but equipped with Rolls-Royce Spey engines as well as some British avionics; the latter would be a development of the Hawker P1127 Kestrel. A tripartite squadron (UK/US/West Germany) was formed in October to evaluate the P1127 Kestrel.

To improve a situation in which there were no long-range stand-off weapons in prospect, and to maintain credibility as a deterrent, the V-force modified its tactics from high- to low-level operations. To make the latter feasible, the Blue Steel had to be modified so that it could be launched from below 1,000ft. The low-yield retarded lay-down bomb, which had been designed for the naval Buccaneer, was being converted into a higher-yield version suitable for use by the V-force. It was also necessary to strengthen the bombers' airframes, since these were originally intended for high-altitude operations. When dropping the new *Yellow Sun* Mk 2, V-bombers would employ a pop-up technique, which involved flying in towards the target at low-level before initiating a rapid climb to release the weapon at a height of about 12,000ft.

A small operation was mounted from Aden in January, following calls for assistance from the Kenyan, Ugandan and Tanganyikan Governments, to help put down Army disturbances in those countries. In each instance, the arrival of British forces by air had the effect of stabilising the situation, and caused an immediate collapse of the mutiny. Frequent violations of Malaysian airspace led, in February, to the creation of an air defence identification zone (ADIZ) running the length of the border. It was policed by eight Hunter FGA9s of No 20 Squadron, and two Javelin FAW9s of No 60 Squadron.

The *Red Pelicans,* flying six Jet Provost T4s from the Central Flying School at RAF Little Rissington, became the RAF's designated aerobatic display team for the season. Also, a team of five yellow-painted Gnat T1s, known as the *Yellowjacks*, was formed in 1964 by No 4 FTS at RAF Valley.

January: The Westland Wessex HC2 tactical support helicopter entered service with No 18 Squadron at RAF Odiham.

5 January: The prototype Short Belfast C1 (XR362) first flew. It was to be two years before production aircraft entered squadron service.

15 January: The new Ballistic Missile Early Warning System at RAF Fylingdales entered the sustained operational phase.

31 January: No 6 Squadron with Canberras at Akrotiri completed 50 years of unbroken service, having been formed at Farnborough on 31 January 1914.

7 March: The Hawker Kestrel V/STOL aircraft, developed from the P1127, made its first flight.

1 April: A unified Ministry of Defence formed. The Air Ministry became the Air Force Department, the Air Council was renamed the Air Force Board and the Secretary of State for Air was henceforth known as the Minister of Defence (RAF).

1 April: A new trade structure was introduced for the RAF.

17 April: The BAC Lightning F6 prototype (XP697) was first flown at Warton. Developed from the F3 it had modified wings and additional fuel capacity from ventral and over-wing tanks. It was the last single-seat interceptor to be produced for the RAF.

September: The RAF took over internal security of British Guyana, operating Whirlwind HAR10s of No 1310 Flight.

September: Whirlwind HAR10 helicopters of No 110 Squadron airlifted equipment for a new radio station 9,000ft up Mount Kinabalu in Borneo.

28 September: The BAC TSR2 prototype (XR219) made its first flight at Boscombe Down.

15 October: A Tripartite Squadron (UK/US/West Germany) was set up at RAF West Raynham to evaluate the Hawker Siddeley P1127 Kestrel F(GA)1 V/STOL strike/reconnaissance fighter.

October: Technician and Craft Apprenticeship Schemes replaced those for (Aircraft) Apprentices (since February 1920) and Boy Entrants (since September 1934) respectively.

December: The first of 20 Hawker Siddeley Dominie T1 twin-jet navigation trainers (XS709) was flown at Hawarden.

December: The Vickers Valiant was withdrawn from service some years ahead of schedule following the discovery of serious metal fatigue.

27 December: The production Beagle Basset CC1 twin-engined light communications aircraft was first flown.

Tony Harold's painting depicts RAF Range Target Towing Launch (RTTL) Mark 2 2757. This 68ft launch was delivered to No 1100 Marine Craft Unit at Alness, Scotland in 1958. After extensive modifications it was transferred to No 1105 Marine Craft Unit, Portrush, Northern Ireland and in 1971 went to RAF Mount Batten, Plymouth. In 1977, it sailed from Mount Batten to the Royal Victoria Dock, London for transfer to the RAF Museum at Hendon, where it now resides outside the main entrance. The painting is reproduced by kind permission of the Royal Air Force Museum.

Range Target Towing Launch by A. C. Harold

Throughout the 1950s and 1960s the Royal Air Force experienced both disappointments and successes in its aircraft procurement programmes. In late 1964 and early 1965, it suffered the cancellation of three types on which it had built up operational plans – the Hawker Siddeley P1154 supersonic V/STOL (vertical/short take-off and landing) fighter, the Hawker Siddeley HS681 STOL tactical transport, and the BAC TSR2, low-level tactical-strike-reconnaissance aircraft intended by the Air Staff as a Canberra replacement. Saved from the axe, the Hawker Siddeley P1127 was developed with the Kestrel FGA1, that equipped a tri-national development squadron, and thereafter into the more powerful, re-engineered Harrier GR1, giving the RAF the distinction of being the first air force in the world to operate a V/STOL fighter.

A new RAF Aerobatic Team was formed in 1965 at the Central Flying School, Little Rissington. Following the impact made by the No 4 FTS *Yellowjacks* in the previous year, the Air Force Board decided to create a new 'permanent squadron' within the CFS as the RAF's premier display team. It was equipped with HS Gnat T1s painted red – hence the name the *Red Arrows,* given to a team that quickly established itself amongst the world's top three military airshow performers. The Hawker Siddeley Dominie T1, a military training version of the already successful HS125 twin-jet executive aircraft, entered service with No 1 Air Navigation School at RAF Stradishall as a navigation trainer.

Following Rhodesia's unilateral declaration of independence, a squadron of Javelins, a mobile air defence radar and an RAF Regiment Squadron were deployed to Zambia in December. Shackletons were sent to Malagasy to help with maintaining United Nations oil sanctions by identifying and intercepting tankers attempting to break the blockade. Transport Command Britannias provided an oil airlift to Zambia, carrying 3,375,500 gallons and 1,000 tons of cargo. The increase in Russian air activity in the areas around the British Isles and out into the Atlantic underlined the Soviet Union's was pursuing a deliberately expansionist policy, which included the probing of defences and the gathering of intelligence. As a result, Britain's air defence Lightning squadrons were increasingly engaged in intercepting and turning away intruders that entered the UK Air Defence Region. To detect and monitor a new class of Russian nuclear submarines moving down through the Norwegian Sea into the Atlantic, Coastal Command had three of its eight Shackleton squadrons based at Ballykelly, three at Kinloss, one at St Mawgan and one in Gibraltar – all with six aircraft apiece.

February: The Defence White Paper outlined plans for Flying Training and Technical Training Commands to merge as a single Training Command (as was the case in 1936–40).

2 February: Most of the RAF's major aircraft replacement programmes were targeted for cancellation (TSR2, P1154 V/STOL and HS681 STOL transport) in favour of ordering American aircraft off-the-shelf (the F-111, F-4 Phantom and C-130 Hercules).

March: Another Westland Whirlwind HAR10 squadron – No 230 – was deployed to Borneo. No 66 Squadron, based in Singapore, was allocated Westland Belvederes, which the disbandment of No 26 Squadron in Aden had made available.

6 April: Cancellation of the TSR2 strike/reconnaissance aircraft was formally announced in the Budget speech.

28 April: The first two-point in-flight refuelling Victor B(K)1A tanker conversion made its maiden flight.

14 May: Hawker Siddeley delivered the 105th and last Gnat trainer to the RAF.

July: The first of 20 Beagle Bassets for the RAF was delivered to the Northern Communications Squadron at RAF Topcliffe.

9 July: The first production Hawker Siddeley Andover C1 (XS594) made its maiden flight from Woodford. Developed from the Avro 748 passenger transport, it was designed to meet an RAF Operational Requirement for a multi-purpose tactical transport with STOL capability.

19 September: Her Majesty The Queen and HRH Prince Philip attended the Thanksgiving Service in Westminster Abbey to mark the 25th Anniversary of the Battle of Britain. About 200 ex Battle of Britain aircrew, plus many next of kin, were present. Later, The Queen watched a flypast of ten Lightnings. A Spitfire and Hurricane flew over the grave of Sir Winston Churchill at Bladon, Oxon.

23 September: The first supersonic fighters to be stationed overseas (Lightnings of Nos 19 and 92 Squadrons) deployed to RAF Gütersloh, Germany.

October: HS Dominie jet navigation trainers entered service with No 1 Air Navigation School at RAF Stradishall.

1 October: The Air Force Department assumed responsibility for the handling of fuels (POL) for all three services (and was in the process of taking over the accommodation stores) as part of a rationalisation programme.

26 November: The first BAC VC10 C1 strategic transport for the RAF (XR806) made its maiden flight at Weybridge.

December: The first Victor B(K)1A refuelling squadron, No 55, became operational at RAF Marham.

December: The Victor SR2 entered service with No 543 Squadron at RAF Wyton, becoming Bomber Command's standard strategic reconnaissance aircraft in place of the Valiant B(PR)1.

3 December: Following the declaration of UDI by Southern Rhodesia, the RAF deployed Javelin FAW9s of No 29 Squadron to Ndola and commenced a massive Transport Command airlift.

David Shepherd's very detailed painting depicts No 5004 Airfield Construction (Light) Squadron in the Radfan during the Aden conflict. It shows a Blackburn Beverley transport landing on a temporary strip amidst a cloud of sand. A Bristol Belvedere is hovering overhead, a Scottish Aviation Pioneer is parked in the background and an RAF caterpillar bulldozer is clearing scrub in the foreground. The painting is reproduced by kind permission of The Commandant, RAF College, Cranwell.

5004 Airfield Construction (Light) Squadron in the Radfan by David Shepherd OBE, FRSA, FRGS, VPGAvA

After the setbacks and cancellations of aircraft and equipment projects in 1965, the RAF was able to take some positive steps in 1966. The Lockheed C-130 Hercules was purchased from the United States as a replacement medium-range tactical transport aircraft, and the first of 66 C-130Ks was delivered in 1966. For the long-range transport role, the initial delivery from the 14 BAC VC10s ordered by Transport Command was made in April. This contributed to the substantial increase in the RAF's airlift capability, along with the 100-ton Short Belfast C1 freighter which entered service with No 53 Squadron at RAF Brize Norton. The latter could accommodate a wide range of bulky military equipment, which would have previously required shipping, demonstrating this ability by helicopter lifts from Guyana and Borneo to the UK, with up to three Whirlwinds loaded in a single Belfast. Larger, Wessex helicopters could also be carried, two at a time, between England, Cyprus, North Africa and Germany. The older Britannias and Comets continued to be employed on scheduled services, exercises and special flights. Arrangements were made with the French for the joint development and production of the SEPECAT Jaguar for use both in operational squadrons and in flying training. Agreement was also reached between Westland in the UK and Aerospatiale in France to produce the Puma, Gazelle and Lynx helicopters.

By the time that the conversion of the RAF's V-bomber force to the low-level role had been completed, only eleven medium bomber squadrons remained: three *Yellow Sun* Mk 2 squadrons at RAF Waddington (Nos 44, 50 and 101) – whose Vulcan B1s were being replaced by B2s; three WE177 (nuclear) bomb squadrons at RAF Cottesmore (Nos 9, 12 and 35) with Vulcan B2s, and five Blue Steel squadrons – three with Vulcan B2s (Nos 27, 83 and 617) at RAF Scampton and two with Victor B2s (Nos 100 and 139) at RAF Wittering. In the months which followed the formal ending of Confrontation (in August), British forces in Borneo were progressively withdrawn, signalling the beginning of a major reduction in British involvement in South-East Asia. As the 1966 Defence Review clearly stated, Britain could no longer afford either to mount a major campaign virtually single-handed, or keep a large permanent garrison overseas, apart from Germany. It was intended, however, to retain the capability to deploy substantial forces to the Far East should the need arise. Cuts in defence spending which had made the shedding of these overseas responsibilities inevitable, also had other consequences for the RAF. Its maritime obligations were greatly increased. With the decision in 1966 not to build any more fixed-wing aircraft carriers, it took over the maritime strike, reconnaissance and airborne early-warning (AEW) roles, formerly fulfilled by Royal Navy squadrons. The RAF's command structure was also drastically simplified. In 1966, Her Majesty The Queen appointed Her Royal Highness Princess Alexandra as Royal Patron and Air Chief Commandant of the Princess Mary's Royal Air Force Nursing Service.

---

3 January: The move of the RAF Technical College from RAF Henlow to RAF Cranwell was completed.

20 January: The Short Belfast C1 heavy-lift strategic transport entered service with No 53 Squadron at RAF Brize Norton.

22 February: Fifty General Dynamics F-111 swing-wing strike aircraft were ordered from the USA as Canberra replacements after cancellation of the TSR2.

21 March: The first of 15 Canberra TT18 (target-towing conversions of the B2) (WJ632) made its first flight.

April: The last front-line transport squadron with Vickers Valettas – No 52 with the FEAF – disbanded at Butterworth, Malaysia.

April: The first of 14 BAC VC10 C1 transports entered service with No 10 Squadron at RAF Brize Norton.

April: Avro Shackletons of Nos 37 and 38 Squadrons began the Beira oil watch from Majunga.

1 April: The Airfield Construction Branch was disbanded and its personnel were transferred to other branches, or to the Royal Engineers.

1 April: The first long-range BAC Lightning F6 entered service at RAF Binbrook. It was the final fighter variant to be produced for the RAF and was to remain in service for more than 20 years.

June: The second Victor tanker squadron, No 57, became operational with three-point Victor K1As at RAF Marham.

June: The Supply Control Centre at Hendon was opened. Its £2.5 million computer made it the largest stock control system in Europe.

11 August: The state of emergency in Borneo was formally ended. During the 44 months of Confrontation, 17 RAF squadrons had taken part. Most were from FEAF in Singapore, including six combat squadrons operating Hunters, Javelins and Canberras, as well as Shackleton MR2s.

31 August: The first pre-production Hawker Siddeley Harrier (XV276) made its initial flight at Dunsfold.

October: The prototype English Electric Canberra T17 electronic countermeasures trainer (WJ977) made its first flight from Samlesbury where the aircraft were converted from redundant B2 airframes.

October: The RAF Technical Branch was renamed the Engineer Branch.

October: The Shackleton MR2 squadron was withdrawn from Gibraltar, the AHQ closed and the airfield reduced to staging post status.

1 December: The Hawker Siddeley Andover C1 medium-range tactical transport entered service with Nos 46 Squadron at RAF Abingdon, and No 52 Squadron at RAF Seletar, Singapore.

December: The Canberra T17 joined No 360 Squadron, a joint RAF/RN electronic warfare trials and training squadron at RAF Cottesmore.

David Shepherd's painting depicts a Comet C4 over Tower Bridge, London. RAF Transport Command received 15 Comets of which five were the C4 version that saw service with No 216 Squadron at RAF Lyneham. The military version of the Comet 4C accommodated 94 passengers, 50 more than the C2. The five aircraft served with No 216 Squadron from February 1962 until June 1975. Two-sixteen Squadron currently operates Lockheed Tristars in the passenger, cargo and tanker roles from RAF Brize Norton. The painting is reproduced by kind permission of the PMC, Officers' Mess, RAF Staff College, Bracknell.

These pages generously donated by The Guild of Air Pilots and Air Navigators of the City of London

De Havilland Comet C4 of No 216 Squadron over Tower Bridge by David Shepherd OBE, FRSA, FRGS, VPGAvA

Up to the time of its withdrawal in 1967, the RAF played a leading part in policing the hinterland of Aden, as part of the general peacekeeping effort in the Southern Arabian and Persian Gulf areas. In the protectorates, and in the Federation when that was formed, except for operations against intruders on the Yemeni border, the RAF acted only on request from Government agents, generally in areas where dissident tribesmen were causing disorders. This barren, mountainous area, where roads were few and ambushes frequent, was ideally suited to a system of air control. Two Squadrons of Hunter FGA9s (Nos 8 and 208) were based at Khormaksar, Aden for much of the period, the former unit having been stationed in Southern Arabia since October 1920.

When introduced into full service, the BAC VC10 C1 substantially increased the capability of the RAF's long-range transport force, which provided a new flexibility and speed of deployment for British forces. Capable of being fitted with 150 seats for operational trooping flights, it could also carry stretchers for casualty evacuation or a mixed cargo/passenger payload. It entered service with No 10 Squadron at RAF Brize Norton, and began operating 'scheduled' services to the Far East and Washington DC.

While the various elements of the transport force were expanding and re-equipping, substantial changes in organisation were also taking place. Air Support Command replaced Transport Command in August. At the same time, No 46 Group was re-formed to assume control of the strategic and tactical forces, while No 38 Group retained the offensive support and helicopter elements. With the time approaching for the Royal Navy's Polaris-equipped submarines to take over Britain's nuclear deterrent task, the contraction of Bomber Command continued. No 12 Squadron, flying Vulcan B2s from RAF Cottesmore, was disbanded in December.

January: Hawker Hunter T7s were issued to No 4 FTS at RAF Valley, to supplement Gnat T1s for pilot advanced flying training.

February: The Defence White Paper announced that Bomber and Fighter Commands would merge in April 1968 to form RAF Strike Command, using the Headquarters of Bomber Command at RAF High Wycombe. The Fighter Command headquarters at Bentley Priory would become the HQ for air defence squadrons of No 11 Group. Nos 1 and 3 Groups in Bomber Command would merge into a single No 1 Group at Bawtry.

February: The first of the RAF's McDonnell Douglas Phantoms, the YF-4M XT852, made its first flight at St Louis.

28 February: The prototype BAC Jet Provost T5 (XS230), a converted T4, made its first flight at Warton.

28–31 March: About 30 Hunters from RAF Chivenor and RAF West Raynham, using bombs and rockets, helped Fleet Air Arm aircraft to break up the tanker *Torrey Canyon*. This had run aground near Land's End, and its cargo of oil was polluting the sea and beaches.

April: The Lockheed C-130K Hercules C1 entered service with No 242 Operational Conversion Unit at RAF Thorney Island.

3 May: The evacuation of service and government families from Aden began. All troops and aircraft were out by 29 November.

23 May: A development of the Comet 4 airliner powered by four Rolls-Royce Spey engines, the prototype Hawker Siddeley Nimrod maritime reconnaissance aircraft (XV148) began flight trials.

11 June: Lightning F6s of No 74 Squadron were deployed to the Far East for the first time – being based at RAF Tengah, Singapore where they remained until 31 August 1971.

July: A Personnel Redundancy Scheme was announced in the Supplementary Defence White Paper.

1 August: No 36 Squadron moved from RAF Colerne to receive its first C-130K Hercules C1 transport aircraft at RAF Lyneham. It became operational as the RAF's first Hercules squadron on 26 September.

3 September: HS Andover C1s began to replace the Beverleys of No 84 Squadron after it had moved from Khormaksar, Aden to Sharjah.

August: Future RAF aircraft purchase plans were confirmed involving orders for Harrier and Jaguar fighter/strike aircraft, F-111K strike bombers (subsequently cancelled), Chinook medium-lift helicopters (also later cancelled) and Jet Provost T5 trainers.

1 August: Transport Command was renamed Air Support Command, and given increased responsibility for long-range strategic and tactical air support/assault roles.

1 August: The last of 258 production Lightnings was delivered.

8 September: No 8 Squadron moved with its Hunter FGA9s and FR10s from Khormaksar to Muharraq Bahrain, with a detachment maintained at Sharjah.

October: The first overseas unit to be equipped with the Hercules C1 – No 48 Squadron – formed at Changi, Singapore. The squadron had converted to the new aircraft at RAF Colerne, before moving to the Far East.

November: Whirlwind HAR10s of No 110 Squadron were the last RAF aircraft to operate in Borneo in support of Malaysian forces.

29 November: Withdrawal from Aden after almost 40 years of RAF responsibility. RAF squadrons based at Khormaksar had either been disbanded or relocated elsewhere in the region (mainly to Sharjah or Muharraq).

December: With the time approaching for the Polaris submarines to take over Britain's nuclear deterrent, Bomber Command continued to diminish in size. No 12 Squadron equipped with Vulcan B2s at Cottesmore was the next to disband, on 31 December.

December: Pressure on the UK's Defence Budget brought about the decision to reduce the number of operational RAF airfields in West Germany to four. It was announced that Geilenkirchen would be handed over to the Luftwaffe in March 1968. The four remaining RAFG flying bases were Brüggen, Gütersloh, Laarbruch and Wildenrath.

The English Electric Lightning was the last single-seat fighter aircraft to serve in the RAF. Roy Huxley's painting depicts two Lightning F6s of No 74 (Tiger) Squadron based at RAF Leuchars, prior to deployment to the Far East in June 1967. No 74 (Reserve) Squadron is currently part of No 4 FTS, flying Hawk T1/T1As for advanced pilot and tactical weapons training at RAF Valley.

These pages generously donated by GEC-Marconi Ltd

BAC Lightning F6s of No 74 Squadron by Roy Huxley

Two famous names disappeared from the RAF's structure in its 50th year, when Bomber and Fighter Commands were merged under the new title RAF Strike Command. The Government announced the decision to withdraw its forces from the Far East (except Hong Kong) and the Persian Gulf by the end of 1971 and to concentrate British defence efforts primarily in Europe and the North Atlantic area. The ground attack and short-range transport squadrons of No 38 Group were earmarked for NATO. The decision to phase out the Royal Navy's aircraft carrier force, after withdrawal from East of Suez, accelerated plans for the formation of maritime air defence and strike squadrons in the RAF and for the transfer of Phantom and Buccaneer aircraft from the Royal Navy. The front-line 'teeth' of the RAF would then be concentrated in Strike Command and RAF Germany. The former now controlled the principal nuclear strike, conventional attack, strategic reconnaissance, air defence, long-range maritime reconnaissance and air-to-air refuelling forces. The 1968 Defence White Paper also announced the decision to purchase 26 Buccaneer S2s, in addition to those taken over from the Navy. In June 1968, Flying Training and Technical Training Commands were amalgamated to become a single Training Command. The first production McDonnell Douglas F-4M Phantom FGR2s were delivered to the RAF, initially to replace Hunter FGA9s and Canberra B(I)8s for ground-attack and Hunter FR10s for fighter-reconnaissance duties. Conversion training of Phantom pilots and navigators was undertaken by No 228 Operational Conversion Unit at RAF Coningsby.

The Defence White Paper also revealed that all British forces would be withdrawn from Malaysia and the newly-independent state of Singapore by the end of 1971, and that only a general reinforcement capability would be retained beyond that date. Air Forces Gulf, which replaced Air Forces Middle East, established two fighter/ground attack squadrons and two tactical transport squadrons at RAF Muharraq, Bahrain. The increasing gap in the RAF's long-range strike and reconnaissance equipment, following cancellation of the BAC TSR2, was recognised and the purchase of 50 General Dynamics F-111s from the United States had been approved. However, this order was subsequently cancelled in response to strong budgetary pressure. Another disappointment was the withdrawal by the French from the Anglo/French Variable Geometry aircraft. The Royal Air Force Museum was established at Hendon as the first national museum devoted exclusively to military aviation and aeronautics. It opened at the historic site in two vintage Belfast truss hangars, which were linked by a new entrance hall and featured eleven display galleries and a large aircraft hall. The galleries cover the history of the RAF, and its predecessors, as well as the general history of aviation.

5 January: The last Handley Page Hastings transport was retired from RAF service. The final operator was No 24 Squadron at RAF Colerne, which re-equipped with the Hercules at RAF Lyneham.

16 January: Sweeping defence cuts were announced including the cancellation of 50 F-111Ks and withdrawal from the Far East (except Hong Kong) and the Persian Gulf by December 1971. The run-down in the number of RAF personnel was to be accelerated during the following four or five years. Jaguar strike aircraft were ordered as part of the on-going joint Anglo-French project.

March: The size of RAF Germany was reduced to four airfields – Brüggen, Gütersloh, Laarbruch and Wildenrath; Geilenkirchen was handed back to the Luftwaffe.

1 April: The Fiftieth Anniversary of the RAF was celebrated by colour-hoisting parades and flypasts throughout the world.

1 April: The RAF's last Gloster Javelin FAW9 all-weather fighters, in service with No 60 Squadron at Tengah, Singapore were withdrawn from service. They had been replaced in FEAF, as elsewhere, by Lightnings.

23 April: The first transatlantic crossing was made by a Harrier GR1 – from RAF Northolt to Floyd Bennett Field, New York.

30 April: Bomber Command and Fighter Command merged to form Strike Command, with headquarters at RAF High Wycombe.

1 June: Training Command was created, with headquarters at Brampton, through the merger of Flying Training and Technical Training Commands.

12 June–9 July: To marks the RAF's 50th anniversary, sixty members of the Queen's Colour Squadron shared guard-mounting duties with the Brigade of Guards at Buckingham Palace, the Tower of London, St James's Palace and the Bank of England.

14 June: Her Majesty The Queen and other members of the Royal Family visited RAF Abingdon to see a Golden Jubilee flying display in which some 150 aircraft took part.

28 June: After 32 years of RAF service the last Avro Ansons were withdrawn from service with the final operating units, the Southern Communications Squadron at RAF Bovingdon and Western Communications Squadron at RAF Andover.

20 July: The RAF's first Phantom FGR2 (XT891) was delivered to RAF Aldergrove. After acceptance, it was flown to No 228 OCU at RAF Coningsby on 23 August.

September: No 100 Squadron, a Victor B2 squadron at RAF Wittering, was disbanded.

1 October: RAF Brize Norton became the main passenger terminal for long-range transport flights of Air Support Command.

11 November: Air Support Command's VC10 C1s were named after RFC and RAF Victoria Cross holders.

21 November: Eight Vulcan B2s, supported by eleven transport aircraft (Britannias, Hercules and VC10s) staged the biggest ever reinforcement exercise to the Far East. They used the westabout route, across the USA and the Pacific.

December: The second, and last, Blue Steel-equipped Victor B2 Squadron – No 139 – was disbanded at RAF Wittering.

The No 10 Squadron BAC VC10 C1 based at RAF Brize Norton in Frank Wootton's painting, is shown taxying in at RAF Changi, Singapore after a scheduled flight from the UK. All VC10s honour winners of the Victoria Cross and this aircraft (XR810) is named David Lord vc. *No 10 Squadron still operates VC10s from RAF Brize Norton today, although with a wider role including air-to-air refuelling. The painting is reproduced by kind permission of The Commandant, RAF Staff College, Bracknell.*

These pages generously donated by No 10 Squadron, RAF

VC10 of No 10 Squadron at Changi, Singapore by Frank Wootton FPGAvA

RAF Signals Command and RAF Coastal Command were absorbed into Strike Command on 1 January and 28 November respectively, becoming No 90 (Signals) Group and No 18 (Maritime) Group. The V-bomber force provided the UK's strategic nuclear deterrent from 1957 until mid-1969, when this role was taken over by the Royal Navy's Polaris submarines. The Vulcans then assumed a tactical nuclear role, to which they were suited, but the Victor was retired from the bombing role. The Vulcan was also tasked for conventional operations, for which its ability to deliver twenty-one 1,000lb HE bombs over a considerable range made it a significant weapon. system

The Hawker Siddeley Buccaneer S2A entered service with No 12 Squadron at RAF Honington in October. A two-seat long-range strike/attack aircraft powered by two Rolls-Royce Spey engines, the Buccaneer had a nuclear capability and carried a wide range of conventional weapons, both internally and on wing stations, for its low-level role. The Hawker Siddeley Harrier GR1 also entered RAF service in 1969, as the world's first fixed-wing vertical/short take-off and landing close support aircraft. It proved capable of operating out of small natural clearings and with an integral auxiliary power unit (APU) supplying all essential electrical power, enabling the aircraft could be held at readiness close to the battle area.

The Nimrod MR1, the world's first land-based all-jet maritime reconnaissance aircraft, which was developed from the Comet 4C passenger aircraft, entered RAF service with the Maritime Operational Training Unit at RAF St Mawgan. In September, the Jet Provost T5, with a pressurised cockpit and powered by a 2,500lb Rolls-Royce Viper 201, entered service with the Central Flying School at RAF Little Rissington. The Bristol Belvedere HC1 twin rotor helicopter, known as 'The Flying Longhouse', which had served with four RAF squadrons, was declared obsolete, when the last squadron, No 66, was disbanded at Seletar, Singapore. There were further reductions in the home-based Vulcan force with No 83 Squadron being disbanded in August while Nos 9 and 35 Squadrons were deployed to Cyprus to replace the Canberras of the NEAF Strike Wing. The McDonnell Douglas Phantom FG1 entered service with No 43 (Fighter) Squadron at RAF Leuchars. With a maximum speed of Mach 2.1, the Phantom possessed a ceiling comparable with that of the Lightning, but could fly further without refuelling, and had improved airborne interception radar.

---

1 January: Signals Command disbanded and re-formed as No 90 (Signals) Group within Strike Command.

6 January: The largest air-to-air refuelling exercise ever mounted by the RAF in which ten Lightning F6s of No 11 Squadron, supported by Victor tankers from RAF Marham, deployed to the Far East for a four-week visit. The Lightnings made 228 individual contacts during which 166,000 gallons of fuel were transferred.

February: The Near East Bomber Wing was reconstituted at RAF Akrotiri, Cyprus with Nos 9 and 35 Vulcan Squadrons.

11 February: The first Hawker Siddeley Buccaneer S2 built to meet RAF requirements was flown for the first time.

March: The Bristol Belvedere HC1 twin-rotor support helicopter was retired from RAF service following the disbandment of No 66 Squadron at Seletar, Singapore.

24 April: The first two-seat version of the Hawker Siddeley Harrier, the T2 (XW174), made its maiden flight from Dunsfold.

7 May: The first Strike Command Phantom FGR2 unit, No 6 Squadron, was formed at RAF Coningsby.

14 May: An agreement was signed with Germany and Italy to develop the MRCA (Panavia Tornado) multi-role combat aircraft as a replacement for the Canberra and as a substitute for the cancelled TSR2 and F-111.

16 June: Four aircraft from No 74 Squadron flew non-stop from Tengah to Darwin, supported by Victor tankers, to make the Lightning's first visit to Australia.

July: The HS Harrier GR1 entered service with No 1(F) Squadron at RAF Wittering.

1 July: Britain's nuclear deterrent responsibility was transferred from the RAF to the Royal Navy. It was announced that Nos 27 and 83 Squadrons were to disband and that No 617 Squadron would convert to the conventional role. Vulcan B2s were released from their strategic commitment. All that remained in the tactical bombing role was the Canberra B(I)8 interdictor force in Germany.

15–21 July: Army reinforcement in Northern Ireland was effected by Air Support Command, which flew 144 sorties carrying 2,431 passengers, 556 vehicles and 78,000lb of freight.

1 September: The RAF's first Phantom FG1 air defence squadron was formed – No 43 Squadron at RAF Leuchars.

3 September: The first BAC Jet Provost T5 basic trainer (XW287) was delivered.

1 October: No 12 Squadron at RAF Honington received the HS Buccaneer S2A, the first to enter service with the RAF.

2 October: The Nimrod MR1 entered service with the Maritime Operational Training Unit (MOTU) at RAF St Mawgan.

29 October: The first SEPECAT Jaguar to be completed in Britain (XW560) made its first flight at Warton.

21 November: A Skynet defence communications satellite was launched from Cape Kennedy.

28 November: Coastal Command merged with Strike Command, becoming No 18 (Maritime) Group, thus completing the reduction of the RAF's Home Commands from eight to four – Strike, Air Support, Training and Maintenance Commands.

Wilfred Hardy's specially commissioned painting 'Air Experience' depicts a young cadet preparing for a passenger flight in a de Havilland Chipmunk T10 of No 3 Air Experience Flight at Filton. Since October 1958, thirteen AEFs located around the UK and in Northern Ireland have been providing flights for the Air Training Corps cadets and members of other similar organisations in some 50 aircraft. Chipmunks are still flown by No 3 AEF from RAF Colerne.

These pages generously donated by Airclaims Limited

Air Experience by Wilfred Hardy

In 1970 it was announced that the order for Anglo-French Jaguars would be altered so as to increase procurement of the operational version of the aircraft and form four additional front-line squadrons in the ground/attack and fighter reconnaissance roles. Jaguars were to replace Phantom FGR2s, thus releasing these F-4Ms to re-equip air defence squadrons where they would ultimately replace most of the Lightnings. A new jet trainer, less expensive than the Jaguar, was to be provided to replace the Hunter and Gnat for the advanced flying training task. The RAF's air-to-air refuelling tanker squadrons, now fully re-equipped with Victor K1 tankers, had the role of supporting the operations and deployments of the shorter-range combat aircraft, both in the NATO area and world-wide. They also provided the training to keep the receiver crews in constant air-to-air refuelling practice. With this support, Lightnings could reach Cyprus in four-and-a-half hours and the Gulf in eight hours. No 12 Squadron became operational in July with former Royal Navy Buccaneer S2A aircraft. The squadron operated in the maritime role in support of the Supreme Allied Commander Atlantic (SACLANT) and was the only RAF Buccaneer squadron with that task until HMS *Ark Royal* was eventually phased out of service. It was then joined by No 208 Squadron. Most of the SACLANT aircraft were eventually equipped to carry the Martel air-to-surface weapon. No 543 Squadron, based at Wyton, continued to operate the Victor SR2 principally for maritime radar reconnaissance and long-range photographic missions. The Avro Blue Steel stand-off bomb was phased out of service by 1970 and the last two Vulcan B2 squadrons equipped with this weapon, Nos 27 and 617, changed to the conventional bomber role with free-fall and parachute retarded weapons. No 27 Squadron also had long-range maritime reconnaissance as an additional task.

A rapid rundown of FEAF's front-line began and by early 1970 five transport squadrons (Nos 34, 52, 66, 209 and 215) together with four strike squadrons (Nos 20, 45, 60 and 64) and the photographic reconnaissance squadron (No 81) had all disbanded. As a result of this contraction, FEAF retained with control of only five squadrons in Singapore and one in Hong Kong. The Supplementary Statement of Defence, published in October, proposed a small contribution by British forces to the defence of South-East Asia in association with Australia, New Zealand, Malaysia and Singapore. The RAF element was to consist of permanent detachments of Whirlwind helicopters and Nimrods, reinforced by visiting units from the UK.

January: The final three Pioneers used for the Forward Air Control of No 20 Squadron's Hunters at Tengah, were withdrawn. These three were the last of 40 that had been supplied to the RAF.

January–February: Three operational FEAF squadrons were disbanded – No 20 Squadron with Hunters and Nos 45 and 81 with Canberras.

8 January: The first production HS Buccaneer S2B to be built specifically for the RAF made its initial flight.

20 January: The HS Nimrod MR1 made its first operational sortie. With a training crew on board, an aircraft from RAF St Mawgan was successfully diverted to find and follow a small force of Russian ships 200 miles south-west of Land's End.

14 February: The death occurred of Air Chief Marshal Lord Dowding, C-in-C Fighter Command during the Battle of Britain.

16 February: Three Harrier GR1s from No 1(F) Squadron made the type's first overseas proving flight to Cyprus.

3 March: Argosy XP444 of No 70 Squadron flew out of El Adem, Libya for the last time.

26 March: The 'GEE Chain' navaid system was shut down.

4 April: The RAF retired its last C-47 Dakota (KN645); it has since been preserved in the RAF Aerospace Museum at Cosford.

A further Dakota subsequently served with the RAE Transport Flight at Farnborough and the Battle of Britain Memorial Flight at Coningsby.

12 April: Deployment stage of *Bersatu Padu* started. This was the largest exercise airlift carried out by RAF Air Support Command. In ten days, VC10s, Britannias, Belfasts and Hercules completed 4,538 flying hours, covered over 1,365,000 miles, carried 2,265 passengers, 1,500,000lb of cargo, 350 vehicles and 20 helicopters.

May: Canberra TT18s joined No 7 Squadron at RAF St Mawgan.

June: The HS Harrier GR1 entered service in RAF Germany with No 4 Squadron at RAF Wildenrath.

June–September: Three squadrons of the RAF Regiment moved to Germany as part of Britain's defence policy of increased involvement in Europe. Bloodhound ground-to-air missiles were also deployed to Germany.

1 July: No 14 Squadron, the first in Germany to be equipped with the Phantom FGR2, was formed at RAF Brüggen.

28 July: The first two-seat Harrier T2 aircraft was delivered to RAF Wittering.

1 September: The first block entry of university graduates to RAF College, Cranwell. With Cranwell's new structure, the traditional Cadet entry was abolished.

14 September: Nimrods took part in NATO manoeuvres for the first time under Exercise *Northern Wedding*.

October: The Defence White Paper announced that four additional Jaguar strike/attack squadrons would be assigned to RAF Germany, with a corresponding reduction in the order for Jaguar trainers. It was also revealed that a replacement advanced jet training aircraft was to be ordered.

1 October: No 15 Squadron formed at RAF Honington. The first Buccaneer S2B squadron destined for RAF Germany, it moved to Laarbruch in January 1971.

November: Operation *Burlap* was conducted to assist with Pakistan flood relief.

Eric Day's painting depicts Westland Whirlwind HC10 XJ407 of No 32 Squadron, based at RAF Northolt, flying over Tower Bridge, London. The squadron had taken over the duties of the former Metropolitan Communications Squadron on 3 February 1969 and received its first Whirlwind in January 1970. In 1993, No 32 Squadron operates HS125s, Gazelles and Andovers from RAF Northolt. The painting is reproduced by kind permission of the Officer Commanding, No 32 Squadron, RAF Northolt.

These pages generously donated by Alenia SPA

Westland Whirlwind of No 32 Squadron by Eric Day

It was announced that more HS Buccaneer S2Bs were to be ordered to equip an additional squadron. Four HS125 Series 400s were delivered to No 32 Squadron at RAF Northolt. The executive jet aircraft would be employed in the high speed/VIP communications role to meet the needs of Royalty, Ministers of State and senior officers, who travel in the UK, the Continent, the Middle East and Far East. Deliveries of the Puma HC1 to the RAF started in January to supplement Wessex HC2s with Strike Command and RAF Germany. The Anglo-French helicopter could carry up to 16 fully-equipped troops at a top speed of 143kt. In 1971, married airwomen were able to serve on units with their husbands, even if there were no other women members of the Service on the station. The first woman to gain promotion to air rank in open competition with her RAF colleagues was promoted to Air Commodore. An Air Loadmaster could be the only female member of the crew of a VC10 or Britannia.

The RAF in Malta had become part of NEAF in 1968 and in 1971 British Forces withdrew from Libya, leaving the RAF in the Mediterranean concentrated on two islands – Malta and Cyprus. The island image of NEAF was further strengthened in 1971 when the Command took over the Gulf staging post of RAF Masirah and assumed RAF responsibilities for the airfield at Salalah, in the Dhofar region of Oman. The Middle East was once again becoming the most volatile and potentially troublesome area in the world. Soviet influence was growing and the USSR had supplied arms on a vast scale, while also sponsoring airfield building in certain countries to a level far above any national requirements. Against this background, the Near East Air Force had both national and international responsibilities. NEAF also had to maintain facilities for Britain to fulfil obligations in the area and to provide an important staging post for the air route to the Far East. Masirah played a major role in the evacuation of refugees from western Pakistan in December. British policy at this time was to encourage the Gulf States to develop their own air forces and provide for their own defence, so allowing Britain to withdraw from the region by the end of 1971. The rundown began at the start of the year, and the last unit to leave the Gulf was No 8 Squadron with Hunter FGA9s. Sharjah closed on 14 December and Muharraq (Bahrain) followed suit on the next day.

January: Buccaneers entered service in Germany when No 15 Squadron moved from Honington to RAF Laarbruch.
January: The Westland/Aerospatiale Puma HC1 entered service with the Air Training Squadron at RAF Odiham.
20 January: Four members of the *Red Arrows* were killed when two Gnats collided while on a training flight from RAF Kemble.
8 March: HRH Prince Charles started five months of training at the RAF College, Cranwell.
April: The HS125 CC1 entered service with the RAF for VIP communications duties with No 32 Squadron at RAF Northolt. Four aircraft (XW788-XW791) were built at Hawarden, Chester and delivered in April and May.
1 April: RAF Gan, the island staging post in the Indian Ocean, was transferred from the Far East Air Force to come under the control of Air Support Command.
4–15 May: Harrier GR1s of No 1 Squadron carried out trials aboard HMS *Ark Royal*.
June: The first Puma HC1 squadron (No 33) was established at RAF Odiham.
30 September: The first of 12 Shackleton AEW2s made its maiden flight at Woodford. Converted from MR2s, they were supplied to No 8 Squadron for airborne early warning duties.

October: It was announced that, by the end of 1972, Air Support Command would be amalgamated with Strike Command, to form a single multi-role operational command.
October: It was confirmed that the RAF was to purchase the Hawker Siddeley 1182 (Hawk) advanced jet trainer, to replace the Hunter and Gnat.
4 October: The first HS Nimrod MR1s arrived in Malta to replace the Shackletons of No 203 Squadron.
21 October: It was decided to order further Buccaneer S2Bs for an additional squadron in RAF Strike Command.
1 November: Far East Air Force disbanded. FEAF had provided air support for the Army and Police in Malaya during the attempt by Communist guerrillas to seize control of the country. An RAF presence was maintained by a small force of Whirlwinds and Shackletons, later to be replaced by Wessex and Nimrods, as part of the Five-Power defence force.
15 November: Flying units of No 90 (Signals) Group were transferred to No 1 (Bomber) Group.
23 November: It was announced that the RAF was to purchase 132 Scottish Aviation Bulldogs as replacements for the Chipmunk with the University Air Squadrons, the Central Flying School and the Primary Flying Grading Squadron. The first Beagle Bulldog had flown on 19 May 1969 – production was taken over by Scottish Aviation at Prestwick after the RAF order was placed.
10–12 December: In 18 sorties between Karachi, Islamabad and Masirah, RAF Hercules evacuated 909 British and friendly nationals from West Pakistan. RAF VC10s flew them on to Cyprus. Other Hercules evacuated 434 people from the bomb-cratered runway in East Pakistan to Calcutta and thence to Singapore.
14 December: RAF Sharjah was formally closed.
15 December: RAF Muharraq was formally closed.
21 December: Withdrawal from the Gulf region was completed, except for the RAF island staging post of Masirah which was retained under the command of HQ NEAF.

Gerald Coulson's painting shows a Short Belfast C1 of No 53 Squadron, Royal Air Force Air Support Command, based at RAF Brize Norton, flying over Hong Kong harbour. The Belfast was the first British aircraft designed from the outset for the long-range military transport role. Only ten were delivered to the RAF, from January 1966, but the type was phased out of service ten years later and No 53 Squadron disbanded. The painting is reproduced by kind permission of The Commandant, RAF Staff College, Bracknell.

These pages generously donated by Bombardier Services

Short Belfast C1 of No 53 Squadron over Hong Kong by Gerald Coulson GAvA

In January, in response to a request from the Maltese Government, the withdrawal of British forces from the island was ordered, pending the outcome of continuing discussions between Britain, Malta and members of NATO. Both Nos 13 and 203 Squadrons temporarily left Malta in early 1972 while further talks took place concerning the military facilities. A new seven-year agreement was signed in London on 26 March under which British forces would continue to be based in Malta. An order for 132 Bulldogs was placed with Scottish Aviation at Prestwick with initial deliveries scheduled for the following year. The Bulldog was to become the standard RAF basic trainer, replacing the de Havilland Chipmunk. Powered by a 200hp Lycoming, the RAF model was structurally strengthened to increase the aerobatic weight and a wider range of instruments and avionics were fitted. No 56 Squadron's Lightning F3s at RAF Akrotiri were replaced by the longer-range F6s in 1972. As in the UK area, the air-defence task in Cyprus was increasingly concerned with warding off Soviet- aircraft intent on probing local air defences.

In the early 1970s, RAF Germany's effectiveness was considerably improved by the introduction of new aircraft. The McDonnell Douglas Phantom FGR2 assumed the battlefield-reconnaissance role from the Canberra and combined it with an effective ground-attack capability. Introduction of the Harrier GR3 and the Buccaneer S2B also occurred, the latter replacing the Canberra B6 and B(I)8 in the interdiction role and providing a greater weapon-carrying capacity, higher performance and enhanced all-weather operating capability. In addition, No 25 Squadron was deployed to Germany and equipped with Bloodhound Mk 2 surface-to-air missiles to enhance the defences of Brüggen, Laarbruch and Wildenrath. It was announced that the low-level defence of these bases, as well as that of Gütersloh, would become the responsibility of the RAF Regiment.

January: No 8 Squadron re-formed at RAF Kinloss as the first RAF Airborne Early Warning Squadron. It was equipped with Shackleton AEW2s.

January: The Helicopter Operational Conversion Flight at RAF Odiham, which had received Pumas in 1971, became No 240 Operational Conversion Unit.

January: With the closure of Muharraq and Sharjah as RAF air bases in the Gulf, only the airfield on the Island of Masirah and the forward landing strip at Salalah were retained. Masirah not only acted as a staging post for aircraft en route to RAF Gan and the Far East, but also became the rear base for RAF units operating from Salalah, further west along the coast of Oman. This was to provide support for the British Forces which were engaged in combat along the western borders of Oman.

January: A decision was announced to withdraw from Malta by the end of March. RAF units involved included No 203 Squadron with Nimrod maritime reconnaissance aircraft and No 13 Squadron with Canberra PR9s. These moved to Sigonella in Sicily and Akrotiri respectively.

19 January: It was announced that additional HS Nimrods were to be ordered to form an extra maritime reconnaissance squadron.

February: Canberra TT18s entered service with No 100 Squadron at RAF West Raynham.

24 February: It was announced that 25 Handley-Page Jetstream twin turboprop-engined aircraft were to be ordered for the multi-engined pilot training role.

1 March: The first Victor K2 flew after conversion at Woodford. The K2 had its wing span reduced to 113ft to help extend fatigue life in its new role.

26 March: A seven-year agreement was signed by the British and Maltese Governments under which British forces would continue to be based in Malta.

23 April: Nimrods of No 203 Squadron returned to RAF Luqa, Malta.

1 May: No 90 (Signals) Group transferred from Strike Command to Maintenance Command.

15 May: HQ No 38 Group moved from RAF Odiham to RAF Benson.

31 May: The body of the late Duke of Windsor was flown by RAF VC10 from Paris to RAF Benson *en route* to St George's Chapel, Windsor.

6 June: After 21 years, the English Electric Canberra was retired from front-line service in its designated role as a bomber, with the disbandment of No 16 Squadron at Laarbruch. HS Buccaneer S2Bs replaced the Canberra B(I)8s.

1 July: No 38 Group was transferred from Air Support Command to Strike Command.

1 September: Air Support Command merged with Strike Command to form a single UK operational command under the latter title. No 46 Group was formed within the new Strike Command.

14–28 September: NATO's biggest ever exercise took place. *Strong Express*, involved 64,000 troops, 700 aircraft and some 300 ships from twelve participating countries. Strike Command aircraft were engaged in every operational facet of the exercise.

29 September: RNAS Lossiemouth was transferred from the Royal Navy to the RAF, to become the UK base for the Jaguar GR1 and the Shackleton AEW2s of No 8 Squadron.

23 October: No 13 Squadron's Canberra PR9s returned to Malta from Cyprus.

15 November: The Royal Air Force Museum at Hendon was formally opened by Her Majesty The Queen.

December: By the end of the year all RAF Germany squadrons had been re-equipped. The force was now made up of four squadrons of Phantom FGR2s, three of Harrier GR1s, two of Buccaneer S2Bs, two of Lightning F2As and one of Wessex HC2s.

Entitled 'Canberras', Rodney Diggens' painting depicts two English Electric Canberra PR7s of No 13 Squadron preparing for flight at RAF Luqa, Malta. No 13 Squadron was based at Luqa, Malta and Akrotiri, Cyprus with Canberra PR7s and PR9s between 1965 and 1972. In 1993, the squadron operates Tornado GR1As from RAF Honington for tactical reconnaissance.

These pages generously supported by Marshall Aerospace

Canberras by Rodney I. Diggens

The Anglo-French Jaguar entered RAF service in September, with the first aircraft being delivered to the Operational Conversion Unit at RAF Lossiemouth. Powered by Rolls-Royce Turbomeca Adour turbofan engines, two versions joined the RAF – the single-seat GR1 and the two-seat T2 operational trainer. The Jaguar carries an impressive war load on four wing stations and a centre-line pylon. External weapons include cluster bombs, rockets and missiles, while two 30mm cannon are housed internally. For self-defence, the GR1 has a comprehensive suite of electronic countermeasures and a radar warning receiver.

Three new types of training aircraft, two fixed-wing and one helicopter, also entered RAF service during the year. The training version of the Westland/Aerospatiale Gazelle was delivered to No 2 FTS at RAF Ternhill, replacing the Westland Sioux for initial helicopter pilot training. Following its first flight in January, production deliveries of the Scottish Aviation Bulldog T1 commenced before the end of the year to the Central Flying School at RAF Little Rissington. The third new type was the Astazou turboprop-powered Scottish Aviation Jetstream T1 which was delivered to the RAF as a replacement for the Vickers Varsity T1 multi-engined pilot trainer. The first aircraft was delivered to the CFS at Little Rissington for trials in July and further aircraft for instructor training from December. The Air Force Board approved an order for two BAC 1-11 jets to replace Andovers with The Queen's Flight – but this order was subsequently rejected by the Government and the turboprops remained in service for nearly 20 more years. There was a new NATO emphasis on conventional warfare, and ground attack capabilities gained fresh importance for army battlefield support. To build up the necessary expertise, two new Hunter FGA9 squadrons, Nos 45 and 58, were formed at RAF Wittering.

A trial installation was made in a Phantom FG1 of threat-warning sensors mounted in a fin-top pod. These radar warning receivers were subsequently incorporated into all Phantoms and other front-line aircraft. Nine Vulcan B2s were converted at Woodford for long-range strategic reconnaissance. Designated B2(MRR), these aircraft had special navigation equipment, cameras and sensors. No 27 Squadron was re-formed at RAF Waddington to operate the aircraft, eventually replacing No 543 Squadron at RAF Wyton with its Victor SR2s. The latter unit disbanded in 1974.

30 January: The first Scottish Aviation Bulldog T1 for the RAF (XX513) made its maiden flight. The Bulldog was ordered as the RAF's standard primary trainer to replace the Chipmunk. Training Command eventually took delivery of 130 Bulldogs, which formed the standard equipment for the 16 University Air Squadrons, the Elementary Flying Training School and the Central Flying School.

March: Operation *Khana Cascade* – the biggest airlift since Berlin – in which Hercules of No 46 Group dropped nearly 2,000 tons of grain, maize and rice to Himalayan villages in Nepal.

April: The SAL Bulldog T1 entered service with the CFS at RAF Little Rissington.

13 April: The first Scottish Aviation Jetstream T1 for the RAF (XX475) made its first flight at Prestwick. Originally designed as a civil aircraft by Handley Page, it was taken over by Scottish Aviation Ltd following the demise of that company. Twenty-six were ordered for the RAF as a multi-engined pilot training aircraft.

30 May: The first SEPECAT Jaguar GR1 was delivered to RAF Lossiemouth for ground crew training.

July: RAF mercy flights to Mali began in Operation *Sahel Cascade*.

17 July: The first Westland/Aerospatiale Gazelle HT3 was delivered to Training Command, where it replaced the Sioux with the CFS at RAF Ternhill. Of 300 Gazelles built for the British armed forces, only 34 examples were supplied to the RAF which mainly used it in the training role. A few were converted to serve as short-range communications aircraft (Gazelle HCC4) and supplied to No 32 Squadron at RAF Northolt. Powered by a 592shp Turbomeca Astazou IIIA, the Gazelle has a maximum speed of 193mph.

26 July: A Jetstream T1 (XX476) was delivered to the Central Flying School at RAF Little Rissington for initial trials.

August: Statistics indicated that Training Command had an inventory of that included 65 Gnats, 25 Bulldogs, 19 Dominies, 22 Hunters, 190 Chipmunks, 195 Jet Provosts, 54 Varsities, 16 Whirlwinds and eight Sioux.

1 September: Maintenance Command became Support Command.

13 September: The first two SEPECAT Jaguar GR1s to be used for flying training were delivered to the Jaguar Operational Conversion Unit at RAF Lossiemouth.

October: Lightning F6s of No 56 Squadron based at RAF Akrotiri, Cyprus, completed the first-ever visit to Iran when a detachment operated from Mehrabad, near Teheran. The Lightnings flew direct Akrotiri-Mehrabad with *en route* air refuelling by Victor tankers of No 214 Squadron. During the week-long detachment, the Lightnings flew training sorties with the Imperial Iranian Air Force.

October: The London University Air Squadron at RAF Abingdon became the first UAS to receive the Bulldog T1, replacing Chipmunks.

1 November: No 27 Squadron – formerly operating Vulcan B2s in the nuclear deterrent role – re-formed at RAF Waddington as the first unit to operate the Vulcan B2(MRR)/SR2 in the strategic reconnaissance role.

December: Nos 22 and 202 Squadrons flew 403 rescue sorties during the year with Whirlwind HAR10 helicopters. More than 200 people were rescued.

December: First instructor training course on the Jetstream T1 commenced at RAF Little Rissington.

A pair of BAC Jet Provost T5s of No 1 FTS tail-chasing over their base at RAF Linton-on-Ouse, North Yorkshire is illustrated in Eric Day's painting. Jet Provost T5s served alongside earlier T3s with No 1 FTS from 1969 until finally replaced by the Shorts Tucano in May 1993. No 1 FTS remains at RAF Linton-on-Ouse. The painting is reproduced by kind permission of the PMC, Officers' Mess, RAF Linton-on-Ouse.

These pages generously donated by Intercapital Brokers Ltd

Jet Provosts of No 1 Flying Training School Tail-chasing by Eric Day

As a result of the establishment of Support Command, the former Maintenance Command stocks of equipment located at four Equipment Supply Depots at Stafford, Carlisle, Quedgeley and Hartlebury were rationalised into three stores with the closure of Hartlebury and the specialisation of Quedgeley. The RAF's reconnaissance units completed their changes during the year. In May, No 543 Squadron was disbanded, six months after No 27 Squadron had re-formed at RAF Waddington in the strategic and maritime reconnaissance role with Vulcan SR2s. At RAF Wyton, the secretive No 51 Squadron retired the last of its Comet C2Rs, having replaced them with Nimrod R1s for electronic reconnaissance. Also at Wyton, No 1 Group had one squadron of Canberra PR9s (No 39 Squadron). A second Buccaneer S2 squadron, No 208 (for long a ground-attack squadron in the Middle East) was re-formed, at RAF Honington alongside No 12 Squadron, for the overland strike and attack role. The Rapier surface-to-air defence missile became operational with RAF Regiment squadrons of No 38 Group. A short-range, low-level, rapid-reaction weapon, guided either optically or by radar, it was initially used for battlefield and point defence.

The Government decided to begin regular surveillance of the off-shore oil rigs and associated fields, demonstrating by the presence of aircraft its interest in a multi-million pound industry in which it had invested heavily. This task was given to various units, such as the communications squadrons, as well as the Nimrod maritime patrol aircraft. A further expansion of the tactical force took place when Nos 6 and 54 Squadrons re-equipped with the Jaguar GR1 at RAF Coltishall. Subsequently, 165 single-seat GR1s and 35 two-seat T2 advanced operational trainers were delivered to the RAF. The latter model was primarily for the Jaguar Conversion Unit established in May 1973 at RAF Lossiemouth – this became No 226 Operational Conversion Unit in October 1974. To improve the wartime survivability of aircraft based at the RAF airfields in Germany, a NATO construction programme of Hardened Aircraft Shelters (HAS) commenced at the three 'Clutch' airfields near to the Dutch border. Each HAS was designed to take one or two aircraft and give protection against all but a direct hit by incoming weaponry. The conspicuous light-coloured buildings which had been such a prominent feature of all airfields in RAFG were re-painted dark green in a process known as 'tone-down'.

---

1 January: RAF Lindholme closed and the Strike Command Bomber School's remaining Hastings were moved to No 230 OCU at RAF Scampton.

1 March: No 208 Squadron re-formed at RAF Honington, to be equipped with Buccaneer S2A/Bs later in the year for low-level strike duties.

29 March: The first operational squadron to receive the Jaguar GR1, No 54 Squadron, formed at RAF Lossiemouth.

April: Harrier GR1s of No 4 Squadron were first employed in the tactical reconnaissance (TacR) role during Exercise *Ash Ramble* in North Germany.

1 April: Air Chief Marshal Sir Andrew Humphrey (former C-in-C Strike Command) became Chief of the Air Staff.

May: The Beagle Basset CC1 was withdrawn from communications squadrons after only nine years, having been plagued by a poor reliability record.

May: No 51 Squadron at Wyton retired its last Comet from the electronic reconnaissance role – they had been gradually replaced by Nimrod R1s from July 1971.

22 May: Thirty-three Canberras of 19 versions assembled at RAF Cottesmore for a celebration to mark the 25th anniversary of the Canberra's first flight.

24 May: Long-range strategic reconnaissance was now provided by Vulcan SR2s of the newly-re-formed No 27 Squadron at Waddington, replacing the Victor SR2s with No 543 Squadron. The latter was disbanded at Wyton.

July: With the entry into service of the Jaguar as the principal tactical ground-attack aircraft, Phantom FGR2s began to revert to pure interceptor duties and replaced Lightnings in all UK squadrons except Nos 5 and 11. The first to commence conversion was No 111 Squadron at RAF Coningsby.

14 August: The first prototype of the European designed Panavia Multi-Role Combat Aircraft (MRCA) was first flown in West Germany. It was to become the RAF's first variable-geometry strike-attack aircraft as the Tornado GR1, destined to replace the Vulcans, and most of the Buccaneers and Jaguars.

21 August: The first HS Hawk T1 (XX154) made its first flight at Dunsfold – and appeared at the Farnborough Air Show a fortnight later. Hawker Siddeley had emerged from a Ministry of Defence competition in October 1971 with a contract to build the HS1182 from which the Hawk T1 evolved as a Gnat and Hunter T7 replacement.

September: The Hunter F6/FGA9 and T7 equipped the newly-created Tactical Weapons Unit at RAF Brawdy.

October: RAF Germany commenced 'hardening and toning-down' its bases to withstand nuclear, biological and conventional attack. It involved the construction of Hardened Aircraft Shelters (HASs) at dispersed sites around the airfields and the repainting of all buildings to match the colour of the surrounding countryside.

30 October: The first of six prototype British-assembled Panavia Tornados (XX946) flew at Warton.

John Young's painting shows a Hawker Siddeley Buccaneer S2B of No 208 Squadron, based at RAF Honington, flying low over the sea and firing a Martel air-to-surface missile. No 208 Squadron, operating in the maritime strike and reconnaissance role, moved to Lossiemouth in July 1983 and remained there until the Buccaneer was retired in early 1994. The painting is reproduced by kind permission of The Commandant, RAF College, Cranwell.

Hawker Siddeley Buccaneer S2B of No 208 Squadron by John Young GAvA

With British overseas defence commitments being reduced in the 1970s, retirement of the 23 Bristol Britannia turboprop transports of Nos 99 and 511 Squadrons at RAF Lyneham commenced towards the end of 1975. They had been in service with the RAF since 1959 as long-range strategic transports, providing rapid deployment for the Army to trouble spots world-wide. By 1975, the RAF's Vulcan bombing force had been reduced to just six squadrons. No 27 Squadron had been disbanded and re-formed as a strategic maritime reconnaissance squadron – and Nos 9 and 35 Squadrons had returned from Cyprus. The latter were replaced by regular detachments of aircraft or full squadrons from the UK, as required. All six bomber units (Nos 35 and 617 at RAF Scampton, and Nos 9, 44, 50 and 101 at RAF Waddington) were operating in the tactical role as part of NATO's strike force. Being capable of delivering free-fall nuclear weapons or conventional bombs, they were fulfilling the role intended for the ill-fated TSR2. By mid-1975, the maritime task had increased with the need to afford greater surveillance and protection for the growing number of offshore installations in the northern waters. The brunt of this fell on Nimrods based at Kinloss and St Mawgan.

The 1975 Defence White Paper announced the Government's decision to withdraw the British contribution to the ANZUK forces in the Far East by April 1976. No 103 Squadron, with eleven Wessex HC2s based at Tengah, Singapore, was disbanded on 31 July 1975 and the Nimrod MR1 detachment was withdrawn. In January, following a government decision to end the declaration of forces to CENTO and reduce numbers in Cyprus, No 56 Squadron returned to RAF Wattisham with its Lightning F3/6s and No 70 Squadron with Hercules was withdrawn to the UK, to join the other Hercules squadrons at RAF Lyneham. The two Vulcan squadrons returned to Lincolnshire. The only unit to remain was No 84 Squadron flying with Whirlwind HAR10s for army support and search and rescue duties. In September, there was a further re-assessment of RAF Germany. Jaguar GR1s had now become available to replace the Phantom FGR2s with Nos 14, 17 and 31 Squadrons in the strike-attack role, and a fourth Jaguar squadron was added at Brüggen when No 20 exchanged its Harriers for Jaguars. Also replaced were the Phantoms of No 2 Squadron, receiving a reconnaissance version of the Jaguar. Phantoms would thus become available to assume the air defence task with Nos 19 and 92 Squadrons, which faced the impending retirement of their Lightning F2/2As.

By early Spring No 38 Group and No 46 Group controlled 227 aircraft – 50 strategic transports, 65 tactical transports, 60 offensive support aircraft and 52 helicopters. Guatemala began to mass troops on the Belize border and reinforcement of Belize from the UK was required. In October, three Westland Puma HC1s of No 33 Squadron were airlifted to the territory, followed in November by six HS Harrier GR3s of No 1 Squadron, which were refuelled eight times on their long flight across the Atlantic. They were followed by an RAF Regiment detachment equipped with the Rapier surface-to-air missile to provide airfield defence.

January: The two Vulcan B2 squadrons based at RAF Akrotiri, Cyprus returned to the UK. No 9 Squadron went to RAF Waddington and No 35 Squadron to RAF Scampton.

15 January: Now based in the UK for the first time since 1919, No 70 Squadron arrived at RAF Lyneham with its Hercules transports.

21 January: No 56 Squadron took up residence at RAF Wattisham with its Lightning F3/6s, following withdrawal from Cyprus.

March: The Wessex HAR2 helicopter entered service in the SAR role, with No 22 Squadron at RAF Manston.

10 March: The Hercules of Lyneham-based No 48 Squadron evacuated civilians from Phnom Penh, Cambodia.

April: Most of Strike Command's 45 squadrons were assigned to NATO's Supreme Allied Commander Europe (SACEUR). Some had a dual assignment.

9 April: The first unit in RAF Germany to begin re-equipping with the Jaguar GR1, No 14 Squadron based at RAF Brüggen, received its initial aircraft. It did not complete replacement of its Phantom FGR2s until November.

30 June: A run-down of the RAF's long-range transport force began with the disbandment of the Comet C4 equipped No 216 Squadron at RAF Lyneham. They had been in service since 1962.

July: The Victor K2 entered service with No 55 Squadron at RAF Marham. The K2 was developed as a replacement for the older K1 and K1A tankers which had served at Marham since 1965. Originally, 29 conversions from B2s and SR2s were ordered, but the number was cut to 24 in April during a Treasury economy campaign. The K2 had its wing span reduced to help extend the fatigue life of the reconditioned airframes.

31 August: No 46 Squadron with HS Andover C1s was disbanded at RAF Thorney Island. The squadron had operated as a tactical transport unit since December 1966.

October: VC10s of No 10 Squadron from RAF Brize Norton evacuated 5,700 people together with 350,000lb of freight from Angola.

November: As a result of invasion threats, Belize (British Honduras) was reinforced by Harrier GR3s of No 1 Squadron and Puma HC1 helicopters of No 33 Squadron.

3 November: No 36 Squadron was disbanded at Lyneham, in a reduction of the number of Hercules squadrons.

December: By this time, the only RAF bases outside the UK and North-West Europe were in Gibraltar, Malta, Cyprus and Hong Kong.

December: Both Bristol Britannia squadrons (Nos 99 and 511) were disbanded at RAF Lyneham.

De Havilland Devon C2 VP981 of No 207 Squadron at RAF Northolt, illustrated by Eric Day, is shown flying over Hillingdon House after taking-off from Northolt. The Devon served with No 207 Squadron after taking over the role from the Southern Communications Squadron in February 1969 until it was disbanded in June 1984. The painting is reproduced by kind permission of the PMC, Officers' Mess, RAF Uxbridge.

These pages generously donated by the Civil Aviation Authority

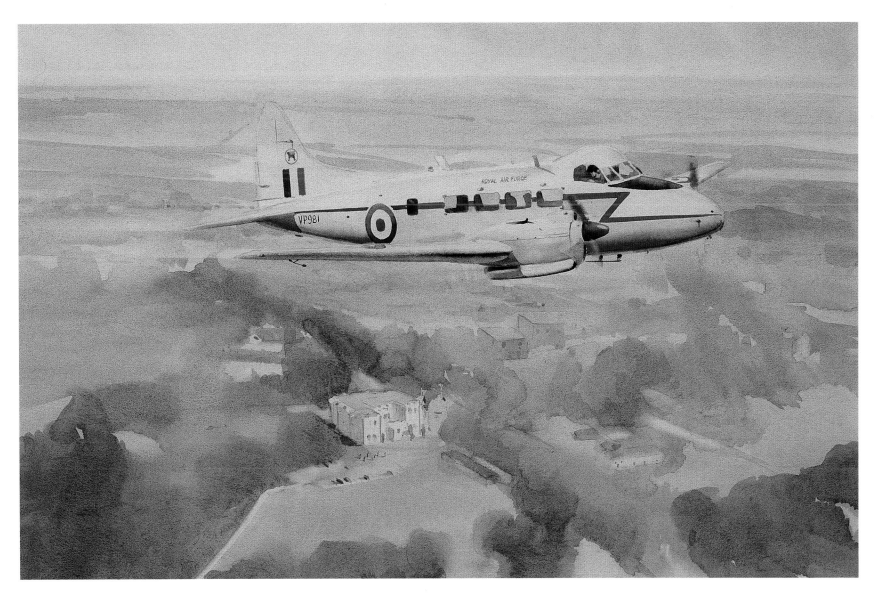

Devon of No 207 Squadron over Hillingdon House by Eric Day

By the mid-1970s, the reduction of the British presence in the Far East, and the introduction of longer range transports, had eliminated the need for Gan (the most southerly island in Addu Atoll, part of the Maldives) as an RAF airfield and staging post. Accordingly, in March, the airfield was closed, and the British military presence ended. By this time, the only RAF squadron permanently based east of Cyprus was No 28 Squadron at Kai Tak, Hong Kong, which had been re-equipped with Wessex HC2s in August 1972. The Near East Air Force was disbanded in April and Air Headquarters Cyprus was formed in its place as an integral part of RAF Strike Command. As a result of all the defence and political changes that had culminated in British forces being withdrawn from Aden, Libya, Bahrain and the Far East, there were inevitable reductions in the long-range regular air services operated by No 46 Group. By 1976, the main destinations still being served were Hong Kong, North America and the two Gulf stations, at Salalah and Masirah.

Following defence cuts announced in 1975, thirteen Hercules were withdrawn from front-line service and a second squadron was disbanded – this left a reduced total of 48 aircraft on the strength of four squadrons that comprised the Lyneham Transport Wing. A further step forward in pilot training occurred in November 1976 with the introduction of the HS Hawk T1 at No 4 FTS, RAF Valley, where it quickly replaced the Gnat in advanced pilot flying training. In the wake of a Defence Review which cut the requirement for multi-engined turboprop pilots with the RAF's transport fleet the newly-delivered Scottish Aviation Jetstream T1s were temporarily redundant. The 26 Jetstreams were placed into storage pending a decision about their future use. By the end of the year, eight had been returned to the training task with No 3 FTS at RAF Leeming. Subsequently, a further four Jetstream T1s joined the Multi-Engine Training Squadron (METS) which moved to join No 6 FTS at Finningley, with the remainder of the Jetstreams going to the Royal Navy. The veteran Vickers Varsity was withdrawn from Flying Training Schools in mid-1976. In July, Phantom FGR2s replaced Lightnings with No 19 Squadron at RAF Gütersloh in Germany – and No 92 Squadron converted in the following January, at which time both squadrons moved to RAF Wildenrath.

The Ministry of Defence announced that the Tornado ADV was to be developed as a replacement for the air defence Phantom. The last three new build Buccaneer S2Bs for the RAF (XZ430-432) left the Brough factory in December with final deliveries being made to RAF Germany.

---

7 January: No 48 Squadron was disbanded at RAF Lyneham, being a victim of 1975 defence cuts that reduced the number of operational Hercules squadrons to four (Nos 24, 30, 47 and 70 Squadrons).
March: The MoD announced that full development of an air defence version (ADV) of the Panavia Tornado was to proceed, as a replacement for the RAF's Phantom interceptors.
29 March: Gan air base was handed over to the Republic of the Maldives. It had been used since 1956 as a staging post for RAF aircraft crossing the Indian Ocean to the Far East.
31 March: The Cyprus-based Near East Air Force was disbanded. It was replaced by the Air Headquarters Cyprus, with the status of a Group within Strike Command.
April: RAF Communications squadrons were halved, with the disbandment of Nos 21 and 26 Squadrons with Devon C2s at RAF Andover and RAF Wyton respectively.
2 April: The Vickers Varsity T1 was retired from the RAF after 25 years of service. Production ceased in February 1954 after 160 had been built for the RAF. Pilots intended for propeller-driven aircraft, such as the Britannia or Shackleton, were sent to convert on Varsities at RAF Oakington. From 1963, the Varsity had equipped No 5 FTS at RAF Oakington, No 1 Air Navigation School at RAF Stradishall, No 2 Air Navigation School at RAF Gaydon and the Central Flying School. From 1970, all navigation training Varsities were concentrated at RAF Finningley.
4 June: The last Hunter ground-attack training wing (Nos 45 and 58 Squadrons) was disbanded at RAF Wittering.
29 June: The UK, Germany and Italy signed a Memorandum of Agreement for production of 809 Panavia Tornados. The RAF was to receive 220 Tornado IDSs (GR1s) to replace Buccaneers and Vulcans and 165 ADVs (F2s) to replace the remaining Lightnings and Phantoms.
14 September: Following defence cuts, the Short Belfast strategic freighter was withdrawn and No 53 Squadron disbanded. The Belfast was the first British aircraft designed from the outset for the long-range military transport role and the first in the world to have a fully automatic landing system.

October: No 2 FTS was established at RAF Shawbury. Equipped with Gazelle HT3s and Whirlwind HAR10s for helicopter pilot training, it had moved from RAF Ternhill.
November: The HS Andover E3, a conversion of the C1 equipped with special electronic devices to calibrate airfield landing and navigation aids, was supplied to No 115 Squadron and operated from Brize Norton. Seven E3s were delivered to permit a phased replacement of the Argosy E1.
25 November: The first Jetstream T1 (XX497) was re-activated at RAF St Athan and issued to No 6 FTS at Finningley.

Wilfred Hardy's painting illustrates three Hawker Siddeley Gnat T1s of No 4 FTS breaking formation and banking over Snowdonia, North Wales. This Advanced Flying Training School operated the Gnat from RAF Valley between 1963 and 1978, when it was replaced by the HS Hawk T1. The same trainer remains in service with No 4 FTS today at Valley. The painting is reproduced by kind permission of Air Commodore G. McA. Bacon, Marshall Aerospace.

These pages generously donated by No 4 Flying Training School

Gnat T1s of No 4 Flying Training School by Wilfred Hardy GAvA

With the retirement of the Victor K1As and replacement by only 24 Victor K2 three-point tankers, No 214 Squadron was disbanded in January 1977, while the new conversions were issued to just two units, Nos 55 and 57 Squadrons, at RAF Marham. Another squadron to disappear was No 203 Squadron at Luqa, Malta. It operated Nimrod MR1s but was disbanded in December as part of the planned withdrawal from Malta. RAF Germany completed the replacement of the ageing Lightning F2/2As by Phantom FGR2s with Nos 19 and 92 Squadrons at Gütersloh. They were then moved to RAF Wildenrath as the F-4s had greater range. The Harriers of Nos 3 and 4 Squadrons, augmented by ex-No 20 Squadron aircraft, were then able to move forward to the former Lightning base at Gütersloh, close to the East German border. Along with the Wessex HC2 helicopters of No 18 Squadron, they were thus better placed to provide close support for the forward elements of the British Army of the Rhine. The Harriers underwent a programme of progressive improvement, updating them to GR3 standard. Weapon carriage and range was improved by fitting more powerful engines – laser ranging marked target seeking (LRMTS) and passive radar warning receiver (RWR) equipment was also incorporated. To further improve defence at the four bases in Germany, hardened concrete shelters were constructed for operation centres and communication facilities. The operational effectiveness of RAF Germany was greatly enhanced by a number of other factors not readily quantifiable – such as the steadily improving association between the member air forces of NATO, the quality of the Command's equipment and its training and operating standards. Also, the development of new tactical concepts played an important part, a field in which the RAF exercised a significant influence within the 2nd Allied Tactical Air Force (2ATAF).

RAF Support Command was created in 1977 from a merger of Training Command and the former Support (Maintenance) Commands. The new unified command had its headquarters at RAF Brampton. This brought about considerable manpower and financial savings without reducing the power of the front-line. In July, continued Guatemalan pressure on Belize prompted the Government to send RAF Harriers and Pumas to guarantee the small nation's security. While Lightnings and Phantoms migrated annually to the Mediterranean for armament practice camps and training exercises, it was decided in 1977 to take advantage of the specially developed US ranges in Nevada. Jaguars, Buccaneers and Vulcans commenced deployment across the Atlantic to Nellis AFB in the Nevada desert.so as to join elements of the US armed forces in *Red Flag* training exercises over the enormous range complex. Gliding training, including the instructors' Central Gliding School at RAF Syerston, underwent a change in 1977 with the first deliveries of 40 new Slingsby Venture T2 powered gliders for operation by ten Volunteer Gliding Schools.

---

28 January: The RAF's tanker force was reduced by one-third when No 214 Squadron with Victor K1As disbanded at RAF Marham. The squadron had operated in this role since 1956, initially with Valiants but with Victors from July 1966.

February: Nimrod MR1 aircraft from RAF Kinloss and RAF St Mawgan began regular North Sea oil and gas rig surveillance duties, under the code name Operation *Tapestry*.

1 March: Jaguar GR1s replaced Harrier GR3s with No 20 Squadron at RAF Brüggen. Originally conceived as a Hunter replacement, it became a successor to the Canberra and Phantom for both ground attack and fighter reconnaissance. It was a flexible ground support fighter with a tactical nuclear strike capability.

31 March: An Airborne Early Warning version of the Hawker Siddeley Nimrod was ordered to replace the Shackleton AEW2. Conversion of surplus Nimrod MR1s to the new AEW3 standard was to be undertaken at Woodford.

12 June: Support Command, with Headquarters at RAF Brampton, was formed through the merger of Training and Support Commands.

30 June: The Handley Page Hastings T5 was finally retired from the Radar Flight, No 230 OCU. This brought an end 31 years of service for the Hastings.

July: RAF Harriers and Pumas returned to Belize to counter the threat of a Guatemalan invasion. Some 700 troops and 750 tons of stores were flown in by VC10s and Hercules.

29 July: Her Majesty The Queen reviewed the Royal Air Force at RAF Finningley, on the occasion of her Silver Jubilee, seeing a static exhibition of 81 aircraft and two missiles and a flying display of 137 aircraft.

6 August: Ten HS Buccaneer S2s and two Vulcan B2s began a four-week operational training exercise (*Red Flag*) at Nellis AFB, Nevada, using the USAF's tactical range.

11 November: The first batch of pilots who received their advanced pilot training on the new Hawker Siddeley Hawk T1, graduated from No 4 FTS at RAF Valley.

December: The last HS Argosy E1s in service with No 115 Squadron, were withdrawn at RAF Brize Norton. They had been used for airfield and navigation aid calibration checking since February 1968 and were replaced by HS Andover E3s.

December: The first of 19 Westland Sea King HAR3 search and rescue helicopters ordered by the RAF was handed over to the trials unit at A&AEE Boscombe Down. It was subsequently introduced into service by the Sea King Training Unit at RNAS Culdrose in February 1978.

31 December: The Malta-based Nimrod MR1 unit (No 203 Squadron) was disbanded. It had been based on the island since February 1969, initially with Shackleton MR3s.

The SEPECAT Jaguar GR1, depicted in Michael Turner's painting, is from No II (AC) Squadron at RAF Gütersloh, flying low on exercises with the Army in NW Germany. No II has been an Army Co-operation Squadron since it was formed in the Royal Flying Corps in May 1912. Currently it is a reconnaissance-strike squadron equipped with Tornado GR1As at RAF Marham.

These pages generously donated by Agfa-Gevaert (UK) Ltd

SEPECAT Jaguar GR1 of No II(AC) Squadron by Michael Turner PGAvA

The RAF had maintained a Search and Rescue (SAR) helicopter capability around the UK since the Bristol Sycamore was introduced into service in 1953. The Sycamore was subsequently replaced by the Westland Whirlwind and the Westland Wessex. In 1978, the much more capable Westland Sea King HAR3 entered service with No 202 Squadron at Finningley. It had a search radar, improved winch, more powerful engines and appreciably longer range than the older helicopters. The new Sea Kings replaced Whirlwind HAR10s at this squadron's detached sites at RAF coastal airfields during the following 18 months. The RAF's intention to re-establish a third air-to-air refuelling tanker squadron was announced in Parliament. There were now four Jaguar GR1 attack squadrons in Germany – Nos 14, 17, 20 and 31 Squadrons. The Jaguar's range superiority over the F-104 and F-5 which equipped other NATO air forces, made it a most valuable tactical offensive asset to SACEUR. It was announced in 1978 that the capacity of the RAF's Hercules fleet was to be considerably enhanced. Nearly half of the C-130Ks, some 30 aircraft in all, were to be 'stretched' by Marshall of Cambridge, the main contractors to Lockheed for the RAF transports. This was to be achieved by inserting two 'plugs' into the fuselage. The lengthened version (designated C3) was 15ft longer, giving it a 40% increase in total payload.

In early 1978, a long-awaited decision was made to order 30 Boeing-Vertol CH-47 Chinooks. The order was subsequently increased to 33 and then to a total of 41.

The twin-rotor CH-47, which had originally flown in 1961 and given sterling service to the US Army and other air arms, was to be known as the Chinook HC1 by the RAF. It could carry up to 55 troops or 24 stretchers. A rear loading ramp, which could be left open in flight, would permit the carriage of extra-long loads or allow the free-fall delivery of cargo and equipment. Later in 1978, experiments were conducted with Phantoms in a revised paint scheme of overall light grey tones to replace the standard grey/green upper-surface colours hitherto used for low-level operations. In addition to the formidable M61 Vulcan cannon, Phantoms were equipped with four infra-red AIM-9D/G Sidewinder and four radar-guided AIM-7E2 Sparrow AAMs; units started being equipped with the improved AIM-9L and Sky Flash versions of these weapons.

RAF Kai Tak, Hong Kong was shared by the RAF with civil airlines and operators, but in June the airport was handed over to the Hong Kong Government and the RAF retained only a small unit to handle transport flight requirements. The resident helicopter squadron, No 28, moved with its Wessex HC2s to its former base at Sek Kong in the New Territories.

The last Fleet Air Arm aircraft carrier, HMS *Ark Royal*, was paid off in December. The RN Buccaneers transferred to the RAF to give a total strength of almost 100 aircraft. These last aircraft were used to form Nos 15 and 16 Squadrons in RAF Germany.

January: It was announced that 30 Hercules were to be modified by Marshall of Cambridge to have their payload capacity increased through by lengthening the fuselage by 15ft.

31 January: Britain signed a contract with Boeing Vertol for 30 Chinook HC1 helicopters for the RAF.

17 February: The RAF's Sea King Training Unit (SKTU) was commissioned at RNAS Culdrose for the training of air and ground crews of No 202 Squadron. The Sea King was the largest helicopter to be used by the RAF until the arrival of the Chinook.

March: Flight Lieutenant David Cyster – a 33-year-old RAF flying instructor – made a 10,000-mile solo flight to Australia in a 1941 Tiger Moth to commemorate the 50th anniversary of the flight made by Squadron Leader Bert Hinkler.

April: A further order for 24 Harrier GR3s was announced.

17 May: No 28 Squadron moved with its Wessex HC2s from Kai Tak, where it had been based since June 1957, to the Army camp and airfield at Sek Kong.

June: Kai Tak airport at Hong Kong was handed over to the Hong Kong Government. The RAF retained a small unit at Kai Tak to handle military transport requirements.

July: Hawk T1s were delivered to the Tactical Weapons Unit at RAF Brawdy for its first course.

July: RAF Cottesmore, which had been under care and maintenance since 1976, was re-opened to prepare for its new role as a training base for the Tri-National Tornado Training Establishment (TTTE) with the Tornado IDS.

August: The first Sea King detached flight of No 202 Squadron was established at RAF Lossiemouth.

3 October: No 13 Squadron with Canberra PR7/9s was withdrawn from Malta and moved to RAF Wyton.

November: The Hawker Siddeley Gnat T1, the RAF's standard advanced pilot trainer, was replaced by the Hawk T1 at No 4 FTS, RAF Valley. The Gnat had been in service here since November 1962.

28 November: The Battle of Britain Museum annexe was opened at the RAF Museum, Hendon.

December: HMS *Ark Royal* was paid off at Devonport and its Buccaneer S2s were transferred to the RAF.

A Westland Wessex HC2 of No 22 Squadron is shown in Eric Day's painting, on a search and rescue mission winching a seaman from a ship that has run aground on rocks in stormy seas. Deployed in small flights at different coastal airfields and tasked with the rescue of downed aircrew, the bulk of No 22 Squadron's SAR missions are to assist civilians in distress. With its headquarters today at RAF St Mawgan No 22 Squadron has Wessex HC2s based at RAF Chivenor (A Flight), RAF Valley (C Flight) and RAF Coltishall (E Flight). The painting is reproduced by kind permission of the PMC, Officers' Mess, RAF Finningley.

These pages generously donated by Alliance & Leicester

Wessex of No 22 Squadron – Search and Rescue Mission by Eric Day

Although *Red Flag* exercises in Nevada provided excellent training, the weather conditions were very different from those usually encountered over the North German Plain. Therefore, in 1979, the RAF became involved in exercises hundreds of miles to the north, at the Canadian Forces Base Cold Lake in Alberta. This offered more appropriate and realistic weather conditions. Exercise *Maple Flag* became an annual deployment where the flying was done over almost uninhabited forest and lakeland; and where snow, low cloud, rain and other familiar European meteorological conditions prevailed. In 1979, RAF Jaguars participated in *Maple Flag* for the first time, with Harriers the following year. Although ground threats could not be simulated in the same way as at Nellis, there were plenty of 'aggressor' interceptors available to ensure that combat conditions were realistically reproduced. After withdrawals from the Middle East and Far East, and with the exception of the bases in Gibraltar, Cyprus, Belize and Hong Kong, the efforts of the RAF now focused on Europe and the threat facing NATO from the Warsaw Pact countries. Its efforts were now focussed towards supporting the many exercises connected directly, or indirectly, with NATO commitments. No 216 Squadron was re-formed at Honington with Buccaneer S2s. The aircraft came from 809 Naval Air Squadron, that had disbanded after the retirement of HMS *Ark Royal*. Two-sixteen was originally a Royal Naval Air Service Bombing Unit but spent the greater part of its RAF career as a transport squadron, most recently operating the Comet C2/C4 from 1956 to 1975.

The first of three Tornado ADV (F2) trials aircraft made its initial flight in October. This was two years before the fighter's Foxhunter radar got airborne in its intended recipient. New weapons to maximise the Tornado GR1's potential were under development. In the anti-airfield role, it would be armed with the Hunting Engineering JP233, an area denial weapon which distributed catering sub-munitions and anti-personnel mines, the latter designed to seriously disrupt repair operations on a target airfield. Studies continued into guided anti-armour and anti-radiation weapons to replace BL-755 and Martel.

Operation *Agila* was set in motion in December. A Commonwealth Monitoring Force, with a sizeable RAF contingent, was deployed to Rhodesia to monitor the country's transition to full independence as Zimbabwe, and to oversee the associated elections. A force of seven Hercules and half a squadron of Pumas was given the task of distributing the ground forces around the country, and thereafter of resupplying the forces, and the tens of thousands of civil war fighters who freely assembled under CMF supervision. The Operation was a complete success, and continued until early March 1980.

January: It was announced that the RAF was to lease 18 Jaguars (two T2s and 16 GR1s) to the Indian Air Force prior to the delivery of new built aircraft.

January: The RAF moved its multi-engined training squadron (METS) from RAF Leeming to RAF Finningley, where it formed part of No 6 FTS.

February: It was announced that the 33 Chinooks on order for delivery from mid-1980 were to be fitted with Ferranti FH32H standby artificial horizons.

February: The Defence White Paper stated that work was to continue on an improved UKADGE (Air Defence Ground Environment) network. This system was to incorporate the eleven radar sites that already existed, plus an additional one in South-West England. It was to be organised into three key sections based at major radar units at Boulmer, Buchan and Neatishead. All twelve stations were to be equipped with three-dimensional L and S band radars, linked together with modern communications equipment.

March: The RAF took delivery of its 100th Hawk T1.

April: The go-ahead was given for British Aerospace to convert nine second hand VC10s and Super VC10s into air-to-air refuelling tankers. These were to equip a new squadron to be based at RAF Brize Norton.

May: RAF Andover E3s operated by No 115 Squadron for radio, radar and navigation aid checking were re-painted in red, white and grey high-visibility colour schemes.

May: The RAF evaluated the use of volunteer RAF Regiment Auxiliary units to defend service airfields in the UK – the evaluations took place at RAF Lossiemouth, Scampton and Honington.

28 May: The new outstation of the RAF Museum, the Aerospace Museum, was officially opened at RAF Cosford.

July: No 216 Squadron was re-formed at RAF Honington. A third of its Buccaneers were previously operated by 809 Naval Air Squadron. The squadron subsequently moved to RAF Lossiemouth.

10 July: The first full production standard Tornado GR1 (ZA319) made its initial flight at Warton.

23 August: The RAF's first rebuilt Nimrod MR2 was delivered to No 201 Squadron at RAF Kinloss.

September: A Vulcan of No 101 Squadron at RAF Waddington won the coveted Blue Steel Trophy – RAF Strike Command's Bombing and Navigation competition.

28 October: The Tornado ADV prototype (ZA254) made its first flight at Warton. Eighteen production F2s were eventually built – eight of them being dual-control F2(T) versions. They were not equipped with the Foxhunter radar.

November: The Government announced that the Vulcan was to be phased out of RAF service by 1981.

December: It became necessary to despatch a Commonwealth monitoring force to Rhodesia/Zimbabwe to oversee the cease fire and subsequent election. During the next four months, the RAF was involved in a major tactical airlift – Operation *Agila* – with Hercules and Pumas.

This Hawker Siddeley Andover E3 of No 115 Squadron, a special radar and navigation aid calibration version, is portrayed by Penelope Douglas, on a check approach to RAF Machrihanish, Argyll. In 1993, No 115 Squadron was based at RAF Benson with Andover E3s prior to disbanding. The task has subsequently been taken over by a civilian contractor. The painting is reproduced by kind permission of the PMC, Officers' Mess, RAF Brize Norton.

Andover of No 115 Squadron at RAF Machrihanish by Penelope Douglas GAvA

Definitive plans were announced for extensive modifications to the UK Air Defence Ground Environment system to ensure that it would be prepared for expected improvements in the Soviet offensive threat during the 1980s. A network of control centres and 12 reporting posts was to be established and commanded from a new Air Defence Operations Centre. For three days in April, No 11 Group was subjected to repeated attacks by aircraft from the US, German, Canadian, Netherlands, Norwegian, Belgian and French Air Forces during a major air defence exercise. The Lightnings and Phantoms of the seven fighter squadrons were supplemented by Hawks and Hunters. Altogether, some 100 aircraft defended UK airspace against 300 aggressors. As the Tornado entered service during late 1980, a decision by the UK Government was awaited on developments or replacements for the Harrier and Jaguar. The competitors were the Harrier GR5 (the 'big-wing' Harrier) and the McDonnell Douglas AV-8B which was being developed as a joint UK-US venture with advanced avionics and composite structures. By 1980, five former BOAC VC10 airliners and four ex-East African Airways Super VC10s were being converted to tanker configuration by British Aerospace at Filton. When in service with the RAF, they would increase the capacity of the air-to-air refuelling fleet by some 50% and would be of particular value to both the Tornado IDS/GR1 and ADV/F2. Conversion of the Nimrod maritime patrol fleet to the improved Mk 2 standard was under way in 1980 by British Aerospace at Woodford. Outwardly similar to the Mk 1, the Mk 2 was refitted with new sensor and communications equipment, plus a Central Tactical Display which made it one of the most advanced long-range maritime patrol aircraft in the world. The EMI Searchwater radar was designed to detect and classify surface targets in high sea states at distances far greater than any other maritime radar. Underwater detection was much improved by the installation of the AQS-901 acoustic system which analyses and classifies data from active and passive sonobuoys. It was announced that the Buccaneer's punch was to be enhanced by the procurement of a new sea-skimming anti-ship attack vessel missile – the P37 Sea Eagle. Nos 12 and 216 Squadrons moved to RAF Lossiemouth so as to be better able to carry out their maritime strike role. However, serious fatigue problems were found in the wings of a number of the older, ex RN Buccaneers. As a result, many aircraft had to be withdrawn, leading in turn to the disbandment of No 216 Squadron. Buccaneer operations were suspended for a six-month period following the discovery that fatigue cracks in the mainplane had caused the mid-air break-up of an aircraft flying in a *Red Flag* training exercise in the USA during February. A modification programme was established by British Aerospace at Brough. Late in 1980, a Hercules of No 70 Squadron was detached to Katmandu to drop over 1,000 tons of rice and wheat to starving villagers in the mountains of Nepal. In Operation *Khana Cascade 80,* the Hercules flew supplies to three remote dropping zones 8,000ft up in the mountainous valleys, showing again the capabilities of this rugged aircraft.

January: RAF given approval for low-level jet training from CFB Goose Bay in Labrador.
February: Anti-submarine operations by RAF aircraft strengthened by the introduction of the US DIFAR sonobuoys – manufactured under licence by Plessey Marine.
March: The maiden flight of the first RAF Chinook HC1 (ZA670) took place at Boeing-Vertol, Philadelphia.
May: The Royal Air Force Aerobatic team the *Red Arrows,* gave its first public display with the Hawk T1, with which it had been re-equipped at the end of the previous season.
June: The RAF ordered a further 18 Hawks. Of the 193 now on order, 130 were in operational service by mid-1980.
1 July: The first two Tornados, a GR1 and a GR1(T), were delivered to the Tornado Tri-National Training Establishment (TTTE) at RAF Cottesmore.
16 July: The maiden flight took place at Woodford of the first BAe Nimrod AEW3 (XZ286). Converted from a Nimrod MR1 airframe, the aircraft was airborne for 3hr 30min. The AEW3 featured bulbous radomes on the nose and tail to house the fore-and-aft radar scanners designed by Marconi. Meanwhile, No 8 Squadron at RAF Lossiemouth continued operating the Shackleton AEW2, pending the arrival of the new aircraft.
1 August: RAF Chivenor was re-activated as a flying station, as the base for No 2 Tactical Weapons Unit which was equipped with Hawk T1As.
2 October: A Sea King HAR3 rescued 22 passengers and crew from the blazing wreck of the Swedish freighter *Finneagle* and flew them to Kirkwall in the Orkney Islands.
14 October: No 230 Squadron equipped with Westland Puma HC1s transferred from Odiham, Hants to RAF Gütersloh, Germany. The Puma replaced Wessex HC2s used for tactical transport and Army battlefield support.
1 December: The last Wessex HC2 based in RAF Germany was retired by No 18 Squadron. After returning to the UK, the squadron was re-equipped with Chinook HC1s in the following year.
2 December: The first Chinook HC1 helicopter was delivered to No 240 OCU at RAF Odiham. The Chinook was to make a much-needed contribution to the RAF's heavylift capability in the battlefield support role.

The RAF Aerobatic Team the Red Arrows, *replaced its scarlet Gnat T1s with Hawker Siddeley Hawks during the winter of 1979, giving their first public display with the new aircraft in April 1980. Wilfred Hardy's painting shows the nine Hawks in characteristic formation at a major air show. The* Red Arrows *continue as the official Royal Air Force Aerobatic Team, based at RAF Scampton, Lincs with Hawk T1As. The painting is reproduced by kind permission of Bournemouth International Airport.*

These pages generously donated by Main Event Catering

The *Red Arrows* on Display by Wilfred Hardy GAvA

The Tornado Weapons Conversion Unit (TWCU) at RAF Honington received its first Tornado GR1s in June. Work then began to train instructors before the start of the first RAF student course in 1982. Essentially a Vulcan replacement, the Tornado had a shorter unrefuelled range which dictated that it be based in Germany. The Vulcan B2 was by now beginning to be retired from service. The question of a Harrier replacement was resolved in 1981 when an agreement between the British and US governments was concluded for the production of up to 100 BAe/McDonnell Douglas AV-8Bs, to be designated Harrier GR5. By 1981, the most numerous RAF Germany aircraft, the Jaguar GR1 (four squadrons – Nos 14, 17, 20 and 31 at Brüggen and No 2 at Laarbruch) had been uprated with Mk 104 versions of the Adour turbofan. Trials began with the modernisation of the navigation and weapons aiming systems, involving the Ferranti FIN 1064 inertial navigation equipment. Plans for extra Lightning squadrons were dropped and it was announced that retirement of obsolete aircraft (Vulcan, Shackleton and Canberra) was to be accelerated. Fourteen ex-airline BAC Super VC10s were purchased for future tanker conversion and to provide spares for the RAF's fleet of 13 VC10 C1s and nine VC10 K2/K3s. They were delivered to RAF Abingdon and Brize Norton for storage. The *Red Arrows* broke all previous sortie-rate and serviceability records during a 31-day detachment that took in six countries – Abu Dhabi, Dubai, Bahrain, Jordan, Cyprus and Greece. The year saw No 13 Squadron with the Canberra PR7/9 disband at RAF Wyton, while Nos 7 and 100 Squadrons with Canberra TT18s amalgamated at RAF St Mawgan.

The June 1981 Government Defence White Paper recommended switching 20 of the Tornado IDS variants on order to the ADV version. Two Phantom squadrons were to be retained in the air defence role after the introduction of the Tornado F2. A further 36 Hawk T1s were to be converted to T1A standard, with provision for Sidewinders (making 72 in all). Additional VC10s were to be converted to tankers. Tornado GR1s were to be deployed to RAF Germany to replace Jaguars and Buccaneers and development of the Hunting JP233 airfield denial weapon was to proceed.

12–16 January: Exercise *Mallet Blow* tested RAF Jaguar, Buccaneer and Harrier pilots in offensive support techniques.

29 January: Formal opening of the Tri-National Tornado Training Establishment (TTTE) took place at RAF Cottesmore.

February: The last flight of the Whirlwind HAR10 with the Search and Rescue Training Unit at RAF Valley. It was replaced by the Wessex HC2.

17 February: The 500,000th Vulcan-force flying hour was recorded by No 230 OCU at RAF Scampton.

1 May: The 50th anniversary of the office of Provost Marshal (RAF).

5–8 May: Exercise *OSEX 3* tested RAF offensive support aircrews and Army forward air controllers.

11–22 May: The first 1981 RAF Germany Harrier field deployment involved aircraft from Gütersloh operating near Lippstadt.

19 May: Flying began on the first Chinook conversion course with No 240 OCU, Odiham.

25 May: The 30th anniversary of the Canberra's entry into service.

1–12 June: RAF teams won three trophies in *Volant Rodeo 81*, the USAF Military Airlift Command (MAC) tactical airlift competition at Pope AFB, North Carolina.

12 June: It was announced that No 360 Squadron and No 231 OCU would be reduced in size.

17 June: The first flight of the advanced Foxhunter air defence radar system in the Tornado F2.

30 June: The formation of first all-RAF Tornado unit at RAF Honington. This was the Tornado Weapons Conversion Unit.

9 July: Two new high-speed launches – HMAFV's *Lancaster* and *Wellington* – joined the RAF Marine Branch.

24 July: The Queen and Prince Philip visited Cranwell for the first Royal Review of the RAF College.

3 August: A Hercules C3 of No 70 Squadron left RAF Lyneham to rescue British residents and holidaymakers stranded in Gambia following an attempted coup. Operating from Dakar, Senegal, the RAF crew evacuated 200 refugees from Banjul airport.

8–18 August: NATO's maritime exercise *Ocean Safari* tested RAF Nimrod crews' anti-submarine warfare capabilities.

19 August: The RAF Regiment received its first *Spartan* and *Scorpion* armoured fighting vehicles. They greatly increased the Regiment's defence capability on front-line airfields.

20 August: The 2,500th SAR sortie was flown by 'C' Flight of No 22 Squadron based at RAF Valley.

24 August: An Anglo-American memorandum of understanding on joint production of AV-8B Harrier II was signed. The RAF would receive 60 aircraft to be known as the Harrier GR5.

12–22 September: The NATO exercise *Amber Express* in Denmark saw the first overseas deployment of the RAF's Chinook helicopters. Also involved were Jaguar and Harrier offensive support aircraft, and Puma and Wessex helicopters.

13 September: The Golden Jubilee of the 1931 Schneider Trophy contest, which was won outright by Flight Lieutenant John Boothman. This major pre-war triumph was marked 50 years later with a commemorative air race over the Solent.

14–25 September: The NATO exercise *Cold Fire 81* provided the RAF Jaguar force with a major test of its capabilities, both in the UK and on the Continent.

9 November: The first Hardened Aircraft Shelter (HAS) to be built for RAF aircraft in the UK was completed at RAF Honington.

30 November: The last RAF Whirlwind helicopters on active SAR duties in Britain were retired from service by 'A' Flight, No 22 Squadron at RAF Chivenor.

11 December: No 617 Squadron's last Vulcan sortie was made by XL318 which flew over the Derwent Reservoir, recalling Lancaster training operations before the Dams Raid in 1943. The Squadron was officially disbanded on 31 December but re-formed with Tornado GR1s in 1982.

14–18 December: The Tornado GR1 made its operational debut in exercise *Mallet Blow* over central and eastern England and the Border country.

Frank Wootton's painting portrays a Westland Sea King HAR3 of No 202 Squadron dropping fodder to wild ponies on Exmoor, Devon during a period of harsh winter conditions. With its headquarters at RAF Boulmer, No 202 Squadron continues to provide a Search and Rescue service from Brawdy, Manston, Lossiemouth, Leconfield and Boulmer. The painting is reproduced by kind permission of Mr Alan Etherington.

These pages generously donated by Industria Engineering Products Ltd

Fodder drop to Exmoor Ponies - Sea King of No 202 Squadron by Frank Wootton FPGAvA

After withdrawing from the turbulent Middle East, it was widely assumed that the days of British military involvement outside the European theatre were over. So, it was something of a shock to conventional defence thinking when Argentine forces seized the Falkland Islands in an unexpected coup on 2 April. A swiftly assembled South Atlantic Task Force set sail from Portsmouth on 5 April. This included HMS *Hermes* with a complement of Sea Harrier FRS1s which included RAF pilots who were on exchange duties with the Royal Navy. In the absence of any friendly land base nearer than 3,900 miles away at Wideawake Airfield on Ascension Island, it seemed that the RAF would make little contribution to Operation *Corporate* – other than by lifting men and equipment between the UK and Ascension. It was, however, soon appreciated that the Argentine air threat to the British Task Force and its operations to re-occupy the Falklands required extreme measures to bring at least some land-based air power to bear. The use of the Victor tanker force made this possible. With air-to-air refuelling having been rapidly improvised for Vulcans, Nimrods and Hercules, a series of remarkable sorties was carried out. Victors reconnoitred the seas around South Georgia prior to its re-occupation. Vulcan strikes (the *Black Buck* raids) were carried out against targets at Port Stanley airfield. Nimrods provided maritime surveillance of the region during certain stages of the operation. Hercules undertook long-range supply-dropping missions to the Task Force. Victors helped Harriers of No 1 Squadron to reach the Falklands in order to assist the Sea Harriers and provide close support for the final land battles. The sole Chinook to survive the sinking of the *Atlantic Conveyor* also played an important part, as did No 63 Squadron of the RAF Regiment. Finally, with the battle won, the RAF was heavily involved in supplying the islands, building up the airfield facilities at Port Stanley, and providing air defence. The four Vulcans which took part in the Falklands War were only three months away from the date when they were due to be scrapped. They were hastily modified with ECM jammers and missile fittings on the mainplane points originally intended for Skybolt. The nose probes and airborne refuelling systems also had to be refurbished. Sorties were also flown by a Vulcan against radar installations using AGM-45A Shrike anti-radar missiles.

6 January: The opening of the Tornado Weapons Conversion Unit (TWCU) at RAF Honington. This was designed to give pilots 32 hours of combat training after transition to type with the TTTE at RAF Cottesmore.

12 February: Eight Nimrods from RAF Kinloss and RAF St Mawgan were involved in rescue operations when the Greek tanker *Victory* broke into two 800 miles west of Land's End.

25 February: No 18 Squadron re-formed at RAF Odiham with Chinooks.

3 March: The expansion of the Royal Auxiliary Air Force Regiment by three squadrons was announced.

3 April: The Falklands War. A major air transport task began as eight Hercules left for Ascension Island. A VC10 also left RAF Brize Norton for Montevideo, Uruguay to collect the Falklands Governor, Rex Hunt, and his family. They had been captured during the Argentine Invasion but were subsequently released.

21 April: The first airdrop was made by a Hercules from Ascension Island to ships of the Task Force in the Southern Atlantic.

1 May: The first Vulcan attack on Port Stanley airfield succeeded in causing some damage to the runway.

1 May: The first Argentine aircraft (a Mirage III) was shot down by an RAF Sea Harrier pilot.

9 May: The first air-to-air refuelled Nimrod sortie was staged from Ascension Island.

20 May: The first Harrier GR3 attack saw three aircraft drop CBUs on a fuel dump at Fox Bay East.

27 May: The *Atlantic Conveyor* was lost with three RAF Chinooks. The surviving aircraft later achieved fame as the Falklands 'Flying Angel'.

28 May: RAF's last photo-reconnaissance Canberra PR9 squadron, No 39, disbanded at RAF Wyton.

1 June: No 63 Squadron (Rapier) RAF Regiment landed at San Carlos.

1 June: No 9 Squadron re-formed at RAF Honington as the RAF's first Tornado GR1 squadron.

3 June: A Vulcan diverted to Brazil after an in-flight refuelling incident involving the loss of its probe on the return leg of an anti-radar strike on the Falklands.

8 June: The first Hercules (XV296) to be fitted out as a tanker aircraft – the C1K – made its maiden flight. Six were eventually converted by Marshall of Cambridge.

13 June: The first laser-guided bomb attack in the Falklands was made by a Harrier GR3. It scored a direct hit on an Argentine headquarters on Tumbledown.

14 June: The Argentine garrison surrendered.

22 June: The first VC10 K2 conversion (ZA141), flew at Filton.

1 September: The second Chinook squadron – No 7 – was formed at RAF Odiham.

4 September: Group Captain Sir Douglas Bader died in London.

October: Phantom FGR2s of No 29 Squadron deployed for the air defence of the Falklands.

12 October: Vulcans, Victors, Nimrods, Harrier GR3s, Hercules and VC10s were among aircraft taking part in a fly-past during the City of London's Salute to the Task Force.

14 December: It was announced that six former British Airways Tristars were to be purchased for the RAF. Five more Chinooks and a squadron of ex-US Navy F-4J Phantoms were all ordered in a post-Falklands spending package.

22 December: It was revealed that the RAF would evaluate the BAe 146's suitability as a replacement for the ageing Andovers of The Queen's Flight.

The Hawker Siddeley Harrier GR3 in Eric Day's painting is shown attacking Argentinian Pucara aircraft and a Bell UH-1 Huey helicopter at Port Stanley airfield during the Falklands War. RAF Harrier GR3s of No 1 (F) Squadron operated alongside Royal Navy Sea Harriers from the aircraft carrier HMS Hermes during the conflict. This painting is reproduced by kind permission of The Commandant, RAF Staff College, Bracknell.

These pages generously donated by Martin-Baker Aircraft Company Ltd

Harrier GR3s Attacking Port Stanley, Falkland Islands by Eric Day

The extensive modernisation programme which began in the early 1980s added the Tornado GR1, VC10 K2/K3, Nimrod MR2 and Chinook HC1 to the RAF's inventory. By May 1983, No 18 Squadron had returned to RAF Gütersloh, Germany re-equipped with Chinook HC1s. In June, No 15 Squadron retired its Buccaneer S2s and in the following month received its first Tornado GR1s at RAF Laarbruch, Germany. The first VC10 tanker was handed over to the RAF for operational trials at A&AEE Boscombe Down. The VC10 K2 and K3 cruise at 560mph and are capable of refuelling large receiver aircraft, such as the Nimrod, from the centre hose and smaller aircraft, such as the Harrier and Tornado, from either the centre hose or, simultaneously, from the two wing hoses. The Falklands War underlined the urgent need for the RAF to possess an adequate air-to-air refuelling capability, not only as a 'force multiplier' for its air defence fighters, but also for long-range deployments by strike/attack, maritime patrol and even transport aircraft. Short term provision of Vulcan tankers and the adaptation of six Hercules helped to lift the burden on the hard pressed Victors in 1982; it was, however, to be late 1984 before the VC10s were in full service with No 101 Squadron at Brize Norton. The first of six HS125 Series 700s was introduced in 1983 for use in the communications role with No 32 Squadron. The decision had been taken to drop the requirement for a Devon/Pembroke replacement and concentrate on the Andover/HS125 fleets for all communications flying in the future. In March, the Chief of the Air Staff, Sir Keith Williamson, flew in Meteor T7 WF791 at RAF Cranwell. The Meteor was, at that date, the longest serving RAF aircraft of all time – 40 years. Also in March, the *Red Arrows* departed from RAF Kemble for Cyprus for their annual training camp, returning to their new base at RAF Scampton. A milestone was reached for the Airbridge to the Falklands when 50,000 flying hours was achieved. In May, Tornado GR1s from the Tactical Weapons Conversion Unit flew across the Atlantic for low-level exercises in Canada. The *Red Arrows* also staged a spectacular tour of North America in the same month. A decision was also announced that the British ALARM missile had been selected for the RAF as the new generation defence suppression weapon. This ended a long sales battle to supply anti-radar missiles for a wide range of existing and future front-line aircraft. Replacement of the RAF's fleet of gliders, mainly used to train ATC cadets, began in 1983 when the first ten Schleicher ASK21 Vanguard T1s arrived to take over from the 60 Sedbergh TX1s and 70 Cadet TX3s at the remaining 17 Volunteer Gliding Schools. At the same time, the Central Gliding School took delivery of modern, high performance equipment in the form of five ASW19 Valiant T1s and two Schempp-Hirth Janus Cs.

January: A Falklands Exhibition was staged by the RAF at the International Boat Show, London.

February: The 100th Tornado was handed over to the RAF by BAe at Warton.

February: Figures released showed the total number of SAR missions flown by the RAF in the previous year to be over 1,100.

March: Ten Buccaneers were detached to Key West in Florida to carry out live firings of Martel anti-shipping missiles.

March: Buccaneers were flown to the Falklands on a long-range deployment exercise.

31 March: Wattisham-based No 23 Squadron was disbanded and its number-plate transferred to the Phantom unit at RAF Stanley in the Falkland Islands.

12 April: The new Bomber Command Museum at Hendon was opened by The Queen Mother.

3 May: Five Chinook HC1s were flown to Gütersloh, Germany marking the return to RAFG of No 18 Squadron. The Chinooks greatly enhanced mobility of the British Army of the Rhine.

16 May: The 40th Anniversary of the Dams raid was marked by No 617 (Dambusters) Squadron which had re-formed as a Tornado GR1 unit at RAF Marham.

14 June: The first BAe 146 CC1 was handed over at Hatfield prior to a two-year evaluation in the transport role at RAF Brize Norton.

1 August: The Tornado Operational Evaluation Unit (TOEU) was set up at A&AEE Boscombe Down with four Tornado GR1s to conduct tactical and weapons trials.

7 August: Chinooks from RAF Odiham flew to Beirut to support the British Army peace-keeping force in the Lebanon. Extra long-range tanks and self-defence equipment were fitted and the aircraft used RAF Akrotiri as their forward base.

29 August: The maiden flight of the Anglo-American AV-8B – British Aerospace-built versions for the RAF were to be known as the Harrier GR5.

31 August: The first Tornado GR1s arrived in Germany, operating alongside Buccaneers with No 15 Squadron at RAF Laarbruch until sufficient numbers were available to permit retirement of the older type

September: No 27 Squadron at RAF Marham completed re-equipment with the Tornado GR1 to become the third UK-based operational squadron.

11 September: Two pairs of Buccaneers from Nos 12 and 208 Squadrons flew low over Beirut as a show of strength. A further pair flew over the city two days later

November: No 1 Group Headquarters moved from RAF Bawtry to RAF Upavon.

18–19 November: A Nimrod MR2 flew non-stop from the Falklands to its home base at Kinloss. It was refuelled in the air several times *en route*.

29 December: AOC No 11 Group presented the first ever Fighter Controller brevets.

Michael Rondot's painting 'Grey Ghost' captures a McDonnell Douglas Phantom FGR2 of No 56 Squadron landing on a wet runway at RAF Wattisham. This air defence fighter had replaced Lightning F6s with the squadron in mid-1976 and continued to serve until 1992. No 56 (Reserve) Squadron is currently the Tornado F3 Operational Conversion Unit at RAF Coningsby.

These pages generously donated by B&Q plc

Grey Ghost by Michael Rondot

The first production Tornado F2 long-range interceptor was rolled out at Warton and delivered to Boscombe Down for development flying. The Tornado ADV was urgently needed to bolster the UK's air defence intercepting Soviet aircraft at long range and countering modern types such as the Su-24 Fencer and Tu-22 Backfire. The operational requirement demanded an interceptor capable of undertaking combat air patrols (CAPs) in all weathers some 350 miles away from base, at high or low altitudes. It would also be able to function in hostile ECM environments and employ the new Sky Flash missile which had a look-down, shoot-down capability, and over 25 miles' range. To achieve this, a new technology radar – appropriately named Foxhunter, with a range of over 100 miles – was specified for the Tornado ADV. The first pair of Tornado F2s was delivered to No 229 Operational Conversion Unit at RAF Coningsby in November. These interim aircraft had less powerful RB199 engines and actually lacked the Foxhunter interception and fire control radar which was suffering delays in the development programme. Thus, the F2 was only used for training purposes and was operated with ballast in its nose. No 16 Squadron phased out the Buccaneer in favour of Tornado GR1s at RAF Laarbruch. In February, Chinooks of Nos 7 and 18 Squadrons evacuated British civilians and members of the peace-keeping force from Beirut to Cyprus. This *BritForLeb* operation continued until the end of March. The DH Devon was retired from communications and VIP transport duties after 37 years of service with the RAF. The last Devons were based at Northolt with No 207 Squadron, which disbanded on 30 June. The veteran continued to be operated in RAF colours with the RAE Transport Flight. Departure of the Hunter F6A, T7 and FGA9 from No 1 TWU, RAF Brawdy left only the T7 and T8 in RAF service as supplementary trainers for Buccaneer crews with 237 OCU and Nos 12/208 Squadrons at Lossiemouth. An order was placed for two BAe 146 Srs 100 jet transports for The Queen's Flight, to replace Andovers that had been in service since the 1960s. Prior to this, a pair of BAe 146s had been operated in 1983 for an intensive evaluation programme, before being returned to the manufacturers. The new 146s would feature special communications equipment and VIP interiors.

---

23 January: A Nimrod of No 206 Squadron, carrying the Secretary of State for Defence, made a record-breaking non-stop flight from the Falklands to RAF Brize Norton. The 8,000-mile flight took 17hr 15min, refuelling three times from Victor and Hercules tankers *en route*.

22 February: The first all-RAF crew flew a Lockheed Tristar 500 as it was introduced on the UK-Cyprus route from Brize Norton.

30 March: The disbandment parade for No 50 Squadron took place at RAF Waddington, marking the end of the Vulcan's operational service with the RAF. It had been extended with a handful of Vulcan tankers as a result of the 1982 Falklands conflict and the need to expand the air tanker fleet pending the availability of VC10 and Tristar conversions.

April: It was decided to axe the RAF Marine Branch in 1986 and to close RAF Mount Batten, Plymouth.

1 May: No 101 Squadron re-formed at RAF Brize Norton with four VC10 K2 air-to-air tankers. Five K3s were added to squadron strength during the following twelve months.

July: The MoD placed a contract with Ferranti Computer Systems Ltd to supply an Air Defence Ground Environment System for use by the RAF in the Falklands.

3 July: The first of five VC10 K3 tankers made its maiden flight at Filton.

1 September: No 31 Squadron re-equipped with Tornado GR1s at Brüggen. The squadron had been flying Jaguars since 1976 and recorded its first Tornado sortie on 14 August – the tenth anniversary of the first flight of the Tornado IDS.

October: The Royal Auxiliary Air Force celebrated its 60th Anniversary. In recent years, the auxiliaries had grown to include six RAF Regiment field squadrons for ground defence of air bases, as well as a movements squadron and an air evacuation squadron. The Maritime Headquarters Units also continued with auxiliary support.

19 October: After an absence of 13 years, No 74 'Tiger' Squadron re-formed as a front-line fighter unit at RAF Wattisham. It was equipped with second-hand F-4J(UK) Phantoms, purchased from the US Navy.

November: Operation *Bushel* – Hercules from Lyneham assisted in the distribution of famine-relief supplies in Ethiopia.

1 November: No 216 Squadron re-formed at RAF Brize Norton, equipped with Lockheed Tristars.

5 November: The first two Tornado F2s were delivered to No 229 OCU at RAF Coningsby, signalling the start of RAF's Tornado ADV training programme.

December: RAF Syerston took delivery of the first Viking TX1 tandem two-seat training sailplanes for use at Volunteer Gliding Schools. The MoD had ordered 100 of these Grob G103 GRP trainers from Germany to replace the elderly Sedberghs and other types and complete modernisation of the Cadet glider inventory.

18 December: It was announced that the final selection of a new trainer for the RAF (to meet Air Staff Requirement 412) would be made between the Shorts-built Embraer Tucano, designed in Brazil, and the British Aerospace-built Pilatus PC-9, designed in Switzerland.

The Boeing-Vertol Chinook HC1 of No 7 Squadron illustrated in Roy Huxley's painting was deployed from RAF Odiham to RAF Akrotiri, Cyprus in August 1983 to support the British Army's peace-keeping force in Lebanon. In February and March 1984, the Chinooks evacuated British civilians and members of the peace-keeping force from Beirut to Cyprus. No 7 Squadron currently operates Chinook HC1s and a Gazelle HT2 at RAF Odiham.

These pages generously donated by Taylor Brothers Bristol Limited – Colour Printers

Chinook of No 7 Squadron in the Lebanon by Roy Huxley

The AOC-in-C Strike Command announced further serious delays in the introduction into service of the Nimrod AEW3 and revealed that the Shackleton AEW2s of No 8 Squadron would remain in service at RAF Lossiemouth for a further undisclosed period. Conversion of Nimrod airframes had been completed by BAe at Woodford but the sophisticated search radar and integrated airborne control equipment had still to meet the required specification, amid rapidly escalating costs. The Secretary of State for Defence announced selection of the Shorts Tucano as the RAF's new basic trainer to replace the Jet Provost from 1987. To give the Tucano the performance demanded by the RAF's exacting training syllabus, a Garrett engine was substituted for the original Pratt & Whitney PT6A. Modifications to the cockpit layout were made to harmonise with the Hawk T1 and other improvements included a vertical air-brake and a strengthened airframe to increase load factors and extend fatigue life. The Tucano was the first new tandem-seat basic trainer for the RAF since the Chipmunk was introduced in 1950. The RAF agreed to provide training expertise to the Sultan of Oman Air Force in support of an order for eight Tornado F3s which were to be diverted from the RAF production line. The Secretary of State for Defence announced in August that Britain, West Germany and Italy had chosen to proceed with the next stage of programme definition for a European Fighter Aircraft (EFA). The aircraft was to be optimised for the air-to-air role, have BVR capability, good supersonic performance and be highly agile in the subsonic regime. The powerplant was to be developed from the Rolls-Royce XG40 turbofan. Subsequently, Spain agreed to participate, with work shared between BAe, MBB, Aeritalia and CASA. In September, it was announced that Saudi Arabia had contracted to buy 48 Tornado GR1s and 24 Tornado F3s for its air force, with deliveries commencing in March 1986. The RAF agreed to defer acceptance of some of its own Tornados to make this possible. BAe announced a contract to update 42 Buccaneer S2Bs to provide for carriage of the Sea Eagle ASM, with modification to the Blue Parrot radar, installation of improved EW equipment and chaff/flare dispensers and an improved automatic flight control system. The RAF Germany Band suffered a tragic loss in February when 19 of its 42 members were killed in a coach crash. The Band was brought back to strength and resumed its programme of engagements in April.

26 January: A Hercules C1 of No 47 Squadron on detachment from RAF Lyneham made the first air-drop of supplies during Operation *Bushel*, over the small town of Rabel at an altitude of about 10,000ft.

1 February: Delivery of the first VC10 K3 to No 101 Squadron at RAF Brize Norton, where it entered service on 20 February, joining five K2s already in service.

13 February: The British Aerospace ALARM defence suppression missile was flown for the first time on Tornado GR1 ZA354.

25 February: Wessex HC2 XT674 of No 22 Squadron 'C' Flight flew the 3,000th search and rescue operation mounted from RAF Valley since 1955. More than 2,000 people had been 'rescued' in 30 years.

April: No 17 (F) Squadron replaced its Jaguars at RAF Brüggen with Tornado GR1s.

1 April: No 2729 (City of London) Squadron, RAuxAF Regiment, was formed at RAF Waddington. Tasked with airfield defence, it was equipped with anti-aircraft guns captured during the Falklands conflict.

30 April: The first flight of the Harrier GR5 (ZD318) took place at Dunsfold.

1 May: No 229 OCU was formally inaugurated at RAF Coningsby to train crews on the interim Tornado F2 and definitive F3.

11 May: A Tristar C2 from No 216 Squadron made its first flight to the Falklands. It set a record of 8hr 22min for the Brize Norton-Ascension leg, 8hr 19min for the Ascension-Mount Pleasant leg and 18hr 28min elapsed time for the whole flight.

June: No 1453 Flight stood down at RAF Stanley. Its Harrier GR3s were returned, in Hercules transports, to the UK and RAFG.

July: No 19 Squadron, RAF Regiment, re-formed at RAF Brize Norton as the third of the Regiment's Short Range Air Defence Squadrons. Equipped with Rapier SAMs and Blindfire radar, it was tasked with the defence of RAF Fairford and RAF Upper Heyford.

9 July: The first flight of Tristar K1 (ZD950) took place at Cambridge after conversion to dual-role tanker-transport configuration by Marshall of Cambridge.

August: Operation *Tapestry* flights by Nimrod MR2s for the surveillance of oil rigs were brought to an end. *Tapestry* flights for fishery protection were to continue, pending the results of a ministerial review.

18 September: Harrier GR3s from Nos 3 and 4 Squadrons at Gütersloh participated in Exercise *Cold Fire*, operating for the first time from a German autobahn. This demonstrated their ability to use a 2km length of one lane as a landing strip. An operations centre was located in a lay-by.

24 September: The last of four VC10 K3s was handed over to No 101 Squadron at RAF Brize Norton.

9 October: Tornado GR1 ZA361 at TTTE Cottesmore completed its 1,000th flying hour – the first Tornado to reach this total.

20 November: The first flight took place at Warton of the initial production Tornado F3, the definitive air defence fighter variant. It was fitted with improved Rolls-Royce RB199 Mk 104 engines and provision for automatic wing sweep.

25 November: The last Hercules C3 conversion (XV299) was delivered by Marshall of Cambridge, bringing the RAF fleet of the stretched version to 30.

Lockheed Hercules C1P XV191 of No 47 Squadron from RAF Lyneham, is depicted in John Young's painting dropping relief aid to starving Ethiopians during Operation Bushel. *The Hercules featured special UN Mercy Flight mission markings. No 47 Squadron remains a tactical transport squadron at RAF Lyneham with the Hercules C1P/C3P. The painting is reproduced by kind permission of The Commandant, RAF College, Cranwell.*

These pages generously donated by Lockheed Martin Aeronautical Systems

Operation Bushel Hercules Dropping Relief Aid in Ethiopia by John Young GAvA

Delays and disappointments with the Nimrod AEW3 reached the point where the Government was obliged to reopen the competition for an airborne early warning aircraft to replace the veteran Shackleton. Bids were sought from alternative suppliers, which included Boeing, Grumman and Lockheed. The Lockheed Tristar tanker conversion entered service in early 1986 with No 216 Squadron at RAF Brize Norton. The RAF Tristars have additional underfloor fuel tanks, twin hose drum units in the rear fuselage, a refuelling probe and a closed-circuit TV system to permit the crew to monitor air-to-air refuelling operations. The K1 can also be fitted with up to 204 passenger seats for the trooping role. All Tristar variants have seating for up to 12 supernumerary crew at its forward end of the cabin. The *Red Arrows* departed RAF Scampton for Exercise *Eastern Hawk*, a six-week tour of the Far East, accompanied by a 68-man support team in two Hercules. The team gave 22 displays in 17 countries and logged 616 flying hours in 565 aircraft sorties – about 57 hours per aircraft. The highlight was participation at the inaugural Indonesia Air Show in June. Other countries visited included Germany, Switzerland, Italy, Saudi Arabia, Oman, Jordan, India, Malaysia, Thailand and Singapore. In December, the Secretary of State announced that the Boeing E-3D had been selected to fulfil the long-standing requirement for a new airborne early-warning aircraft. Further development of the Nimrod AEW3, with its troublesome GEC radar systems, was to be stopped immediately. An contract for six E-3Ds was placed for initial delivery in 1990, with an option for two more to be purchased later. The RAF aircraft were to be powered by CFM International CFM56 engines and have Loral ECM equipment in wing-tip pods, as specified for the Nimrod AEW3. The Westinghouse radar was to be similar to that in E-3s flown by the USAF, NATO and Saudi Arabia. They were to be fully compatible with the 18 NATO E-3s already in service at Geilenkirchen. The eleven Nimrod airframes already modified to AEW standard were declared redundant and eventually scrapped. No 229 OCU, the first operator of the Tornado F3, was declared operational at RAF Coningsby in the air defence role with the 'shadow' identity of No 65 Squadron.

---

8 January: The RAF Marine Branch disbanded at RAF Mount Batten, Plymouth.

14 February: The first flight, at São José dos Campos, Brazil, of the Tucano in RAF configuration, with a Garrett TPE331-12B turboprop engine.

5 March: A flypast was made over London by BBMF Spitfire PR19 PM631 to mark the 50th anniversary of the first flight of the Spitfire.

4 April: No 232 OCU, responsible for training aircrew for the Victor K2, was disbanded at RAF Marham.

11 April: The first flight in the UK by Shorts Tucano (G-14-007) after its transfer from Brazil.

16 April: The British Aerospace EAP (Experimental Aircraft Programme) demonstrator (ZF534) was rolled out at Warton. Aircraft testing was to provide data for the forthcoming European Fighter Aircraft.

23 April: The first of two BAe 146 CC2s for The Queen's Flight at RAF Benson was handed over by British Aerospace at Hatfield.

12 May: The US Ambassador to Great Britain unveiled a memorial in Grosvenor Square to the first RAF Eagle squadron – formed in 1940 by American volunteers.

30 May: Delivery of the last BAe Hawk T1A (XX256), modified at Dunsfold to war role configuration, with provision for two AIM-9L Sidewinder missiles.

July: The first operational Plessey Watchman display system for an RAF airfield was handed over at RAF Waddington. The system was the first of nearly 40 to be installed over a three-year period to update RAF air traffic control facilities.

July: No 5 Squadron, flying Lightning F3As and F6s from Binbrook, became RAF *Top Guns* for 1986 by winning the Seed Trophy. The award was based on scores achieved by nine air defence squadrons during its annual APC deployments to Cyprus.

16 July: The MoD sanctioned the acquisition by BAe and McDonnell Douglas of long-lead time items for the production of a further batch of Harrier GR5s.

4–8 August: The Tactical Fighter Meet 1986 brought aircraft of the Belgian, Canadian, Danish, French, Dutch, West German and US forces to RAF Waddington for the first of these NATO events to be held in the UK.

October: No 9 Squadron, operating Tornado GR1s, moved from RAF Honington to Germany, becoming the seventh Tornado-equipped unit in RAFG.

21 November: For the first time, a fully-loaded passenger-carrying RAF transport was air-refuelled. Carrying 129 troops from 5 Airborne Brigade to participate in Exercise *Saif Sareea*, a VC10 C1 of No 10 Squadron rendezvoused over Sicily with a VC10 K2 tanker of No 101 Squadron. It completed the non-stop 1,200 mile flight in 9hr 30min.

16 December: Supermarine Spitfire PR19 PS915 made its first flight at Samlesbury after a 30-month refurbishment by British Aerospace. This aircraft had left the RAF in 1957 and subsequently appeared in the film *Battle of Britain* before becoming a 'gate guardian' at RAF Brawdy. A modified Rolls-Royce Griffon engine previously used in a Shackleton was fitted. It returned to the RAF to serve with the BBMF in 1987.

30 December: The maiden flight, at Belfast, of the Shorts Tucano T1 (ZF135), the first of 130 to be built for the RAF.

Hawker Siddeley Nimrod MR2P XV253 of the RAF Kinloss MR Wing, shown here in Eric Day's painting, is shadowing a Russian Victor 1 nuclear submarine on the surface in the Northern Approaches. Today, the RAF's fleet of maritime patrol Nimrods is operated by Nos 120, 201, 206 and 42 (R) Squadrons at RAF Kinloss. The painting is reproduced by kind permission of the PMC, Officers' Mess, RAF Finningley.

These pages generously donated by Lady Humphrey OBE on behalf of The Air League

Nimrod Shadowing a Russian Submarine by Eric Day

In November, No 29 Squadron at RAF Coningsby became the first front-line air defence unit to become operational with the Tornado F3. It was simultaneously declared to NATO. The F3 was designed to combat the bomber threat in an intense ECM environment and in all weathers. The RAF played a vital part in the massive air and sea rescue operation after the *Herald of Free Enterprise* capsized at Zeebrugge. A joint forces team of helicopters, divers and paramedics was quickly scrambled to assist. Yorkshire University Air Squadron at RAF Finningley claimed to be the first UAS to recruit girls and the first to send a girl solo in the Bulldog. With the second annual intake, there were 100 female UAS cadets undergoing flying training – and most of them expressed a wish to follow their two years with the UAS by entering the RAF for training as aircrew. A VC10 tanker of No 101 Squadron broke the record for non-stop flying time between the UK and Australia, completing the 9,000-mile flight in just over 16 hours – thus beating by 2hr 4min 30sec the record set by a Vulcan in 1963. Introducing the Defence White Paper, the Defence Secretary said 508 aircraft had been ordered for the RAF since 1979 – and in real terms the defence budget was 20% higher than in 1978/79. He said "The RAF was in the midst of a major modernisation programme and that the Tornado programme alone was costing nearly £10 billion more than Trident". The Flying Selection Squadron at RAF Swinderby, best known as the home of the School of Recruit Training, was renamed the Elementary Flying Training Squadron (EFTS). It was the first such unit to be formed in the RAF since No 21 EFTS disbanded at Booker in 1950. The squadron was the largest single operator of the Chipmunk in the RAF, with eleven T10s, including WB550, the oldest Chipmunk still in RAF service and the second off the production line in 1949. RAF fire tenders began reverting to a red paint scheme. In the early 1970s, all service vehicles, including fire tenders, had to meet 'tone-down' requirements and were painted olive drab. The camouflage was so effective that fire vehicles could not be easily seen, so a yellow longitudinal stripe was added to their sides. This offered only a marginal improvement in visibility so it was decided to re-introduce the 'fire-engine' red paint scheme. In August, the Lightnings of No 5 Squadron's detachment took-off from RAF Akrotiri and headed for home at the end of the fighter's final armament practice camp in Cyprus. The squadron re-equipped with Tornado F3s in January 1988.

January: RAF Halton received a gate guardian – Hunter F6 (XF527), that had been first delivered to the RAF in September 1956.

February: Debut of the Tornado F3 on the Aberporth Ranges, producing outstanding performance in Sky Flash firing tests.

March: RAF Germany received an Andover C2 (XS793), which joined No 60 Squadron at RAF Wildenrath as a replacement for the unit's Pembrokes. XS793 had been with The Queen's Flight at RAF Benson until replaced by a BAe 146.

April: No 360 Squadron at RAF Wyton took delivery of the first Canberra T17 in the new hemp/grey colour scheme. The squadron celebrated its 21st birthday in April and has operated the T17s throughout its life.

April: Biggin Hill's historic gate guardians, Hurricane IIc LF738 and Spitfire XVIe SL674, left for RAF Abingdon following the decision to replace them with plastic replicas, that could better withstand the weather.

1 April: The Queen Mother attended the farewell to RAF Hendon, one of the service's most historic bases, on the occasion of its closure.

May: No 228 OCU's 18 Phantom FGR2s moved from RAF Coningsby to RAF Leuchars.

July: The RAF took delivery at Dunsfold of the first of 62 Harrier GR5s (ZD324).

July: No 1 (Fighter) Squadron, normally land-based at RAF Wittering, deployed on HMS *Ark Royal* for Exercise *Hardy Crab*. Five Harriers, together with 65 personnel, spent a week training for operations against land and sea-based targets from the ship.

July: A pair of No 74 (Tiger) Squadron Phantoms from Wattisham broke the record flight time from London to Edinburgh on the 70th anniversary of the Squadron's formation. They recorded a time of 27min 3sec for the 340-mile journey, travelling mostly over the sea off the east coast and reaching a speed of 1,150mph.

September: Tornado ZE155 from Boscombe Down was the first F3 to make a transatlantic crossing, supported by a Tristar tanker of No 216 Squadron, RAF Brize Norton.

24 September: The first unrefuelled transatlantic crossing was made by a British fighter. Returning to the UK after completing successful hot weather trials in Arizona, Tornado F3 ZE155 covered the 2,200 nautical miles from Canada in 4hr 45min.

October: Meteor T7 WF791, built in 1951, was restored to flying condition after storage, joining the *Vintage Pair* display team.

1 November: The first RAF front-line Tornado F3 unit, No 29 Squadron at RAF Coningsby, was declared operational to NATO.

28 November: The Victor celebrated 30 years of operational service with the RAF. The first Victor B1 entered service at RAF Gaydon – three decades later, the type was still in service (as a tanker) with No 55 Squadron at RAF Marham, the last of the V-bombers to remain operational.

The No 1 School of Technical Training hangar at RAF Halton, featured in Michael Turner's painting, shows Jaguars, Gnats, Jet Provosts and a Wessex being used to instruct RAF engineering apprentices and craftsmen. This task will be transferred to RAF Cosford in 1994. The painting is reproduced by kind permission of the PMC, Officers' Mess, RAF Halton.

These pages generously donated by No 1 School of Technical Training, RAF Halton

No 1 School of Technical Training at Halton by Michael Turner PGAvA

The BAe Harrier GR5, developed jointly by Britain and the United States, entered service during the year. Derived from the McDonnell Douglas/British Aerospace AV-8B, the GR5 has a new wing, a more powerful Rolls-Royce Pegasus engine, increased bird strike protection, a new Aden 25mm cannon, additional electronic countermeasures equipment, increased range and load-carrying capabilities and an improved cockpit including a moving map display. It has since been further upgraded to undertake low-level missions at night as the GR7.

It was announced in 1988 that the proposed civilian take-over of the Search and Rescue Service had been rejected. The Minister for the Armed Forces stated that wherever there was a military requirement for SAR it would continue to be provided by the RAF and RN. In May, the Royal Aircraft Establishment was retitled the Royal Aerospace Establishment. The RAE came into being in 1918, having previously been known as the Royal Aircraft Factory since 1912. Also in May, it was announced that a further 34 Harrier GR5s had been ordered for the RAF, bringing the total purchase to 96. The retirement of the Lightning took place in 1988 when No 11 Squadron laid up its colour, pending its

re-formation as a Tornado F3 squadron at RAF Leeming on 1 July 1988. The Lightning entered RAF service in July 1960 with No 74 Squadron. The RAF announced a new policy to further the preservation of its historic aircraft. Spitfire gate guardians were to be removed and some would be replaced by glass fibre replicas. Some of the original aircraft were subsequently sold and restored to flying condition. By 1988, the RAF still had over 100 aircraft as gate guardians, but this number was to be reduced. In July, a flypast by four Tornado F3s from No 11 Squadron marked the transformation of RAF Leeming to a front-line fighter station, following a £142 million rebuilding programme. It had previously been a Support Command training base. The first Shorts Tucano was officially handed over in September to the Central Flying School at RAF Scampton, heralding a new approach to flying training in the RAF. The last operational sortie by an RAFG Jaguar was flown in December, bringing to an end 13 years of continuous Jaguar operations by the RAF on the continent. The last Jaguar belonged to No 2 (AC) Squadron, which claims the distinction of being the oldest flying squadron in the RAF. It subsequently became the first Tornado GR1A reconnaissance squadron.

January: A and B Squadrons of the A&AEE at Boscombe Down amalgamated to form the Fixed Wing Test Squadron with three Flights. At the same time, D Squadron was renamed the Rotary Wing Test Squadron.

January: The fastest non-stop flight between Britain and the Falklands was achieved by a No 10 Squadron VC10 C1. It took 15hr 45min and was refuelled twice from a VC10 K3 of No 101 Squadron.

January: The last Red Top missile to be fired on a Missile Practice Camp was discharged from Lightning XR754 over Cardigan Bay.

February: The RAF took its first Air Combat Simulator on charge. Designed and built by BAe, it enabled fighter crews at RAF Coningsby to train and practice air-to-air combat.

February: The MoD concluded a long lease with Kent International Airport, enabling RAF Manston to continue as an operational RAF airfield.

March: Phantom FG1 XV582 of No 43 Squadron, one of the original airframes to enter RAF service in 1969, became the first Phantom to accumulate 5,000 flying hours in RAF service. It also set a new speed record by covering the length of Great

Britain in 46min 44sec at a speed of 760mph.

March: Jet Provost T3A XN501 was withdrawn from active flying service at RAF Scampton, the first retirement in anticipation of replacement by the Tucano T1. It was taken out of use after flying 8,340 hours in 28 years and went to No 2 School of Technical Training at Cosford for ground instruction.

5 May: RAF St Athan returned one of the world's first rocket-powered fighters to its former owner. Messerschmitt Me 163 Komet 191904 was handed over to the new Aviation Heritage Centre at Oldenburg.

June: Two Nimrod crews from No 206 Squadron at RAF Kinloss conducted a 14-hr low level operation at the North Pole. Two refuelling contacts were provided by VC10s of No 101 Squadron. The mission was to provide support to two RN nuclear-powered hunter submarines which had surfaced at the Pole.

June: RAF Akrotiri received a new gate guardian in the shape of a Lightning F6 which flew direct from RAF Binbrook to Cyprus in 5hr 15min, requiring ten air-to-air refuelling contacts. The aircraft is now displayed in a natural metal finish, with the markings of No 56 Squadron, which was the air

defence unit based in Cyprus.

30 June: The last flight was made by RAF Lightnings when F6s XS898 and XS923 were flown from Binbrook to a private buyer at Cranfield.

September: The Strike Attack Operational Evaluation Unit (SAOEU) at Boscombe Down received the first of three Harrier GR5s.

November: The Government announced an order for a further 26 Tornado GR1s and 15 Tornado F3s to sustain the RAF's Tornado force into the next century.

December: The RAF Fire School moved from RAF Catterick to RAF Manston and became known as the RAF Fire Service Central Training Establishment.

John Young's painting depicts two Panavia Tornado F3s from No 29 Squadron at RAF Coningsby intercepting a Soviet Tupolev Tu-95 Bear-F long-range maritime reconnaissance patrol aircraft. Tornado F3s were regularly scrambled to intercept these long range aircraft which were probing NATO defences over the North Sea. The painting is reproduced by kind permission of The Commandant, RAF College, Cranwell.

These pages generously donated by Lucas Aerospace

Tornado F3s of No 29 Squadron Intercepting a Russian *Bear* by John Young GAvA

The first operational Cruise Missile Wing at RAF Molesworth closed under the terms of the Intermediate Range Nuclear Forces Treaty of December 1987. The massive bunkers for the 60 ground-launched cruise missiles were closed. The last Jet Provost T4s in service with the RAF were retired from the Central Air Traffic Control School at RAF Shawbury. It was confirmed in July that, for the first time since the RAF was formed on 1 April 1918, women were to be recruited to the service as pilots and navigators. The first group of female aircrew applicants attended the Officer and Aircrew Selection Centre at RAF Biggin Hill in the following month. The first of the new female aircrew students commenced navigator training with No 6 FTS at RAF Finningley in September. One of the world's largest military hangars was opened at RAF Waddington for the servicing of the RAF's new Boeing E-3D Sentry. The introduction of a smoking ban was announced on all RAF VC10 and Tristar flights of up to three hours' duration, following a trial on aircraft chartered from Britannia Airways. No 13 Squadron at RAF Honington was the latest Tornado GR1 squadron to form and was the second Tornado squadron dedicated to the reconnaissance role. It was also the last of eleven front-line squadrons to receive the Tornado, in this case GR1As, under the current plan. The first major overseas deployment of the Harrier GR5 took place when aircraft from No 3 Squadron at RAF Gütersloh, Germany flew to Cyprus for combat training with Phantoms from Nos 19 and 92 Squadrons. The 'prototype' of a batch of twelve replica historic aircraft was installed on a plinth at Biggin Hill in February. Carrying the markings of No 92 Squadron, the most famous of Biggin Hill's Battle of Britain squadrons, Supermarine Spitfire 'N3194' occupies pride of place outside St George's Chapel of Remembrance. This was the first glass fibre replica to be installed under the policy to rescue historic aircraft from permanent outside display. A replica Hawker Hurricane, in No 79 Squadron markings, subsequently joined the Spitfire at Biggin Hill.

January: Several hundred airmen continued to take part in the clearing-up operations following the terrorist bombing of the PanAm Boeing 747 with the loss of 270 lives near Lockerbie on 21 December 1988.

8 January: Three helicopters ferried survivors to hospital after a British Midland Airways Boeing 737-400 crashed on the M1 motorway near Kegworth in Leicestershire. Sea Kings from RAF Leconfield and RAF Brawdy and a Wessex from RAF Coltishall were quickly on the scene. RAF Mountain Rescue teams from Stafford and Leeming helped survivors from the wreckage.

February: The Queen Mother laid a wreath in the RAF Chapel at Westminster Abbey to dedicate a memorial to leaders of the Royal Air Forces of Great Britain and the Commonwealth in WW2.

1 February: The basic flying school at the RAF College Cranwell was given the title No 3 Flying Training School.

18 March: The last Hercules Airbridge sortie was flown from RAF Lyneham to the Falklands. Since 1982, a total of 650 flights, each involving a round trip of 14,600 miles and 30 hours flying, had taken place. The task was taken over by the Tristars of No 216 Squadron at RAF Brize Norton.

13 May: The 40th anniversary of the first flight of the English Electric Canberra was celebrated at Wyton, which was the home base for the four units operating the RAF's remaining examples. A line-up of 40 Canberras was assembled and two aircraft were painted in the blue colour scheme worn by the first prototype.

June: RAF Chivenor received its 100th fighter training course since re-opening in 1980. At that date, No 2 Tactical Weapons Unit had trained 1,390 students.

July: The roll-out of the first Boeing E-3D Sentry AEW1 for the RAF took place in Seattle.

July: During a four-day detachment at RAF Valley, the new BAe Harrier GR5s of No 1 Squadron at RAF Wittering carried out the first live firing of AIM-9 Sidewinders by operational squadron aircraft.

September: On Sennelager military training area in Germany, the Harrier GR5 made its first field deployment on the Continent in the hands of the newly-equipped No 3 Squadron at Gütersloh.

September: An RAF Hercules from Belize flew relief supplies to Antigua and Montserrat following the devastation caused by Hurricane *Hugo*. It recorded 24 sorties in two weeks, airlifting 520,000lb of freight and 400 personnel.

September: One of the world's largest military hangars was opened at RAF Waddington. It was to be used for the servicing of the new E-3D Sentry AEW1.

October: No 54, a new Squadron of the RAF Regiment, equipped with the BAe Rapier surface-to-air missile system for defence against low-flying aircraft, was formed at RAF Leeming.

October: It was announced that a third BAe 146-100 was to be purchased and delivered in 1990 for The Queen's Flight, replacing the remaining Andover at RAF Benson.

29 November: The BAe Harrier GR7 night-attack aircraft made its maiden flight at Dunsfold.

December: At RAF Church Fenton No 42 Basic Flying Course became the first to be trained on the new Shorts Tucano T1, commenced formal flying instruction.

December: No 25 Squadron became fully operational and was declared to NATO. Thus, with Nos 11 and 23 Squadrons, RAF Leeming's Tornado Air Defence Wing was completely equipped.

Ronald Wong's painting illustrates a Westland Puma HC1 of No 33 Squadron, based at RAF Odiham, landing in poor light on snow-covered terrain whilst on Exercise Hardfall in Northern Norway. No 33 Squadron remains a helicopter support squadron at RAF Odiham. The painting is reproduced by kind permission of the PMC, Officers' Mess, RAF Strike Command, High Wycombe.

These pages generously donated by Racal Electronics plc

Hardfall by Ronald Wong BSc(Hons), GAvA, GMA, ASAA

*O*ptions for Change, a Government paper outlining proposals affecting three armed services as a result of the ending of the *Cold War*, was presented to Parliament in July. Ironically, this was just one week before the sudden demands of the Gulf crisis emerged. The proposals included substantial cuts. For the RAF, there was to be a reduction in front-line strength, accompanied by a cut in personnel numbers from 89,000 to 75,000, the lowest figure since 1938. When the Iraqi Army invaded Kuwait on 2 August 1990 and the Saudi Arabian Government requested assistance, air power was the only means available to the British Government to ensure a timely response and prevent Saddam Hussein's threatened invasion of Saudi Arabia. Because of that, the RAF was at the forefront of the British effort from the outset and remained so throughout. The RAF's contribution to Allied air power in the Gulf, both in crisis and conflict, was second only in importance to that of the United States. Under Operation *Granby*, in addition to the original 18 Tornado F3 fighters deployed, the RAF sent 45 Tornado GR1s, six GR1As, 12 Jaguar GR1s, 17 Chinooks and 19 Puma support helicopters plus a detachment of four Nimrod MR2P maritime patrol aircraft. Tanker support came from a total of 17 VC10, Victor and Tristar aircraft, and in-theatre transport support was undertaken by seven Hercules with communications by an HS125. Later in the campaign, the attack force was supplemented by 12 Buccaneers to provide laser designation of targets for Tornados bombing from medium level. The amount of logistic support required to deploy and sustain this large force 3,000 miles from its main operating base was immense, and much of the responsibility fell on the RAF Air Transport Force of Hercules, VC10 and Tristar aircraft. A number of ground units were also deployed, including eight RAF Regiment air and ground defence squadrons. In addition, medical and aeromedical evacuation teams were despatched to the Gulf region, together with other supporting units. At the peak of hostilities, some 5,500 RAF regular and reserve personnel were supporting RAF operations in the Gulf.

January: A new Military Area Services Operations Room opened at the London Air Traffic Control Centre, West Drayton. Controllers then had access to twelve country-wide radar heads.

January: The 800th production Tornado, an F3, was delivered to No 43 Squadron at Leuchars.

January: No 3 Squadron at Gütersloh flew its last sortie with the Harrier GR3.

5 January: The first flight of the RAF's first Boeing E-3D Sentry AEW1 (ZH101) took place at Seattle.

February: BAe won a £100 million contract to convert five former British Airways Super VC10 aircraft into flight refuelling tankers for the RAF. This would bring the total of VC10s employed in the air-to-air refuelling role to 14.

February: It was announced that the RAF was to receive 14 new Harrier T10 training aircraft. Based on the US Marine Corps TAV-8B, they would incorporate operational features of the Harrier GR7.

March: The RAF's Hercules recorded one million flying hours in service.

May: The last course of student pilots to fly the Jet Provost at No 7 FTS concluded at RAF Church Fenton.

May: Twelve SNCOs, training at the NATO base at Geilenkirchen as aircrew for the Sentry AEW1, were the first recipients of the RAF's newest aircrew brevet. This was 'AT' – Airborne Technician.

June: History was made when the *Red Arrows* crossed the former Iron Curtain for the first time. They displayed at Kiev and Budapest.

July: The first of seven E-3D Sentry AEW1s (ZH102) arrived to join No 8 Squadron at RAF Waddington.

July: The Secretary of State for Defence announced *Options for Change*, the proposals for a 'New Look' to Britain's armed forces.

July: The RAF Regiment's UK-based Light Armoured Squadrons were reduced to three when No 15 Squadron disbanded at RAF Hullavington.

2 August: Iraqi forces invaded Kuwait.

11 August: Tornado F3s on APC at Cyprus relocated to the Saudi Arabian Air Force Base at Dhahran. On the same day, 12 Jaguar GR1As from Nos 6, 41 and 54 Squadrons at RAF Coltishall departed for the Omani Air Force Base at Thumrait. Operation *Granby* had commenced.

12 August: Three Nimrod MR2Ps departed from RAF Kinloss for Oman, to be based at the coastal civil airport at Seeb.

23 August: It was announced that 12 Tornado GR1s from RAFG would be deployed to Bahrain. No 14 Squadron at Brüggen was the core of the composite unit which left for Muharraq, Bahrain on 27 August.

November: The RAF deployed 15 Puma helicopters to the Gulf from No 33 Squadron at RAF Odiham. As with many RAF aircraft despatched to the region, they received a sand-coloured paint scheme. They were followed by Chinooks from No 7 Squadron.

November: The first Tucano T1 (ZF144) was delivered to RAF Cranwell for use by No 3 FTS.

13 November: It was announced that the RAF bases at Gütersloh and Wildenrath would close within two years as part of the *Options for Change* restructuring programme.

December: Four Victors from No 55 Squadron at RAF Marham deployed to Bahrain.

23 December: The *Atlantic Conveyor* left Southampton Docks with eight Chinooks and four Puma helicopters. Also on board were twelve RN Sea Kings.

'Tens', painted by John Dimond, illustrates a BAC VC10 K2 of No 101 Squadron on a training flight with No 241 OCU refuelling, from its fuselage hose, a BAC VC10 C1 of No 10 Squadron. All three units are based at RAF Brize Norton. The VC10s of No 10 Squadron are being modified as C1K tankers. The painting is reproduced by kind permission of the Officer Commanding, No 241 Operational Conversion Unit, RAF Brize Norton.

These pages generously donated by No 241 Operational Conversion Unit

Tens by John Dimond

The diplomatic effort to persuade Iraq to withdraw from Kuwait culminated in UN Resolution 678 which authorised the 'use of all necessary means' to evict Iraq from Kuwait after a deadline set for 15 January. When Operation *Desert Storm*, the air campaign against Iraq, started on 17 January, RAF Tornado GR1s were amongst the first aircraft in action. Equipped with JP233 airfield denial weapons, 1,000lb bombs and ALARM anti-radar missiles, the Tornados attacked a number of the Iraqi Air Force's huge airfields. Most of the Tornado GR1 sorties during the first week of operations were flown at low level and at night. By day, RAF Jaguar GR1As attacked a variety of targets including Iraqi supply lines, SAM and artillery sites, naval vessels and Silkworm anti-ship missile sites. In addition to 1,000-lb bombs, the Jaguars used the Canadian CRV-7 rocket to great effect. Tornado F3s flew combat air patrols to protect Saudi airfields against an expected Iraqi Air Force counter-attack which did not actually materialise. The RAF aircraft were refuelled by VC10, Victor and Tristar tanker aircraft, which also supported a number of aircraft from other coalition nations. The overwhelming success of the offensive counter-air campaign against the Iraqi airfields created the opportunity to change Tornado tactics, and for the next three weeks the Tornado GR1 force flew both day and night missions against a variety of interdiction targets. The deployment of a squadron of Buccaneers equipped with Pave Spike laser designators enabled the Tornados to use Laser-Guided Bombs (LGBs) with great precision during daylight raids on strategic targets and airfields. The Tornado's capability was further enhanced with the delivery of a small number of experimental Thermal Imaging Airborne Laser Designator (TIALD) pods which gave the Tornado an enhanced precision night attack capability. A total of six Tornado GR1s was lost in action, four of which were involved in low-level attacks with 1,000lb bombs and one which was flying a low-level JP233 mission. Tornado GR1s completed some 1,500 operational sorties. Six Tornado GR1A reconnaissance aircraft flew 140 operational sorties, while Jaguars, operating in daylight, logged 600 operational sorties, many of which involved battlefield air interdiction. Nimrods maintained a complete surface plot of all merchant shipping in the Gulf, and challenged 6,552 ships. They also flew in support of the USS *Midway* task group in the northern Gulf, detecting Iraqi surface vessels and aircraft and directing attack aircraft to their targets. Puma and Chinook support helicopters were used extensively in the casualty evacuation and logistics support roles, flying over 1,700 sorties from desert bases. Operation *Granby/Desert Storm* was the UK's largest military operation since the end of WW2 – an offensive which stands as one of the most successful air campaigns in history.

---

17 January: Operation *Desert Storm* commenced. Tornado GR1s took part in Allied air strikes, concentrating on anti-airfield operations with JP233 cratering weapons.

17 January: Jaguar GR1As from Muharraq made day raids on targets in Kuwait. Newly-received CRV-7 rocket pods were used for the first time.

21 January: It was announced that Tornado tactics had changed with most missions now being flown at medium level.

24 January: Buccaneers from RAF Lossiemouth were sent to Muharraq to operate in target-designation role.

27/28 January: Night operations included Tornado GR1s using ALARM missiles in direct support of Saudi Tornado IDS bombing raids.

29 January: Jaguars continued to attack Silkworm sites, in conjunction with Allied naval forces' attacks on the Iraqi Navy. American CBU-87 cluster bombs were used for the first time.

30 January: Two Jaguars sank a Polnochney C-class landing craft with CRV-7 rockets and 30 mm guns.

2 February: Combat debut of the Buccaneer S2B. Using the Westinghouse AN/AVQ-23E Pave Spike laser designation pod, a bridge over the River Euphrates was successfully marked for six Pave Way laser-guided bombs dropped by two Tornado GR1s.

10 February: Service debut of Tornados with TIALD (Thermal Imaging and Laser Designation) pods. Four bridges were destroyed, together with an aircraft inside a hardened shelter.

24 February: Allied coalition ground offensive launched; all British air, land and sea forces involved.

26 February: Iraq withdrew from Kuwait.

28 February: Allied offensive military operations ended. Operation *Desert Storm* concluded.

May: Measures to restructure the RAF in Germany were announced. These included the withdrawal of the two Phantom air-defence squadrons and reducing the number of Tornado GR1 squadrons in RAFG to four.

June: Flight Lieutenant Julie Ann Gibson became the first woman in the service to receive her pilot's wings. She subsequently joined No 32 Squadron flying Andovers.

1 July: The Shackleton AEW2 was finally retired.

31 July: No 85 Squadron, which had operated the Bloodhound surface-to-air missile at West Raynham since 1975, was disbanded.

6 September: The first BAe Hawk T1A was delivered to No 100 Squadron at RAF Wyton. The squadron, which provides aerial target facilities, commenced re-equipment, having flown Canberras since 1972.

11 September: Implementation of *Options for Change* began with the disbanding of No 16 Squadron at RAF Laarbruch. This was the first of three RAF Germany Tornado GR1 squadrons to be disbanded.

October: The last ex-operational Bloodhound Mk 2 surface-to-air missiles left West Raynham.

2 October: The Quick Reaction Alert (QRA) by RAFG fighters was discontinued. The changed security situation meant that it was no longer necessary.

3 December: No 2 (AC) Squadron, equipped with Tornado GR1As, moved from RAF Laarbruch to RAF Marham.

The Panavia Tornado GR1 depicted in Ronald Wong's Gulf War painting is dropping laser-guided bombs on a bridge over the River Euphrates in Iraq during Operation Desert Storm. *The HS Buccaneer S2B flying alongside is designating the target with a laser for the Tornado. The painting is reproduced by kind permission of the PMC, Officers' Mess, RAF Strike Command, High Wycombe.*

These pages generously donated by Defence Evaluation and Research Agency

Laser Surgery - Iraq 1991 by Ronald Wong BSc(Hons), GAvA, GMA, ASAA

The contribution made to NATO by RAF Germany embraced a whole range of missions that would have been carried out in war – counter-air, interdiction, ground attack and tactical support helicopter operations. With the unification of Germany and the demise of the Warsaw Pact, air defence of the 2 ATAF area over Germany – previously the Command's responsibility – passed to the Germans. From the early 1990s, Britain's contribution to NATO was reorientated towards the new regional rapid reaction forces. In response to these changes, the RAF's presence in Germany was reduced to approximately half of its 1991 level. Direct support to the Army remained the task of two squadrons of Harrier GR7s that were moved to RAF Laarbruch, but tactical support was reduced from a squadron of Chinooks and one of Pumas to a combined squadron. The Tornado force was reduced to four squadrons, all concentrated at RAF Brüggen. RAFG's No 60 Squadron, used for communications, was disbanded, with its aircraft and crews being absorbed by No 32 Squadron at Northolt. RAF Regiment force levels were also cut, with No 16 Squadron at Wildenrath, No 58 Squadron at Catterick and No 63 Squadron at Gütersloh all being disbanded. The Officer and Aircrew Selection Centre moved from Biggin Hill to RAF Cranwell in September. The Centre assesses the suitability for training of any candidates for cadetship, scholarship, commissions and aircrew service. RAF Church Fenton closed, with the last course completing training at No 7 Flying Training School. The airfield was retained as a Relief Landing Ground (RLG), but the School's Tucanos were allocated to other units and the Jet Provosts retired. The RAF announced a two-year programme to re-title most of the operational conversion units and allocate 'new' reserve squadron numbers to these and some advanced flying training units. This was done in order to preserve the 'number plates' of recently disbanded but historically significant squadrons. The last two Phantom FGR2 units, Nos 56 and 74 Squadrons, both based at RAF Wattisham, were disbanded and their number plates allocated to training units. RAF Chivenor was transferred from RAF Strike Command to Support Command. At the same time, No 2 TWU was redesignated No 7 FTS with the added task of advanced flying training in the new pilot training programme. It was announced that the two 'shadow' squadrons (Nos 63 and 151 Reserve Squadrons) would assume the identities of the recently disbanded Nos 19 and 92 Squadrons respectively.

14 January: A new £5.2 million building for the Air Navigation School was opened at RAF Finningley.

February: It was announced that BAe had been contracted, with Flight Refuelling Ltd, to modify No 10 Squadron's VC10 C1s to air-to-air tanker configuration. An order for six additional Westland Sea King HAR3s was also confirmed.

February: RAF St Athan took on the major servicing of VC10s from RAF Brize Norton and third-line maintenance of Hawks and Jaguars from RAF Abingdon.

March: It was announced that RAF recruiting staff were to be integrated to form the Directorate of Recruiting and Selection based at RAF Cranwell.

1 April: The Tornado GR1s operated by the TWCU at Honington became No 15 (Reserve) Squadron. Both the previous unit title and the shadow designation (No 45 (Reserve) Squadron) ceased to be used.

1 June: No 60 Squadron formed at Benson with Wessex HC2s.

July: No 229 OCU at RAF Coningsby, which was previously No 65 (Reserve) Squadron, was retitled the (Tornado) F3 Operational Conversion Unit, No 56 (Reserve) Squadron. No 242 OCU at RAF Lyneham became the Hercules Operational Conversion Unit, No 57 (Reserve) Squadron.

6 July: Four Tornado F3s left RAF Coningsby, routing via Ascension Island to the Falklands, where they replaced Phantoms of No 1435 Flight.

15 July: It was revealed that RAF Honington would become the RAF Regiment Depot after the Tornados are redeployed to Lossiemouth in 1993/94.

31 July: RAF Abingdon closed and the station's flying units – the Oxford and London University Air Squadrons plus No 6 Air Experience Flight – moved to RAF Benson.

31 August: All flying training ceased at RAF Brawdy as part of the reorganisation of advanced flying and tactical weapons training. The base remained open to parent residual commitments, including SAR.

September: Three Tornado GR1s and three GR1As drawn from Nos 2, 27 and 617 Squadrons flew from RAF Marham to Dhahran to assist US forces in upholding the air exclusion zone over Southern Iraq, south of the 32nd Parallel.

21 September: The RAF's last airworthy Vulcan B2 (XH558) was retired after its last airshow appearance at Cranfield.

30 September: No 42 Squadron, the last Nimrod MR2 unit based at RAF St Mawgan, disbanded. The number plate was transferred to the Nimrod OCU at Kinloss – previously No 38 (Reserve) Squadron.

1 November: No 38 Group was re-formed at HQ Strike Command at High Wycombe with responsibility for all RAF transport and air-to-air refuelling operations, bases and training.

November: The RAF took delivery of the first of eight additional Tornado F3s (ZH552–ZH559). Originally ordered by Oman, they raised the RAF's total of F3s purchased to 152.

November: RAF Colerne was reactivated to accept Bristol UAS Bulldogs and No 3 AEF Chipmunks, which had been based at RAF Hullavington.

12 December: Two Hercules and four crews left RAF Lyneham to participate in Operation *Vigorous* – the support of Somali relief efforts.

16 December: The last 'military' flight by three Lightning F6s (XP693, XR773 and XS904) took place at BAe's Warton airfield. They were flown by British Aerospace test pilots

Eric Day's painting portrays two generations of RAF airborne early warning aircraft flying together. The veteran Avro Shackleton AEW2, of which twelve were converted for No 8 Squadron at RAF Lossiemouth, served from January 1972 to 1991. It was replaced by the Boeing E-3D Sentry AEW1 which became fully operational with No 8 Squadron at RAF Waddington when the seventh and last aircraft was delivered in May 1992. The painting is reproduced by kind permission of Wing Commander R G Thompson RAF.

These pages generously donated by the Boeing International Corporation

Sentry and Shackleton of No 8 Squadron by Eric Day

As part of Operation *Provide Comfort* the British element Operation *Warden* at Incirlik Air Base in Turkey enforced the 'No-Fly Zone' in Northern Iraq, north of 36°N. It comprised some 200 personnel supporting eight Jaguar GR1As manned by the three squadrons at RAF Coltishall. Two VC10 tankers were also provided by No 101 Squadron at RAF Brize Norton. Laarbruch became the home of the No 2 Group's (formerly RAF Germany) Support Helicopter Force with No 18 Squadron moving in from Gütersloh, alongside the Harrier GR7s of Nos 3 and 4 Squadrons.

In the first award by the MoD to a commercial organisation, a contract to train student pilots for the RAF and Royal Navy was won by Hunting Aircraft. It covered the operation of a Joint Elementary Flying Training Squadron (JEFTS) at RAF Topcliffe where student pilots receive basic flying instruction on a fleet of Slingsby T-67 Firefly aircraft. In April No 231 Operational Conversion Unit at RAF Wyton disbanded after more than 41 years operating the Canberra. Three Victors from No 55 Squadron and 16

Buccaneers from Nos 12 and 208 Squadrons flew over Buckingham Palace for the Queen's Birthday Flypast on 12 June, being the last occasion for both types before they were withdrawn from service. On 29 December a Hercules of No 47 Squadron flew the 1,000th humanitarian relief mission into Sarajevo, bringing the total load carried to nearly 15,000 tonnes (more than carried during the Berlin airlift of the early 50s). An RAF Hercules flew an average of three sorties a day from Ancona in Italy, each lift conveying 15 tonnes.

RAF, RN and HM Coastguard rescue helicopters and mountain rescue teams assisted 1,473 people in distress in Britain during 1993. The busiest SAR Unit was 'D' Flight, No 202 Sqn at RAF Leuchars. Overall the 14 SAR Units around the UK were called out by the RAF Rescue Co-ordination Centres at Edinburgh and Plymouth to 2,150 incidents, slightly more than in 1992. More rescues were carried out at night by RAF crews in 1993 because of the increasing use of the latest night vision goggles.

---

19 January: The first of 33 Chinook conversions to a common standard with the US Army's CH-47D plus standard for the RAF, Chinook HC2 ZA718, was rolled out at the Boeing Defense and Space Group Helicopter Division, Philadelphia.

March: Six Tornado F3s were deployed from RAF Leeming to Italy to help UN forces monitor the 'No Fly Zone' over Bosnia.

31 March: RAF Hullavington closed and was formally handed over to the Army.

1 April: Her Majesty The Queen presented a new Colour to the Royal Air Force to mark the 75th Anniversary of the founding of the Service, at RAF Marham.

1 April: Headquarters RAF Germany disbanded after 34 years, having been formed in October 1959 from the former 2TAF.

2 April: Harrier GR7s of Nos 3 and 4 Squadrons replaced Jaguars on Operation *Warden* over Northern Iraq.

20 May: Flypast of 14 aircraft at RAF Linton-on-Ouse to mark the retirement of the Jet Provost in the 'through-jet' training role.

29 May: First flight at Warton of the Tornado GR4 (XZ631) development aircraft for the GR1/1A mid-life update programme.

June: 18 Tornado F3s were grounded at RAF St Athan after being severely damaged during servicing by a private company under a £7m contract.

19 June: A VC10 C1K from No 10 Sqn at RAF Brize Norton was involved in the first air to air refuelling 'trail', following the delivery of the squadron's first VC10 transport equipped for the additional tanking role.

24 June: After 72 years of apprentice training at RAF Halton, the graduation of the 155th and final entry, marked the end of an era.

30 June: RAF Gütersloh, Germany closed and was transferred to the Army as the Princess Royal Barracks.

July: 12 Jaguar GR1As of No 6 Sqn at RAF Coltishall flew to Italy to participate in NATO operations to enforce a No-Fly Zone over Bosnia, as part of Operation *Deny Flight*.

6 July: RAF Jurby Head, the smallest RAF base in the British Isles employing eight servicemen and two civilians, was closed on the Isle of Man.

6 July: The last three Harrier GR3s in RAF squadron service left Belize, exactly 16 years after the first deployment arrived in Central America.

30 July: The first VC10 K4 tanker (ZD242), converted by British Aerospace from a former British Airways Super VC10 airliner, made its maiden flight at Filton.

1 August: The Army took over Upavon after 75 years of RAF stewardship, following the move of HQ No 1 Group to RAF Benson.

14 August: Jet Provosts were retired from service at RAF Finningley after 22 years' use as a navigation trainer.

31 August: No 100 Sqn moved with its Hawks from RAF Wyton to RAF Finningley.

September: RAF Wattisham was formally handed over to the Army Air Corps although the SAR Sea King HAR3 flight of

No 202 Squadron remained.

October: No 12 Squadron at RAF Lossiemouth retired its Buccaneer S2Bs.

1 October: The 'numberplate' of No 27 Sqn was transferred from RAF Marham to RAF Odiham, where it became No 27 (Reserve) Squadron, the Puma/Chinook OCU.

15 October: The last RAF Victor K2 tankers, operating with No 55 Squadron at RAF Marham, were withdrawn from service. The squadron number plate was transferred to No 241 Operational Conversion Unit.

19 October: RAF flight checking of military landing and radar aids was transferred from No 115 Sqn at RAF Benson to Hunting Aviation Services at East Midlands Airport, who continued to operate the four Andover E3s.

30 November: Victor K2 XH672 *Maid Marian* made the RAF's last V-Bomber flight from RAF Marham to RAF Shawbury. The aircraft was dismantled and moved to the RAF Cosford Aerospace Museum.

17 December: RAF Swinderby was closed, the Joint Elementary Flying Training Squadron having transferred to RAF Topcliffe.

Specially commissioned by No 1(F) Squadron, Royal Air Force Wittering, Michael Rondot's painting shows a British Aerospace Harrier GR7 about to take-off for a night attack Army support mission. The squadron has been operating Harriers from Wittering since July 1969.

These pages generously donated by British Aerospace Defence Ltd

Night Attack Harrier by Michael Rondot

There were a number of Tornado developments and changes. The GR1s of No 12 Squadron left RAF Marham on transfer to RAF Lossiemouth, where the unit formed half of the former Buccaneer maritime strike/attack force. Later No 617 Squadron joined No 12 in place of No 208 Squadron's Buccaneers. It was announced that No 14 Squadron based at RAF Brüggen would be designated the TIALD target marking squadron, replacing No 617 Squadron.

The first Tornado GRIB with an interim capability of launching the BAe Sea Eagle anti-shipping missile was delivered to No 617 Squadron at RAF Marham, prior to the squadron's transfer to Scotland. In April, the full integration of women into the Royal Air Force took place and the title Women's Royal Air Force and the post of Director were disestablished. Also in that month, two new RAF Commands were established – Personnel and Training Command at RAF Innsworth and Logistics Command at RAF Brampton, which replaced the former RAF Support Command. A major new NATO command headquarters was opened at RAF High Wycombe – named HQ Allied Forces North Western Europe (AFNORTHWEST) the new HQ would, in wartime, command a wide range of national and international defence formations.

For the first time, the RAF took part in the US Army's Exercise *Air Warrior*, when Harrier GR7s from Nos 1, 3 and 4 Squadrons used the facilities at Nellis Air Force Base and the top secret ranges in Nevada. Six Tornados deployed from RAF Brüggen to the Gulf Region, in response to the build-up of Iraqi forces close to the border with Kuwait. Proposals to move the *Red Arrows* from RAF Scampton to RAF Marham were outlined in a consultation document. The MoD announced an order for 25 Lockheed C-130J Hercules for delivery to the RAF – the remainder of the RAF requirement possibly to be met by a subsequent order for the Airbus Future Large Aircraft (FLA).

---

7 January: Ten Tornado GR1s of No 12 Squadron left RAF Marham on transfer to RAF Lossiemouth.

31 January: The UK's last airworthy Phantom FGR1 XT597 was retired following its use by A&AEE Boscombe Down as a calibration chase aircraft.

1 February: RAF Honington ceased to be a regular flying base when the Tornado GR1As of No 13 Squadron moved to RAF Marham .

26 February: After nearly 80 years service, No 23 Squadron was disbanded at RAF Leeming. Its Tornado F3s were reallocated to other air defence squadrons.

25 March: DRA Farnborough ceased flying on 25 March and commenced its move to Boscombe Down.

27 March: The Buccaneer S2B came to the end of 25 years of service with the RAF when No 208 Squadron disbanded at RAF Lossiemouth.

31 March: The RAF Headquarters and accommodation at West Drayton, the London Air Traffic Control Centre, closed after 60 years' service.

1 April: Full integration of women into the Royal Air Force took place and the title Women's Royal Air Force and the post of Director were disestablished.

1 April: Two new RAF Commands were established – Personnel and Training Command at RAF Innsworth and Logistics Command at RAF Brampton, replacing the former RAF Support Command.

6 April: The BAe constructed British prototype of the Eurofighter 2000 made its first flight at Warton. On the following day the BAe Harrier T10 was airborne for the first time at the same airfield.

27 April: No 617 Squadron, equipped with Tornado GR1/1B strike/attack aircraft, left RAF Marham to join No 12 Squadron at RAF Lossiemouth, to assume the anti-shipping role in place of No 208 Squadron's Buccaneers.

30 June: The Berlin Station Flight at Gatow was disbanded and its two Chipmunk T10s withdrawn.

30 June: The RAF ensign was lowered at RAF Catterick for the last time. The RAF Regiment Depot transferred to RAF Honington.

1 July: A major new NATO command headquarters, HQ Allied Forces North Western Europe (AFNORTHWEST), was opened at High Wycombe.

1 July: 'A' Flight of No 22 Squadron at RAF Chivenor received two Sea King HAR3 helicopters to replace its Wessex HC2s.

21 July: After 30 years of helicopter Search and Rescue operations at RAF Coltishall, No 22 Sqn B Flight moved to Wattisham.

31 July: The Pumas of No 1563 Flight, Belize ceased flying after 16 years of operational service in Central America, marking the closure of the RAF's last operational unit in Belize.

7 September: RAF Gatow finally handed over to the Luftwaffe.

22 September: Two RAF Jaguars were called into action in Bosnia. A retaliatory attack involved the Jaguars each dropping a 1,000lb bomb on a Bosnian Serb 155 tank which had entered the Sarajevo heavy weapons exclusion zone.

30 September: No 7 FTS (formerly No 2 Tactical Weapons Unit) at RAF Chivenor closed. Its advanced flying training role was passed to No 4 FTS at RAF Valley.

October: The RAF's first female Air Electronics Operator graduated after spending a year at the Air Electronics, Engineer and Loadmaster School at RAF Finningley.

31 October: No 360 Squadron, based at RAF Wyton stood down after 28 years of continuous service. A joint RN-RAF Squadron it was equipped with the veteran Canberra T17 and T17As, which provided air defence operators of all three services with realistic electronic counter measures (ECM) training.

November: No 84 Squadron at RAF Akrotiri converted from Wessex HC5s to grey-painted Wessex HC2s for its dual SAR/Support Helicopter roles in Cyprus.

December: The purchase of new TIALD laser designator pods, to be shared between 10 upgraded Jaguar GR1Bs and two Jaguar T2Bs at RAF Coltishall was announced. The MoD also announced an order for 25 Lockheed C-130J Hercules.

December: The RAF's first woman Tornado pilot, Flt Lt Jo Salter, achieved 'combat ready' status with No 617 Squadron at RAF Lossiemouth.

Wilfred Hardy's painting Low Down The Lake – Again *showing a Sea Eagle-equipped Tornado GR1B of No 617 Squadron, was specially commissioned by The Royal Air Force Benevolent Fund to mark the 50th anniversary of the raid on the German dams by Lancasters of No 617 Squadron in May 1943.*

These pages generously donated by British Aerospace Defence Ltd

Low Down The Lake – Again by Wilfred Hardy GAvA

The E-3D Sentry AEW1 component of the NATO Airborne Early Warning (AEW) Force, based at RAF Waddington, was declared fully operational, though it had been involved in UN operations over the former Yugoslavia since 1992, when Operation *Maritime Monitor* commenced. The first of the RAF's six new Sea King HAR3A search and rescue helicopters (ZH540) – the most advanced SAR Sea King – made its maiden flight at Westlands, Yeovil.

The new Harrier T10 two-seat trainer entered operational service with the Harrier OCU/No 20 (Reserve) Squadron at RAF Wittering. The RAF received 13 T10s, the two-seat version of the GR7 day/night all-weather capable aircraft, that is fully equipped to train pilots for day and night attack missions. Modified to take the TIALD thermal imaging and laser designation pod, the first Jaguar GR1B was formally handed over to the RAF by the DRA at Boscombe Down. The GR1B can also be equipped with a 1,000lb laser-guided bomb, Phimat chaff dispenser and ECM pod. Eight Jaguars were converted to GR1B standard and two T2 trainers were similarly modified to T2B standard. A hundred years of British military ballooning came to an end with the disbandment of the RAF's Balloon Operations Squadron. Based at RAF Hullavington since the 1950s, the gas balloons were replaced by a Short Skyvan aircraft operated by a private contractor.

The Queen's Flight disbanded at RAF Benson after more than 50 years service and the aircraft and aircrew became part of No 32 (Royal) Squadron, restructured into three flights at RAF Northolt. To celebrate the 50th Anniversary of VE and VJ days the International Air Tattoo was designated by the MoD and RAF as The Victory Airshow – this being the most ambitious and successful event organised by the RAF Benevolent Fund Enterprises. The RAF's new Air Warfare Centre was opened at RAF Waddington. The Thomson building enables the key areas of tactics, electronic warfare, scientific research and analysis and air warfare, to be joined in a single centre for the first time.

January: The E-3D Sentry AEW1 component of the NATO Airborne Early Warning (AEW) Force, based at RAF Waddington, was declared fully operational.

February: The first of the RAF's six new Sea King HAR3A search and rescue helicopters (ZH540) made its maiden flight at Yeovil.

March: Flt Lt Elaine Taylor became the RAF's first fast jet navigator with No 25 Squadron at RAF Leeming flying on air defence duties.

March: A Harrier T10 made its first operational sortie with the Harrier OCU/No 20 (Reserve) Squadron RAF Wittering.

31 March: RAF Stanbridge closed as a self accounting unit and became a satellite of RAF Henlow.

31 March: The last Andover was retired from RAF service, although one remained with the Defence Research Agency for 'Open Skies' Monitoring.

31 March: The RAF's Balloon Operations Squadron, used for parachutist training, was closed at RAF Hullavington, having been based there since the early 1950s.

31 March: The Queen's Flight disbanded at RAF Benson. The aircrew and aircraft became part of No 32 (Royal) Squadron at RAF Northolt.

1 April: RAF Wyton ceased as an independent station and became part of RAF Brampton.

1 April: The Joint Elementary Flying Training School (JEFTS) with 18 civil registered Slingsby T67M Fireflies, moved from Topcliffe to RAF Barkston Heath.

1 April: Two further Tucano operators, the Central Flying School and No 6 FTS (navigator training) moved from Scampton and Finningley respectively to RAF Topcliffe.

1 April: The RAF's two Operational Evaluation Units (the F3 OEU at RAF Coningsby and the Strike/Attack OEU at Boscombe Down) were renamed as elements of the Air Warfare Centre.

1 April: RAF Newton's 55-year history as a flying and ground training unit came to an end when it was reduced from station to enclave status.

16 May: A Nimrod R1 electronic reconnaissance aircraft of No 51 Sqn ditched off Lossiemouth when both starboard engines caught fire during a test flight following major servicing at RAF Kinloss.

22 June: The first of 24 RAF Tornado F3s being leased to the Italian Air Force (ZE832/MM7202) was flown after preparation at RAF St Athan.

1 August: More than 5,000 hours of flight operations in support of the UN Protection Force in the former Yugoslavia had been accumulated by Jaguars from the Coltishall Wing detached for Operation *Deny Flight* since 1993, when they were replaced by Harrier GR7s of No 4 Squadron.

15 August: The first modified Dominie navigation trainer (XS728) was delivered from Marshall of Cambridge to DTEO Boscombe Down for pre-service trials.

25 August: VC10 C1K XV103 *Major Edward Mannock* made the last of No 10 Squadron's twice-weekly scheduled flights from Brize Norton to Washington, DC.

6 September: A Closure Day Ceremony was held at RAF Swanton Morley, the service's largest grass airfield, before the station was handed over to the Army.

21 September: No 100 Squadron, along with its complement of Hawk T1As arrived at RAF Leeming on relocation from RAF Finningley. With the closure of Finningley the Joint Forward Air Control Training & Support Unit (JFACTSU) also relocated to Leeming.

1 October: The final Dominie T1s and Jetstream T1s were transferred from RAF Finningley as the build up of No 3FTS at RAF Cranwell was completed. Twelve of each type joined the Bulldog T1s already in residence.

26 October: RAF Chivenor was handed over to the Royal Marines on 26 October.

30 October: The Franco-British Euro Air Group, a new alliance between the air forces of Britain and France, was inaugurated.

23 November: The *Red Arrows* left RAF Scampton for the last time when they set off on a world tour. On return to the UK they moved to RAF Cranwell, although continuing to use Scampton's airspace for training flights.

This new painting by Ronald Wong shows a pair of fully armed Jaguar GR1s en route to an Operation Deny Flight *patrol over Bosnia, with one of the aircraft receiving fuel from a Tristar KC1 of No 216 Squadron.*

These pages generously donated by Cobham plc

Deny Flight Patrol by Ronald Wong Bsc(Hons), GAvA, GMA, ASAA

In January the last RAF relief flight was made into Sarajevo under Operation *Cheshire*, the United Nations humanitarian effort into Bosnia. In an internal reorganisation of Strike Command, No 1 Group moved its HQ from RAF Benson to High Wycombe. Headquarters No 2 Group at Rheindahlen, the last RAF HQ on mainland Europe, was closed down and moved to Strike Command at High Wycombe. No 11 Group, controlling the RAF's air defence forces, and No 18 Group responsible for maritime and electronic warfare operations, were combined as No 11/18 Group, while maintaining their individual headquarters at Bentley Priory and Northwood respectively. The control of transport and tanker elements was transferred to No 38 Group from Strike Command HQ at High Wycombe on 31 March. The last Hercules tanker aircraft returned to RAF Lyneham from the long term detachment with 1312 Flight at Mount Pleasant Airfield in the Falkland Islands and the Hercules tanker force was disbanded. The Chipmunk's long association with the Air Cadets ended when the aircraft was retired from RAF service, just two months before the 50th anniversary of its first flight. The Defence Secretary announced that the BAe Nimrod 2000 would be the RAF's replacement maritime patrol aircraft, and a total of 21 Nimrod 2000s were to be converted from the existing MR2 fleet. The Armed Forces Minister announced that a joint venture between three private companies would operate the new tri-service Defence Helicopter Flying School, to be operated at Shawbury from April 1997. No 28 (AC) Squadron vacated its base at RAF Sek Kong and flew its six Wessex HC2s to Kai Tak International Airport, Hong Kong where it was to be based until the hand-over in June 1997. Sek Kong, the last RAF base on mainland Asia then closed. The Eurofighter programme moved another stage forward with a reaffirmation of full commitment to its development by all four partner nations at the end of the year.

---

8 January: The Implementation Force (I-FOR) was inaugurated. Four additional Chinook HC2s from No 7 Squadron at RAF Odiham joined the detachment in Bosnia.

9 January: The last RAF relief flight was made into Sarajevo under Operation *Cheshire*, the United Nations humanitarian effort in Bosnia.

February: The *Red Arrows* arrived at RAF Cranwell, its new base, after a record-breaking five-month tour of three continents.

4 March: In an internal reorganisation of Strike Command, No 1 Group moved its HQ from RAF Benson to High Wycombe and took on the functions of No 2 Group.

24 March: RAF Hospital Wegberg closed down after 43 years service to British Forces Germany.

31 March: The Hercules tanker force was disbanded following the return of the last aircraft from its long term detachment with 1312 Flight at Mount Pleasant Airfield in the Falklands.

31 March: The Chipmunk's long association with the Air Cadets ended when the aircraft was retired from RAF service – two months before the 50th anniversary of its first flight.

31 March: The RAF ensign was lowered for the last time at Princess Alexandra's Hospital, Wroughton.

31 March: No 34 Squadron RAF Regiment disbanded in Cyprus, where it had been based for 40 years. The Squadron deployed first to Nicosia in 1956 and then moved to RAF Akrotiri in 1960.

31 March: An 81-year link with military flying came to an end when RAF Turnhouse closed.

1 April: No 23 Squadron, which disbanded as a Tornado unit after the Gulf War, was re-formed at RAF Waddington, with responsibility for E-3D Sentry aircrew training and an operational role.

1 April: Two Twin Squirrel helicopters (ZJ139 and ZJ140) were handed over at RAF Northolt, for use as VIP transport with No 32 (The Royal) Squadron.

1 April: RAF Boddington closed and No 9 Signals Squadron transferred to become part of RAF Innsworth. RAF Ash also ceased to exist as a station on the same day.

5 April: The first of 25 Lockheed C-130J-30 Hercules II ordered for the RAF made its maiden flight from Dobbins Air Reserve Base at Marietta, GA.

20-21 July: The RAF Benevolent Fund's IAT, the world's largest military airshow held annually at RAF Fairford was given the Royal prefix, becoming The Royal International Air Tattoo.

31 July: No 48 Squadron RAF Regiment ended its 18-year association with Lossiemouth when the squadron moved to RAF Waddington to form a new combined regular and reserve unit.

August: Control of Operations *Jural* and *Warden* was handed over from HQ Strike Command to the Permanent Joint Headquarters. Since the inception of Operation *Jural* in 1991, the RAF had flown more than 5,500 operational sorties in policing an exclusion zone in southern Iraq. Aircraft engaged on Operation *Warden* (previously Operation *Haven*) over the skies of northern Iraq, had flown more than 7,000 operational sorties.

24 September: The new NATO Maritime Headquarters opened at Northwood.

26 September: No 14 Maintenance Unit at RAF Carlisle closed after 58 years of operation.

October: The last VC10 C1K (XR808) converted by Flight Refuelling Ltd for two-point refuelling with underwing FRL Mk 32B hose-drum pods, was delivered back to No 10 Sqn at RAF Brize Norton.

19 October: The last three RAF Andover E3s, that had been used for calibrating landing aids and radar at British military airfields, were retired from service. Based at East Midlands Airport, the aircraft had been operated under contract by Hunting Aviation Services, but flown by RAF crews.

1 November: The Dominie Squadron of No 3 Flying Training School became No 55 (Reserve) Squadron at RAF Cranwell.

1 November: The Sea King Operational Conversion Unit at RAF St Mawgan became No 203 (Reserve) Squadron, equipped with Sea King HAR3/3As.

1 November: No 28(AC) Squadron vacated its base at RAF Sek Kong and flew its six Wessex HC2s to Kai Tak International Airport, Hong Kong.

Wilfred Hardy's Royal Squadron – Royal International Air Tattoo, *depicting a British Aerospace BAe 146 CC2 of No 32 (The Royal) Squadron flying overhead RAF Fairford in July 1996, has been specially commissioned to mark the granting of the 'Royal' prefix to the RAF Benevolent Fund's International Air Tattoo.*

These pages generously donated by British Aerospace Defence Ltd

Royal Squadron – Royal International Air Tattoo by Wilfred Hardy GAvA

The Implementation Force serving in the former Yugoslavia was replaced by the new Stabilisation Force (SFOR) which assumed the NATO peace-building role. It ensured the parties continued compliance with key military aspects of the peace agreement. The RAF Logistics Support Services Defence Agency was officially launched at RAF Wyton, which will strengthen RAF and MoD operational capability by providing effective and specialist military aerospace logistics support and logistics consultancy services. The RAF Personnel Management Centre at Innsworth became a Defence Agency on 1 February, as part of the Government's 'Next Steps' initiative. Bracknell became home to Joint Services Command and Staff College courses until a new tri-service college at Shrivenham is up and running. Operation *Warden*, based at Incirlik, Turkey – which continued to be an essential part of the post – Gulf conflict policy of policing the no-fly zone over northern Iraq, became known as *Northern Watch* following the withdrawal from theatre by the French. A new Reserve Forces Act came into being on 1 April which included a new power of call-out for peace-keeping, humanitarian and disaster relief operations; new categories of reserve; and a range of safeguards for reservists and their employers. Sixty years of tradition ended when the RAF Volunteer Reserve amalgamated with the Royal Auxiliary Air Force. The first of 142 Tornado GR1/1A aircraft to be upgraded to the new GR4/4A standard by BAe made its maiden flight from the company's Warton airfield – delivery to front-line squadrons will begin in 1998, with all 142 aircraft due to be upgraded by 2002. The Government announced that Royal Auxiliary Air Force pilots and navigators were to fly Tornado F3s for the RAF – almost 40 years after the politicians decreed that fast jets were too complicated to have auxiliaries in their cockpits.

January: IFOR in Bosnia was replaced by SFOR (Stabilisation Force).

February: Three Nimrod MR2s, which had been in deep storage at RAF Kinloss, were transported by air aboard an Antonov An-124, to Bournemouth Airport for rebuilding by FRA, as part of the £2 billion contract for the RAF's new Nimrod 2000 maritime patrol aircraft.

11 February: The last two Westland Wessex helicopters of No 60 Squadron left RAF Benson and flew to the RNAY at Fleetlands.

March: No 18 Squadron's Puma Flight completed its move from Laarbruch to join No 72 Squadron at Aldergrove, as a result of the restructuring of the RAF's support helicopter force and the withdrawal of the Puma from Germany.

30 March: No 2 Flying Training School, based at Shawbury, disbanded for the fifth time since it formed in 1920 at Duxford. It handed over the ab-initio helicopter aircrew training task to the new tri-service Defence Helicopter Flying School two days later.

1 April: The Search and Rescue Training Unit at RAF Valley became part of the Defence Helicopter Flying School (DHFS), which formed this day at RAF Shawbury.

1 April: No 60 Squadron disbanded as an operational flying unit at RAF Benson. It reformed later in the month as a training unit at Shawbury as No 60 (R) Squadron.

1 April: The new Operations Support Branch was established with five specialisations: air traffic control, fighter control, intelligence, RAF Regiment and the new specialisation of flight operations.

12 May: The new Sea King HAR3A Search and Rescue helicopter entered RAF operational service with A Flight, No 22 Squadron, Chivenor.

June: It was announced that the RAF was to recruit reservist air traffic controllers for operational and instructional duties at seven airfields in Personnel and Training Command.

3 June: The six Wessex helicopters of No 28 (Army Co-operation) Squadron made a final flight around Hong Kong, before they were handed over to the Uruguayan Air Force. No 28, the last RAF squadron in Hong Kong, was disbanded.

13 June: Pumas from No 33 Squadron flew into RAF Benson on transfer of their base from Odiham.

July: The last two Chinooks of No 18 Squadron left RAF Laarbruch, Germany. August: After nearly 20 years, the final air-to-air gunnery sortie was flown from No 4 FTS at RAF Valley.

August: The first group of Hercules reserve aircrew completed its re-familiarisation training with No 57(R) Squadron at RAF Lyneham.

August: The Westland Gazelle, which had served as the RAF's basic helicopter trainer since 1973, was retired from the service on 31 August, being replaced by Squirrel HT1s at the DHFS.

30 September: The RAF's long-standing association (since 1970) with flying training in Sardinia ended when the last air weapons detachment finished at Decimomannu.

14 October: On the 50th anniversary of the first supersonic flight, Squadron Leader Andy Green, an RAF Tornado F3 pilot, became the first person to set a supersonic land speed record in the jet-powered Thrust SSC. Thrust produced an average speed of 763.035mph across the Nevada Desert.

October: Flight Lieutenant Ian Black of the Royal Auxiliary Air Force became the first reserve fighter pilot to fly with the RAF since 1957.

31 October: The first Tornado GR4 conversion was delivered to the RAF at DERA Boscombe Down.

31 October: The Queen presented RAF Halton with a new Colour, the first to be awarded to the RAF since 1969.

November: The Government announced the formation of four new Royal Auxiliary Air Force squadrons to support front-line operations or humanitarian duties – to be based at Cottesmore, Marham, Brize Norton/Lyneham and Leeming.

12 December: The Rescue Co-ordination Centre at Plymouth closed as part of a major reorganisation. Plymouth handed over responsibility for its southern military and aeronautical co-ordination area to its northern counterpart, the RCC at Kinloss, on 1 December.

Specially commissioned to mark the opening of the new Defence Helicopter Flying School on 1 April 1997, this painting by Roger Middlebrook shows a Bell Griffin HT1 and a Eurocopter Squirrel flying over RAF Shawbury.

These pages generously donated by FBS Limited (FR Aviation, Bristow Helicopter Group and Serco Defence)

Defence Helicopter Flying School by Roger Middlebrook GAvA

Lest We Forget by Frank Wootton FPGAvA

This page generously donated by
Lloyds Bank plc

Opposite page:
*Anthony Cowland's specially commissioned
painting shows a newly delivered Lockheed
Martin C-130J-30 Hercules C4 making an
ultra low-level airborne delivery while on a
test flight from Boscombe Down.*

The page opposite generously donated by
Lockheed Martin Aeronautical Systems

Testing the Hercules by Anthony Cowland BA(Hons), GAvA, FSAII

ACKNOWLEDGEMENTS

The Royal Air Force Benevolent Fund wishes to extend its warm and grateful appreciation to the following companies and organisations for their most generous support of the Fund by sponsoring pages within this book:

Adwest Group plc
Agfa-Gevaert (UK) Ltd
Airclaims Limited
The Aircrew Association
Alenia SPA
Alliance & Leicester
Arkell's Brewery Ltd
Aviation Leathercraft
B&Q plc
Boeing International Corporation
Bombardier Services
British Airways PLC
British Aerospace Defence Ltd
Civil Aviation Authority
Cobham plc
Courage Ltd

Defence Evaluation & Research Agency
DTZ Debenham Thorpe
Ercol Furniture
Ernst & Young
FlyPast Magazine
GEC-Marconi Ltd
The Guild of Air Pilots and Air Navigators
of the City of London
Haynes & Cann Limited
Imperial Tobacco Limited
Industria Engineering Products Ltd
Intercapital Brokers Ltd
Jeppesen
Kodak Limited
Lloyds Bank plc
Lockheed Martin Aeronautical Systems

Lucas Aerospace
Main Event Catering
Marshall Aerospace
Martin-Baker Aircraft Company Ltd
Morgan Grenfell Asset Management
Motorola
Music For Pleasure
Provident Mutual
Racal Electronics plc
Rolls-Royce plc
SNECMA
Taylor Brothers Bristol Limited
Timet UK Ltd
Vickers PLC
Lady Humphrey OBE on behalf of
The Air League

and to the following current and former Royal Air Force Squadrons and Units who have also graciously sponsored pages:

No 1 School of Technical Training
No 4 Flying Training School
No 10 Squadron
No 14 Squadron

No 17(F) Squadron
No 60 Squadron
No 84 Squadron
No 201 Squadron
No 241 Operational Conversion Unit

The Royal Air Force College, Cranwell
Course members of No 85 Advanced Staff Course,
RAF Staff College, Bracknell
The Officers of Royal Air Force Waddington

and finally to the following personnel and organisations who have provided invaluable help and assistance in the compilation of this book:

Mr James Binnie
The Guild of Aviation Artists
Imperial War Museum, Department of Art
Air Historical Branch, Ministry of Defence

Mr David Ring LBIPP
The Royal Air Force Club
Royal Air Force Museum, Department of Research
and Information Services

Commandant, Royal Air Force College, Cranwell
Presidents of Mess Committees of
Royal Air Force Officers' Messes
Director of Public Relations, Royal Air Force

THE CONTRIBUTING ARTISTS

C J ASHFORD GAvA FCIAD

Diploma student at Wakefield and Glasgow Schools of Art in the 1930s, he served in camouflage development units during World War 2 in the Middle East, visiting airfields in North Africa and Italy. After the war, exhibited paintings in London galleries and produced illustrations for magazines and advertising. One of the full and founder members of the Guild of Aviation Artists, specialising mainly in historical aviation subjects. Also a member of the Canadian Historical Aviation Society. Paintings in a number of national and private museums, also RAF Stations in Britain, Canada and the USA, including the RAF Museum, Hendon; The Shuttleworth Trust, Old Warden; The Greenwich National Maritime Museum; and the Ashmolean Museum, Oxford.

GERALD COULSON GAvA

Born at Kenilworth, Warwickshire, Gerald Coulson is a self-taught artist. He began drawing at around 16 or 17 years of age but professionally trained and qualified as an aircraft engineer. He served in the Royal Air Force for eight years and later used his technical knowledge and drawing ability for a successful career illustrating technical manuals for civil and military aircraft and associated equipment. Gerald qualified for a pilots licence in 1960, fulfilling a boyhood ambition. A love of flying and most anything connected with aviation motivated the desire to put on canvas the sky and all its various moods. He became a full-time artist in 1969 and since then his paintings have featured many times in the Fine Art Group top ten best-selling prints. They can be seen in many establishments and collections around the world, and quite naturally in RAF stations, museums and exhibitions.

ANTHONY R G COWLAND BA(Hons), GAvA, FSAII

Anthony Cowland was born in June 1956 and brought up in Barbados and Singapore before returning to the UK by sea, over several months, in 1966. After boarding school in Warwickshire, he studied Art at Brighton College of Art, went on to Design and Architecture and gained a First Class BA (hons) degree. His working life began in Design/Architecture and he worked in New York, Germany, Italy and Switzerland and the UK. Anthony became a director of a major design group in 1986. He kept up his painting/illustration, but in 1988 made the break to become a full-time freelance artist. His aviation paintings are regularly seen in major UK museums and many are in private collections worldwide. He is a Full Member of the Guild of Aviation Artists, a Fellow of the Society of Architectural and Industrial Illustrators and a Member of the Chartered Society of Designers.

ERIC DAY

Eric Day was born in Warwickshire and studied art in London. During World War 2 he served in Bomber Command, after which he spent some time painting in South Africa. Returning to the UK in 1949 he settled in Cornwall painting the Cornish landscape and a number of commissioned portraits. Painting in both oil and watercolour the last few years have been spent working in watercolours. A selection of his work is on permanent exhibition at the RAF Staff College, Bracknell and various messes throughout the Royal Air Force.

RODNEY I DIGGENS GAvA

Born on 2 August 1937 in Dulwich, South London, he was evacuated to North Green Parham, Suffolk during World War 2, living in a small cottage adjacent to the USAAF air base that was the home of the 390th BG. Much time was spend on and around the airfield, this time having a lasting effect. He studied art at the Central and the Camberwell Schools of Art. Served with the 1st Royal Tank Regiment during National Service, which included the Suez crisis and a tour of Hong Kong. Took up a career in advertising and printing before taking up painting full time. A keen interest in motorsport led to racing saloon cars in the late fifties and sixties. He paints in gouache acrylic and oil and was greatly influenced by the Victorian painters, notably J W Waterhouse and Alma Radema. Has exhibited widely and has completed many commissions world wide. A founder member of the Guild of Motoring Artists.

JOHN DIMOND

Initially self taught, John received no formal art training, but instead developed a natural aptitude for painting over many years. His love of painting and a life-long fascination for flying led to a specialisation in aviation art. He was accepted into the Guild of Aviation Artists in 1980, and subsequently benefited from the influence and tuition of many leading professional artists. Turning professional in 1986, John has enjoyed a wide range of subject matter. His work has been exhibited widely at venues which include the Qantas Gallery, London; Carisbrooke Gallery, London; RAF Museum, Hendon; Hull & Kingston City Gallery; Coventry City Gallery and the Collectair Gallery in North California, USA. One of his framed prints was presented to The Duke of Edinburgh by No 120 Squadron during their 70th anniversary celebrations. Developments in John's career have attracted periodic press interest, and he recently appeared in a Central Television filmed interview and report featuring his aviation paintings. Based in Coventry, John is married with two daughters. He is a volunteer motor gliding instructor with the RAFVR(T) and holds a Private Pilots' Licence.

PENELOPE DOUGLAS GAvA

Penelope Douglas started painting aircraft at the time of the 50th anniversary of the RAF. She is a founder full member of the Guild of Aviation Artists, and works in oils. She has been commissioned for many paintings for the Royal Air Force and privately, the largest collection of seven 36" x 48" paintings being at RAF Brize Norton, one of which is the HS Andover E3 of No 115 Squadron at RAF Machrihanish. Another collection of six paintings is at RAF Akrotiri, Cyprus. Through her commissions for the Armed Forces, she has visited many places, including Cyprus, Germany, Gan, Masirah, Gibraltar, Ascension Island and Kenya. Penelope Douglas' work includes the RAF Odiham and Support Helicopter Force stained glass window at All Saints Church, Odiham. She has completed many commissions for the Army and Navy, and also paints landscapes and animal portraits. She is also an author.

ALAN FEARNLEY GAvA

Alan was born in 1942 and paints all forms of transport subjects in oils on canvas. A member of the Guild of Aviation Artists and winner of the Flight Tankard and Qantas Trophy for aviation painting, he is also a member and past Chairman of the Guild of Railway Artists and is now mainly concerned with the depiction of motoring and motor sport subjects.

FRED GROVES

Fred Groves is a Canadian who lives and works in Yorkshire. He trained as an artist in Montreal after wartime service in the Royal Canadian Air Force. He is represented in collections in Canada, the USA and Britain.

WILFRED HARDY GAvA

Born in London, 7 July 1938. Both his father and uncle were artists. With no formal art training he went straight from school into a series of London art studios, eventually specialising as an illustrator. He became a freelance in 1966, working mainly in magazines and advertising. Since 1975 he has been associated with the RAF Benevolent Fund and its International Air Tattoo organisation. He has also worked with the RAF Association and is proud of his association with the RAF and its charities. His work is to be found in military and civil establishments and museums in many parts of the world. A Full Member of the Guild of Aviation Artists, in 1991 he was awarded the prestigious Roy Nockolds Trophy for the most popular painting by public vote.

TONY HAROLD GAvA

Born on 21 March 1944, Anthony Christopher Harold was educated at Reading Blue Coat School and Berkshire College of Art, from which he graduated in 1964 with a National Diploma in design. He joined the design team of the embryo RAF Museum in 1970. His international reputation as an artist was recognised in 1985 by his promotion to Keeper of Fine Art and in 1988 he was appointed as Keeper of Visual Arts, leading eventually to the post of RAF Museum senior curator. In 1990 he was awarded an MA in museum studies by London University and was elected Vice-President of the Guild of Aviation Artists. Tony was tragically killed on 11 April 1991 when the Avco Lycoming-powered Nieuport 24 replica N153JS he was flying crashed during rehearsals for the Great War Combat Team at North Weald. He is survived by his wife and two daughters.

AIR VICE-MARSHAL NORMAN HOAD
CVO, CBE, AFC*

Norman Hoad entered the Royal Air Force in 1941 and retired from it 37 years later in the rank of Air Vice-Marshal. During World War 2 he flew Lancasters until shot down and taken prisoner in October 1944. He has been drawing since childhood but after studying part time at the York College of Art 1950/52 started painting military and aviation subjects. He is a Founder Member of The Guild of Aviation Artists. While serving in Paris during the late 1960s he became interested in the racing scene and his work now includes all aspects of Equestrian Art. He took a leading role in forming The Society of Equestrian Artists and was its Chairman for seven years.

ROY HUXLEY GAvA

Roy Huxley was born at the time of the 'Battle of Britain' and at present lives and works in Buckinghamshire. During 30 years as an artist, he has painted many subjects and began aviation paintings as a result of being commissioned to illustrate aircraft for model kit boxes. Gradually this has developed and his aviation paintings have become well known at home and overseas. He finds skies fascinate him with their ever changing moods and this he has combined with an interest in aircraft. Roy is a member of the Guild of Aviation Artists and was the recipient of the Aviation Painting of the Year Award in 1990.

GEOFFREY E LEA GAvA

A resident of Leeds and an ex-Merchant Navy Radio Officer, Geoff now paints in oils, portraits, landscapes, marine and aviation subjects full-time after leaving middle-management with British Telecom. Most of his work has been commissioned by serving and ex-serving members of HM Forces and adorn the walls of many clubs, officers mess ante rooms and private collections both at home and abroad. A number of Geoff's paintings have been published as fine art prints and he is currently working on a number of portraits and scenes of significant importance in military history. He exhibits annually in the summer and other GAvA exhibitions and in local art and militaria galleries.

KENNETH McDONOUGH GAvA

Born in February 1921, Kenneth McDonough studied at Regent Street Polytechnic, London. He served for five and a half years in the Army during World War 2 in North Africa, Italy, France and Germany. He was the last regular artist working on the Illustrated London News. He paints in oils and gouache and prefers the impressionistic approach to painting; this can clearly be seen in his work exhibited at the Royal Air Force Museum, Fleet Air Arm Museum and other collections.

ROGER H MIDDLEBROOK GAvA

Born 1929 Roger studied at the Slade School of Fine Art. He is a full member of the Guild of Aviation Artists and twice winner of the Guild's SBAC and Wilkinson Sword Trophies. He still has strong connections with Sweden where he lived for many years working for Volvo cars as a technical illustrator. In 1980 he became a freelance artist and illustrator. He has exhibited aviation paintings in the UK, Sweden and America. In Sweden he was honoured with a one-man show at the Swedish AF Museum in 1995.

EDMUND MILLER DLC, CEng, MRAeS, GAvA

Born in July 1929 Edmund Miller was educated at Sale Grammar School. He served for two years National Service in the Royal Air Force, then studied Aeronautical Engineering for four years at Loughborough College of Technology, qualifying in 1954. He joined the de Havilland Aircraft Company as an Aircraft Structural Designer working on various airliners and in the Airworthiness Department, before taking early retirement as Principal Airworthiness Engineer in 1988. He has been involved with aviation art since the mid-1950s, exhibiting with the Society of Aviation Artists and then with the Kronfeld Aviation Art Society until the formation of the Guild of Aviation Artists. He has paintings on permanent exhibition in museums, airports and private collections. His other interests include aviation history, vintage transport, and portraiture and gliding. He is married with two daughters.

MARK POSTLETHWAITE GAvA

Born on 11 August 1964 in Enderby, Leicestershire and educated at Lutterworth Grammar School, Mark went into the Audio Visual Industry at the age of 18 and trained as a Rostrum Camera Operator before ending up as a professional photographer. Mark started painting aircraft at the age of 18 and became the first ever Artist in Residence at the RAF Museum, Hendon, in 1987, in what was the first major exhibition of his work. He turned professional as an artist in February 1992, specialising exclusively in aeronautical subjects. In 1991, Mark was elected to full membership of the Guild of Aviation Artists, thereby becoming the youngest artist ever to receive this distinction.

MICHAEL RONDOT

Michael Rondot was born in Windsor, Ontario and spent 25 years in the RAF from August 1967 to July 1992. He flew Canberras, Hunters and Jaguars, achieving over 5,000 flying hours, before returning to become a professional aviation artist and formed Collectair Limited Editions. He kept his painting skills throughout his Service career and aircraft began to creep in as subjects from 1969 and they have remained in the portfolio ever since. He was a founder associate member of the Guild of Aviation Artists in 1971 and his paintings have been exhibited in London shows since 1971, and are in private, corporate and military collections and museums worldwide. His artistic philosophy is that if an aircraft looks right, it flies right; paintings that look right, are right. Having been a pilot is a great help in understanding the technical details of airframes and undercarriages, etc, and helps to give his paintings realism and atmosphere without fussy detail.

DAVID SHEPHERD OBE FRSA FRGS VP GAvA

David Shepherd's early career was, to quote his own words, "a series of disasters". After failing to be a game warden in Africa which was his first ambition, he turned to his second choice, painting – and was promptly turned down as "not worth training" by the first art school he tried to enter. They said he had no talent. David owes all his subsequent success to the man who trained him, Robin Goodwin. He started his career as an aviation artist and it was soon that the Royal Air Force started noticing his work. Whilst he has never served with the RAF, they started flying him around the world as their guest and commissioning paintings from him. It was as a result of such a trip to Aden and then on down to Kenya

in 1960 that his life changed. It was the RAF in Nairobi who commissioned him to do a couple of paintings for the Officer's Mess at RAF Eastleigh. They said, "We don't want aeroplanes. We fly those things all day. Do you paint elephants?" That is what started it all and he claims he has never looked back since and he is now regarded by many as one of the world's leading wildlife artists.

ROBIN SMITH

Born in Louth in Lincolnshire in December 1949, Robin has always had a keen interest in aviation from the moment he first saw Avro Lincolns operating from Manby airfield. Serving as an apprentice at Rolls-Royce in Derby from 1966 to 1971, he learned to fly with the Merlin Flying Club and took an interest in catching aircraft in paint. He joined the Guild of Aviation Artists in 1987 and at the time of publishing, organises and runs the East Midlands Region of the Guild of Aviation Artists. His particular interest is in the older types of aircraft and all aspects of sport aviation, from microlights to Sopwith Camels.

CHARLES J THOMPSON GAvA ASAA

Charles J Thompson was born in Poona, India the son of a British Army sergeant. Educated at La Martiniere College, Lucknow and returned with the family to England in 1949 where he joined the staff of Briggs Motor Bodies as a trainee draughtsman. Served as an airframe mechanic in the RAF for his National Service (1955-56) before returning to Briggs which had now become part of the Ford Motor Co. Moved to the Styling Department where he rose to become Executive Designer responsible for the Mark I Cortina, Corsair and Zephyr/Zodiac models. He took early retirement in 1986. A lifelong aviation enthusiast, he began painting in oils 15 years ago. Became an Associate member of the Guild of Aviation Artists in 1982, elected a full member in 1984. A Founder member of the Guild of Motoring Artists and an Artist Fellow of the American Society of Aviation Artists. Happiest just painting for pleasure, exhibitions and commissions. His book 'Wings' on World War 2 aircraft was published by Pan Books in 1990. Married with two sons and one daughter.

RAY TOOTALL GAvA

Ray Tootall was born in 1913 in a suburb of Manchester, and he spent most of his working life in that city in the studio of a family-owned advertising agency, retiring as art director. He left school at

14 and followed that by two years of full-time formal art training. Much of the agency work involved technical accounts and as Ray had a natural ability in that direction it served him well when World War 2 began. In late 1939 he embarked on a Government Training Course of Draughtsmanship at the end of which he joined the drawing office of the Daimler No 2 Engine Factory in Coventry, engaged in the production of Bristol Hercules engines. After the war Ray rejoined his pre-war firm, but it was only after retirement in 1973 that painting became a serious pursuit, and with a great affection for aeroplanes he became an associate member of the Guild in 1977 and was elected to full membership in 1980.

MICHAEL TURNER GAvA

President of the Guild of Aviation Artists, Michael Turner was born at Harrow, Middlesex in March 1934. Fired with a boyhood enthusiasm for aircraft and the Royal Air Force he studied at the Heatherley School of Fine Arts, London having chosen a career in art. His continuing fascination for aviation found expression through his painting, specialising also in motor sport and associated mechanical subjects after turning freelance in 1957. To enhance his understanding of the subject, he has flown in a wide variety of service aircraft from Tiger Moth to Tornado and flies his own ex-RAF Chipmunk. A founder member and twice chairman of the Guild of Aviation Artists Michael is also a founder member of the International Racing Press Association and a member of the Guild of Motoring Writers. His paintings hang in permanent collections at the Science Museum, the Fleet Air Arm Museum and many more collections in Britain and around the world.

BRIAN WITHAMS GAvA

Brian Withams has been a professional freelance artist for the past 20 years, initially working mainly as an aviation artist and book cover illustrator, and is one of the founder members of the Guild of Aviation Artists. Before going freelance Brian worked for many years as a chief draughtsman and technical illustrator, skills he has used to striking effect in his paintings. He has exhibited his work and sold commissions worldwide, especially in the Americas. In the UK he has exhibited work at the RAF Museum, Hendon; Fleet Air Arm Museum, Yeovilton; and annually for the past 20 years at the Guild of Aviation Artists. His work is very diverse in subject and style, ranging from aviation and marine to portraiture and landscape.

RONALD WONG BSc (Hons) GAvA GMA ASAA

Ronald Wong is a long-standing member of the Guild of Aviation Artists. He gained his BSc Degree (Honours) in Biochemistry at Hatfield Polytechnic and subsequently worked in the Health Service in London,. At that stage, painting was a self-taught hobby which was quite separate from his other interests, which included aviation and aircraft modelling. In 1974 one of his early aviation paintings won the SBAC Trophy. Two years later, after much thought and with considerable regret, he left his scientific career and embarked on an artistic one. Since then his aviation work has continued to win prizes. In 1987 he gained the Nockolds Trophy as well as the Wilkinson Sword Poignard, both for oils. As well as the Guild of Aviation Artists, he has exhibited with the Royal Society of Marine Artists and the Society of Wildlife Artists in London and his work sells through prominent galleries in London and the US. He has worked very closely with RAF, and in particular USAF, personnel in this country, and his work can be seen at many military bases. Ronald lives in St Albans, Hertfordshire with his wife and daughter.

KEITH WOODCOCK GAvA

Keith Woodcock was born in April 1940 and educated at Belle Vue Grammar School, Bradford and Salford College of Art. After pursuing a career in industry he became a freelance graphic designer and illustrator in 1969. But a lifelong enthusiasm for aircraft finally persuaded him to devote his entire time to aviation art in 1982. Lately, however, he has also added motoring subjects to his repertoire and is now a full member of the Guild of Motoring Artists. Keith is a past winner of the prestigious Aviation Painting of the Year Award organised annually by the Guild of Aviation Artists. Painting in both gouache and oils, his work is frequently used for fine art prints, book jackets, magazines and cards. His paintings have been commissioned by companies and individuals worldwide.

FRANK WOOTTON GP GAvA

Eminent among aeronautical artists, Frank Wootton, a Sussex man born and bred, was, in the words of a leading art critic, "destined to become the first artist to be inspired by the awe and wonder of aviation and by the transcendent beauty of the element that is its challenge". Frank Wootton, who volunteered for the RAF in 1939, has flown in most of the aircraft that he has so vividly painted. At the invitation of the then Air Commodore Peake, Director of Public Relations at the Air Ministry, and subsequently Chairman of the RAF Benevolent Fund, he toured RAF Stations in 1940 and 1941 to record for history the endeavours of those critical years. Later he served as an official war artist in France and Belgium and in South-East Asia. He has continued from those days until the present to express on canvas his love for aircraft and, in 1979, was awarded the much-prized trophy of the Air Public Relations Association. Mr. Wootton's work in his studio in the Cuckmere Valley in his native Sussex, by the sea, continues to chronicle the story of the Royal Air Force.

DAVID WRIGHT

Born in 1926 in Aberdeen, David Wright was educated at Robert Gordon's College. He joined the RAF in 1946, flew as a pilot from 1952, flying Meteors, Canberras, Valiants, Vulcans during which time he was involved in flight refuelling. Subsequently he flew Britannias with Transport command. Leaving the RAF in 1968, he joined Caledonian Airways (eventually BCAL) flying BAC 1-11s, Boeing 707s and DC-10s as Captain until he retired in 1986. He has painted for many years and joined the Guild of Aviation Artists in 1979. David is now involved in local landscape painting, aviation and wildlife art, frequently exhibiting in galleries and holding occasional one-man exhibitions.

JOHN YOUNG GAvA

John Young was born in Bristol in 1930 and educated at the Royal Grammar School and the School of Art in High Wycombe. Inspired by the visit of Sir Alan Cobham's National Aviation Day air display to a farmer's pasture near his home in Chesham, his love affair with flying machines began. John has painted professionally since 1950 when employment in the studio of an advertising agency enabled him to translate an intense interest in aviation into a style of painting which combined portrayal of technical subjects with natural, atmospheric situations. Having established a career in illustration for many aviation manufacturers, airlines, air forces, and publishers, John went freelance in the early 1960s to expand his capabilities and move toward the world of fine art. To this end, he exhibited in the inaugural and subsequent exhibitions of the Society of Aviation Artists, later to become the Guild of Aviation Artists. John is a founder member of the Guild and recently completed a term as its Chairman. He was awarded the Guild of Aviation Artists Medal in 1983 and was the first member of the Guild to receive the Flight International trophy for the Best Professional Aviation Artists three times. John lives with his wife Barbara in the village of Chesham, the same small town where he grew up.

THE GUILD OF AVIATION ARTISTS

The Guild of Aviation Artists, which was founded in 1971, incorporates The Society of Aviation Artists. This latter organisation had held its first exhibition in 1954 at London's Guildhall, but by 1958 a number of professional members had become somewhat disenchanted with the new society and turned their attention to a small social club catering for light flying and gliding enthusiasts, called the Kronfeld Club, who were keen to put on an exhibition of aviation art at their Victoria premises. So it was that top professionals like Wootton, Turner and Young hung their work alongside artists who actually flew the aeroplanes. It is the same today and from these small beginnings the Guild now has over 200 members and a like number of 'friends' who too are mostly artists. An annual open exhibition is entitled 'Aviation Paintings of the Year' and is sponsored, amongst others, by British Aerospace and Rolls-Royce. It attracts a prize of £1,000 for the artist of what is judged the best exhibit. Other exhibitions are organised to commemorate many of the important events in our aviation history and members work continues to be sought by historians, publishers and collectors alike. Their paintings are hanging in service messes and clubs, museums, galleries and aviation offices throughout the world.

Enquiries regarding paintings, exhibiting or membership should be made to:
The Secretary, The Guild of Aviation Artists,
Unit 516, Bondway Business Centre,
71 Bondway, Vauxhall Cross, London SW8 1SQ.
Telephone: 0171 735 0634.